Pioneer Priests and Makeshift Altars

Fr. Charles P. Connor, S.T.L., Ph.D.

Pioneer Priests and Makeshift Altars

A History of Catholicism in the Thirteen Colonies

EWTN PUBLISHING, INC.
Irondale, Alabama

Cover design by LUCAS Art & Design, Jenison, MI.

On the cover: *Allegorical Painting of Cecil Calvert Presenting the Acts of Toleration to Governor William Stone*, oil painting, 1853, by Tompkins Harrison Matteson (1813–1884).

EWTN Publishing, Inc.
5817 Old Leeds Road, Irondale, AL 35210

Distributed by Sophia Institute Press, Box 5284, Manchester, NH 03108.

Library of Congress Cataloging-in-Publication Data
Names: Connor, Charles P. (Charles Patrick), author.
Title: Pioneer priests and makeshift altars : a history of Catholicism in the Thirteen Colonies / Fr. Charles P. Connor, S.T.L., Ph.D.
Description: Irondale, Alabama : EWTN Publishing, Inc., 2017. Includes bibliographical references.
Identifiers: LCCN 2017041256 ISBN 9781682780329 (pbk. : alk. paper)
Subjects: LCSH: Catholic Church—United States—History—17th century. Catholic Church—United States—History—18th century.
Classification: LCC BX1406.3 .C66 2017 DDC 282.7309/032—dc23 LC record available at https://lccn.loc.gov/201704125

In memory of my father,
Joseph N. Connor (1922–2014),
whose Catholic faith would be the envy
of all the personalities in this book

Contents

Foreword

In his more than twenty-five years of priestly ministry, Father Charles P. Connor of the Diocese of Scranton has shared his gifts with the Archdiocese of Baltimore as a professor of systematic theology and Church history at Mount St. Mary's Seminary and University in Emmitsburg and with the Eternal Word Television Network (EWTN), where he has helped to produce several series on Church history and Catholic spirituality. In this latest book, he has displayed not only his skill as a historian but his deep love of the Church.

The publication of *Pioneer Priests and Makeshift Altars* is an occasion for grateful reflection. In its pages is related the early history of the Church in this country, beginning with the arrival in 1634 of the first English Catholic settlers in the colony of Maryland and ending in 1790 with the election of George Washington as the nation's first president and the consecration of John Carroll of Baltimore as its first Catholic bishop. The story of what happens in between may come as a surprise to many, and Father Connor provides us with an incisive account. We learn how the conditions for Catholics in post-Reformation England, when the Church had been suppressed and Her members persecuted for not abandoning the Faith of their ancestors, followed them to the colonies. So pervasive was this anti-Catholic feeling that all thirteen colonies would enact laws that either discriminated against Catholics or forbade them from entering their borders altogether. This deep-seated feeling persisted until the American Revolution, when the contributions of Catholics to the Patriot cause, along with the critical French alliance, did much to improve relations.

Such an environment discouraged Catholics from immigrating, and, as a group, they represented less than 1 percent of the total population by the end of the colonial period. Maryland was home to nearly two-thirds of the Catholic population, its members having been attracted by the promise of religious toleration that had been extended by the colony's founder, the Catholic Lord Baltimore. Within sixty years this "pious enterprise" had come to an end, and Catholics became subject, once again, to discriminatory laws. Pennsylvania and Delaware had the second largest community of Catholics. There, under the protection of William Penn's policy of religious toleration, they worshipped publicly and without fear of persecution—the only place in the English Empire where they were free to do so. Small numbers of Catholics were found in New Jersey, New York, and Virginia. All were served by the Jesuit missionaries of the English Province, who had been placed in charge of the Catholic mission to the Thirteen Colonies.

It is unclear why the Catholic experience in the Thirteen Colonies has been largely forgotten. What this book makes clear is that it is a story of trial and adversity, persecution and discrimination. Above all, however, it is a story of faith and perseverance. It is my hope that readers will look at the events of our past not only with historical interest, but with a newfound appreciation for the struggles and challenges our colonial Catholic forbearers confronted. May their witness inspire us with the same courage to remain steadfast in our faith and proclaim the love of Christ through the example of our lives.

—Archbishop William E. Lori

Pioneer Priests and Makeshift Altars

Chapter 1

The Reformation Heritage

In the mid-nineteenth century, Blessed John Henry Newman gave a series of conferences to his fellow Birmingham Oratorians. As a leader of the famed Oxford Movement[1] and a recent convert to Catholicism, Newman was describing the current state of affairs for his coreligionists in England. His opening observation is telling:

> I am going to inquire why it is, that, in this intelligent nation, and in this rational nineteenth century, we Catholics are so despised and hated by our own countrymen, with whom we have lived all our lives, that they are prompt to believe any story, however extravagant, that is told to our

[1] Begun in the 1830s at Oxford University, and led by such individuals as Newman, E. B. Pusey, and John Keeble, the Oxford Movement sought to intensify religious fervor, and interiorly strengthen the Church of England. By advocating a return to a serious study of the Fathers of the Church, many of its members began to see the inherent fallacies of the Established Church, and converted to Catholicism. In 1845, Newman himself became a Catholic at Littlemore, a few miles from Oxford, where he was serving as Anglican vicar. The movement spread to the United States and, as in the Mother Country, attracted large numbers of converts.

> disadvantage; as if beyond a doubt we were, every one of us, either brutishly deluded or preternaturally hypocritical, and they themselves, on the contrary were in comparison of us absolute specimens of sagacity, wisdom, uprightness, manly virtue, and enlightened Christianity.[2]

To answer that inquiry, one must return to the source: the Protestant Reformation in Europe, officially begun in 1517, but with centuries of historical antecedents. That movement would find its way to England later in the sixteenth century, and from there to the Thirteen Colonies in British North America. Only with this background can the story of the Catholic Church in those colonies be understood.

Humanism: Precursor to Upheaval

The Reformation in sixteenth-century Europe had roots in the previous two centuries. Beginning with the Renaissance and continuing with the advent of humanism, the configuration of the Protestant revolt against the Church of Rome gradually took shape.

The Renaissance followed the Middle Ages, during which an individual's state in life was clearly determined by his position—monk, professor, mason, soldier, craftsman, peasant. This would change drastically by the fifteenth century, when the prevailing sentiment in Europe prioritized personal freedom and individual development. In other words, subjectivity had assumed priority, and man was quickly becoming the measure of all things. This is not to say the Renaissance ignored religion entirely; the innovators found much inspiration in the Christian notion of the dignity of human nature and the necessity of each person's salvation.

[2] John Henry Newman, *The Present Position of Catholics in England* (London: Longmans, Green, 1908), 1.

> At the same time the Renaissance introduced a new set of ideal values (or set an ideal value on human activities) which were not necessarily secular but were essentially natural and belonged to the sphere of free human activity. No doubt Thomism had already prepared the way for this by introducing the Aristotelian ethics and the Aristotelian idea of intellectual contemplation as man's highest good. But in Thomism these values were strictly subordinated to religious and supernatural ends, whereas the humanists regarded them as ends in themselves and gave them an autonomous significance. Thus there arose the ideals of "pure scholarship," "pure art" and "pure science" which were to have such a great importance for the development of modern culture.[3]

Humanism was not a uniform philosophy. Rather, it was a popular current of thought, originating largely in Italy, and spreading through the Continent for a century and a half. It dealt with most areas of the mind but found expression especially in areas such as literature, grammar, rhetoric, style, and philology. A key element was the *studia humanitatis*, or the "science of the spirit," which described the development of man's moral, physical, intellectual, religious, and aesthetic possibilities. The prominent humanist Pico della Mirandola, for example, believed there was nothing more important and more perfect than man; thus, man was to be educated. For this task, all the knowledge that had been accumulated throughout history could be useful. This knowledge included Christianity, but only as one type or subset of the sum total of human knowledge.

Humanism would not hesitate to use pagan or other religious images. Many humanists tried to reread paganism in light of

[3] Christopher Dawson, *The Dividing of Christendom* (New York: Sheed and Ward, 1965), 45–46.

Christianity in order to find the true and worthwhile elements even in the ancient traditions. The humanist worked from the basic theory that man can be educated intellectually, morally, and religiously, and that in doing so he is fulfilling his potential and thus giving glory to his Creator—whoever or whatever that might be. This was done by a return to the original sources of all disciplines, such as Plato and Aristotle in philosophy, and reading them in their original language. By studying the original, it was thought, one could formulate the purest interpretations of the classics rather than simply accepting earlier Scholastic thought.

Within the wide range of humanistic studies, the work of Erasmus of Rotterdam assumes special significance. Born about 1466, he was educated by the Brethren of the Common Life, a fifteenth-century pietist religious community, but had no particular inclination to religious life nor any special interest in medieval, Scholastic thought. He was essentially a literary man, an individualist comfortable among the leisure class. He would be found among a growing number of scholars and churchmen friendly to the newer modes of thought—people such as John Colet, Thomas More, Bishop John Fisher, and Archbishop William Warham. He came to be considered the greatest humanist produced by Northern Europe because he

> became the exponent of a form of Christian Humanism very different from the contemporary humanism of Italy. This movement, which has been called "Biblical Humanism", sought the reform of religion by a return to the sources, above all to the New Testament in the original Greek, and secondly to the study of the writings of the Fathers of the Church. As the Italian Humanists had made classical antiquity the pattern of culture and the only standard of literary and artistic merit, so now Erasmus and his friends and disciples

> set up the ideal of Christian antiquity as its counterpart in the spiritual realm and made it the standard of moral and religious values.[4]

Erasmus's Christian philosophy was quite novel. He reproved the Scholastics because of the complexity of their thinking, finding it contrary to simplicity. At the same time, he argued, their reasoning tended to be too general; putting forth such proofs had the danger of watering down the true meaning of the Gospel and substituting it with man-made legalisms and formulas. He felt that the entirety of the Christian life should reflect the simplicity found in the early Church, making it understandable to the simplest of minds and winning many adherents to the truth. Further, Erasmus wanted to emphasize personal piety—a real affection for the God-Man, Jesus Christ, Whom we all want to follow and to imitate in His humility. Christ is at the heart of *pia doctrina* (pious learning): We are to know Him personally as the center of our spirituality. We are to follow His example in living a life of charity and modesty, and then we must teach others to follow His example. Erasmus had a strong belief in the educability and the goodness of man, and he would come to oppose strongly Martin Luther's position that every person is inherently corrupt and evil. Erasmus clearly stood apart from his secular counterparts and would not have befriended the reforming theologies that followed so soon after. His was a reformation from within, a cleansing where cleansing was needed.

[4] Ibid., 56–57. Christopher Dawson strongly emphasized the importance of Erasmus because he "seems to represent the meeting of two great forces which changed Western culture in the sixteenth century: the revival of learning and the reformation of religion." Ibid., 60.

Luther Fires the First Shot

There are both parallels and differences to be found between humanism and the Protestant Reformation. Both the humanists and the Reformers strongly criticized the ritualism, superstition, and intellectual abstruseness of the church in general. (However, humanism never attacked the Catholic Church in Her claim as a Divine Institution.) Both sharply attacked medieval Scholasticism, and insisted on the reform of the universities and their pedagogical methods. Both insisted on the study of the biblical languages as being necessary to reach a better understanding of the original source material, and both stressed the individual over the community (including the Church). Differences were also sharp and can be seen in the contrast between Erasmus and the later Protestants. Erasmus stressed the *pietas*—that is, the importance of an active, integrated, ministerial faith—while the Reformers went after doctrine and its formulation. He also focused on the image of the human Christ, but the Reformers who followed stressed a divine Christ, who both changes and justifies man. Erasmus thought man capable of reforming and renewing himself; the Protestants (especially Luther) stressed the idea of man as a lost being, sinful, and without any capacity to restore himself. One might say that Erasmus laid the egg of Protestantism that was later hatched by Luther, though this is a contentious point among students of Christian humanism.

It is always difficult to assign exact dates to historical movements. Many have taken the 1517 nailing of the Ninety-Five Theses of Martin Luther to the door of the Wittenberg Cathedral as the beginning of the Protestant Reformation. At the same time, they assign 1565 as its close, the year of the death of Father Diego Laynez, S.J., the second General of the Society of Jesus, who had been sent by Pope Pius IV to the closing session of the Council of

Trent, which marked the height of the Catholic Church's response to the Reformers—what has come to be called the Counter-Reformation. Within that time frame may also be listed the conclusion of the Council of Trent and the beginning of the application of its teachings; the publication of the Thirty-Nine Articles by the newly established Church of England, and the deaths of the first generation of Reformers—Luther, John Calvin, and Ulrich Zwingli.

As a movement, the Reformation is also said to have four geographic centers: (1) Wittenberg, Germany, where Luther taught, and where it was quite easy for his teachings to travel into Scandinavia; (2) Basel, Switzerland, the city of Martin Bucer and later, even more significantly, Ulrich Zwingli; (3) Geneva, Switzerland, where the influence of John Calvin is the strongest; and (4) England in the time of the Tudor and Stuart monarchs, beginning with Henry VIII. But it is to Germany that one must first look to appreciate the reform climate that eventually affected the American colonies.

Martin Luther initially did not view himself as a Reformer and rather disliked the term when it was applied to him. His early life seemed the model of faithfulness. Born in Eisleben, Germany, in 1483, he was educated at the University of Erfurt, where he eventually became an Augustinian monk and was later ordained a priest. He became a lecturer at the University of Wittenberg, where he was awarded a doctorate in 1512. He went on to write commentaries on the book of Psalms, St. Paul's Letters to the Romans and the Galatians, and the Letter to the Hebrews.

The Lutheran Reformation had roots in the practice and preaching of Penance in medieval times. Luther regarded this from the perspective of his pastoral experience. He questioned how one could have confidence in a merciful God and how one could do enough or live in such a way as to obtain His mercy. Even more personally,

Luther was very concerned with how he saw *himself* in God's eyes. From this, he wanted to establish a practical doctrine of Confession based on the necessity of an interior disposition motivating one's request for God's forgiveness. That disposition, he felt, was far more important than the exterior action of Confession; the absence of this disposition rendered the act of Confession an empty gesture. Luther was not saying that man should not do penance, but rather that doing penance was not for God's satisfaction; instead, the interior disposition was what God desired, and this could be achieved only in faith inspired by His grace. This was at the heart of Luther's grievances over the abuses that had crept into the Church in the buying and selling of indulgences; the practice could easily separate the external act of giving the indulgence from the interior disposition of the penitent.

These thoughts, coupled with others he would eventually make public, were the beginning of what became a total transformation, albeit difficult to place in specific time slots:

> The traditional picture of Luther's discovery of justification by faith makes it a story of agonized turmoil and release, a dramatic adventure of conversion that has been much imitated in the spiritual experience of evangelical Christians. Conversion has indeed subsequently become something of a required element in evangelical religion, with Luther's conversion standing in a succession of dramatic sudden turns.... [His] turning point has been linked to the picturesque tale of a "tower experience", drawn from his own account long afterwards in 1545, and remarkably difficult to fit into a definite chronological point in his life.[5]

[5] Diarmaid MacCulloch, *Reformation* (London: Penguin Books, 2003), 118.

By Luther's own admission, the "tower experience"—that is, the moment of apparent clarity that he experienced while studying in a tower at Wittenberg—was not mystical; it was theological, exegetical, and, to some degree, psychological. It underscored his developing thought on the necessity of faith in living the Christian life: One was not saved by good works, but rather by faith in Christ. Luther felt he had at last discovered objective truth.[6] Such truth was found in Scripture, and must be received subjectively; we must, Luther thought, let the Scriptures speak to each of us individually. Prior to this, he had developed the idea of the "Iustitia Dei activa," the idea that all our good works are actively inspired by God's power since we are corrupted sinners and He is perfectly just. Between God and man there was the Law that man had to obey in order to be justified. The problem was the sinfulness of man that prevented him from fulfilling the law. God, who is just, would therefore be angered and punish him. Even if man tried to lead a blameless life, it would prove impossible because of his inherent depravity.

As a result of the "tower experience," Luther's view of a God who was angry and who quickly punished evolved into a God who is merciful and justifies. The gift of God's mercy or grace, and not anything we could ever do on our own, is what makes man just. Man needs only to have faith, and to accept passively the mercy of God acting in his life. In place of the Old Testament Law that only condemns, there is the New Covenant, the Gospel of Mercy. Now God's justice saves rather than condemns man. But man must remain passive in order to believe, and in this "sweet commerce" God takes our sins on Himself and communicates His justice to us. Man is not the central player; in fact, he need only be a receiver.

6 Specifically, he felt he had discovered what St. Paul had meant in Romans 1:17.

Luther's primary contributions, each wielding significant influence, were three. The *Address to the Nobility of the German Nation* is one of his strongest antipapal statements. He added little new to condemnations of the past, but reemphasized that the Pope was not what he claimed to be, but an imposter placed by the devil. If this were true, civil representatives had a right and indeed an obligation to discipline, if not overthrow the papacy for the future security of the Continent. The whole clerical system as then understood, Luther claimed, was a travesty, existing for the benefit of the few. The discipline of celibacy imposed on clerics must be abolished, if for no other reason than that it was, in the Reformer's mind, an unnatural way for man to live.

This was followed by *The Babylonian Captivity of the Church*, in which he redefined the notion of a sacrament. He spoke of "scriptural sacraments," which bore little resemblance to the seven sacraments traditionally understood. From his reading of Holy Writ, a sacrament consisted of a divine promise indicated by a divine sign, both of which were to be found exclusively in the Bible, and could include only Baptism, the Eucharist, and Penance. No sooner had he developed this theme than he began seriously to reconsider the notion of Penance, and quickly dropped it from the list. Since the Eucharist was also being rethought by some contemporaries, Luther felt the Catholic understanding of the Mass, especially the mystery of transubstantiation, had to be re-explained. He argued that

> Christ's sacrament should not be viewed through Aristotle's eyes, and treated as an object for rational analysis, but instead it should be accepted by faith through the plain words of Scripture. 'This is my body… this is my blood' In these simple statements quoting Christ's words recorded in the gospels of Matthew, Mark and Luke, lay a time bomb which … soon blew apart any unity in Protestantism. There

> was still more to Luther's analysis of the Eucharist. If he hated Aristotle, he also hated the idea that good works or human merit had value in God's eyes. So he insisted that the Mass could not be a work, therefore its performance could not be a sacrifice, or be manipulated for any one human intention. It was a road of communication from the divine to the human, a channel of God's love: "the word of divine promise in this sacrament sets forth the forgiveness of sins"—Christ on the cross had been the only sacrifice. A sacrifice is done by a priest, and so Christ had been the only priest, sacrificing himself. No sacrifice, no priest: so the clergy who ministered communion were not set aside to be special priestly beings; that idea was part of the Roman cheat. Every faithful Christian was a priest, although only those called by the community or by a superior should exercise priesthood.... Clergy were just servants ... "ministers" of the church.[7]

Finally, *The Freedom of a Christian*, far less strident in tone, came back to the uselessness of good works in meriting salvation. Luther tried to answer the question "Why be good?" Admitting the impossibility of keeping the commandments properly, Luther assured his readers that God does not condemn any of us for this; indeed, He came in anguish to take all our anguish upon Himself. Our good works as followers of Christ come very naturally to us as expressions of gratitude for the loving and saving grace Christ has freely imparted to us. It was an optimism he hoped his followers would seize upon, thereby leading zealous lives and bringing others to a joyous appreciation of what Christ had done, and continues to do for them, if only they would deepen their receptivity.

[7] MacCulloch, *Reformation*, 130.

The Reformation Radicalizes: Zwingli and Calvin

After Germany, the next scene of reforming theology was to be found in Zurich, Switzerland—and what emerged was something very different from what now might be called Lutheranism. Crowds had become agitated for some time by any number of popular preachers, and were ripe for the teaching of Ulrich Zwingli, the city's foremost reform spokesman. Zwingli, a Catholic priest who had entered into a clandestine marriage that he kept secret from diocesan authorities, finally had his opportunity to disclose all to the local bishop and offer his advice that a clerical marriage was far better than priests openly living with women while claiming to be true to their sacred calling. Having set aside one of the most important components of priestly life, he was even better positioned to analyze Luther's theology and substantially deviate from its tenets.

> A great division was being born in Zurich in the 1520's, which would widen and come to distinguish the Reformed from the Lutheran branches of European Protestantism. For this was not just an abstract debate; the consequence of ... preaching was that Zurichers started pulling down images from churches and from the roadside. This frequently involved disorder, and disorder has never appealed to the Swiss.[8]

Such actions moved the city council of Zurich to action. The first area of concern was the Mass: If images were being dismantled for being idolatrous, might not the same be said of the action Catholics had considered central to their Faith? In 1524, religious images were banned; the following year, the public offering of the Mass suffered a similar fate. Such was indicative of the Zurich Reformation: The traditional decision-making procedures of the Church were ignored, and lay authority alone held sway.

[8] Ibid., 146–147.

Zwingli, for his part, took on Luther's arguments on the Eucharist. Though he did not interpret the words of consecration in the Mass in the same way the teaching Church always had (and the Council of Trent strongly affirmed), Luther had still taken a literal view of Christ's words up to a point. Zwingli went much further, arguing that since Luther did not accept the Mass as a sacrifice, and denied the concept of transubstantiation, could he not see the illogic in maintaining that Christ was present in the Eucharist in any way after the words of institution had been uttered? "Christ could hardly be on the communion table," Zwingli wrote, "when Christians know He is sitting at the right hand of God."

With that argument, Zwingli then had to answer the question of whether the Eucharist constituted a sacrament, as that term had traditionally been understood, or even as it was understood by Luther. He argued that the Latin root, *sacramentum*, had a military meaning, connoting the oath Roman soldiers took upon entering service. From this, he derived that the Eucharist could not be understood as some sort of mystical representation of Christ's body, but rather a *symbol* of the believer's faith. The only way in which it could be construed as a sacrifice was as one of faith and thankfulness on the part of the individual believer to God. In like manner, Baptism was a way of welcoming children into God's family and did not involve some mystical forgiveness of sin. From all this it quickly followed that if the Eucharist did not involve a spiritual matter, outward signs of bread and wine were unnecessary; and if Baptism were a mere welcoming gesture, why should it be given to small children who had not the ability to grasp its significance? Such ideas began to take hold in many of the Swiss Cantons (provinces) beyond Zurich in the 1520s and radically altered the Protestant landscape.

Such proposals not only divided Christendom but sparked considerable debate and much acrimony. Without a doubt, it cleared the way for further speculation into sacramental matters, Church governance, and especially the nature of salvation. Luther's view of man's depravity, while somewhat tempered in later years, was to be challenged by the far more threatening theory of "double predestination" put forth by John Calvin. Calvinistic theology developed far beyond what the Geneva reformer envisioned and had ripple effects throughout Western Europe, later becoming a theological mainstay in nearly all the thirteen American colonies. Because of this, Calvin has traditionally been viewed as far more hostile to and threatening for Catholic theology, Catholic interests, and Catholic peace and tranquility in the new world.

Born in 1509, John Calvin was a French theologian and pastor during the Reformation. He would become well known for his views on predestination and the absolute sovereignty of God in the salvation of the human soul. He was trained as a humanist lawyer and broke with the Catholic Church sometime around 1530. His most famous work, *Institutes of the Christian Religion*, written in 1536, is often thought to be an in-depth theological tome, but Calvin actually meant it to be a book of elementary instruction for anyone interested in Christianity from the "reformed" point of view. He was a tireless polemical and apologetic writer, and, experiencing the backlash against Protestants in France, he fled to Geneva, Switzerland, in hopes of reforming the Church there. For some of his fierier polemics, he was expelled and then went to Strasbourg to serve as minister to a church of French refugees. His return to Geneva some years later provided opportunity to implement ideas he had been developing with a precision that Luther would not have prioritized.

He referred to his plan as the Ecclesiastical Ordinances of the Church of Geneva. It was to be a spiritual government, instituted by God's word. The city-state of Geneva and the Church were not *identical* but *co-extensive*. Between the two, there was both tension and collaboration. Differing from Luther, both civil and ecclesiastical government were seen to be under the governance of Christ. The spiritual government resembled, but was not exactly, a theocracy. It was a government based on the Bible, a "Bibliocracy," where Scripture governed the city, both in the temporal and spiritual realms. Since God ruled all of reality, the secular order was to be Christianized. There was a pronounced unity between both branches, unlike Luther's government of the "right and left hand," in which the Church was not to interfere in matters of state.

Within the Church were four specific ministries, not hierarchically arranged, but equivalent in stature. Each performed a distinct but necessary function in the community; Calvin did not want to refer to them as *sacraments*, as if they were instituted by Christ, though he did stress all four ministries were scripturally based.

"Pastors" were to preach the word of God and administer the sacraments (only two: Baptism and Eucharist). Also, they were to maintain discipline, and be totally orthodox to the tenets of reformed thought in their sermons. Some have suggested that pastors functioned like priests in light of their ordination to ministry, but their ordination was anything but sacramental, though it did appear to give them a stable function in the community. "Doctors" were those who were to teach theology and Scripture, while "elders"—laymen and members of the community—were to keep strict surveillance on the moral code of the community and those living in it. They seemed to be always looking for scandals and heresies from which to free the people as they sought to maintain good order and fear of God among all. Finally, "deacons" were those who administered the goods of the Church and took care of the sick and the poor.

Calvin's theory of double predestination, which condemned to perdition most of contemporary society in general and the majority of individuals in particular, derived from Luther, and to a degree from a pessimism found in St. Augustine. He surely felt that only a minority would be saved, though he shied away from any specifics. On Calvin's account, the only sort of evidence indicating divine favor was to be found in a successful life; those who, for example, amassed enormous fortunes did so through hard work and God's smiling on their efforts. Every minute of every day was to be given to God in the form of hard, industrious work. A life of contemplation, seclusion, prayer, and so on, was considered futile, if not outright sinful. To live in this way was not professing one's faith, trust, or fear of the Lord in an adequate manner. As George Grant, a Canadian philosopher and observer of a culture dominated by a Calvinistic ethic has commented, contemplation "never crossed the ocean." Nor should it have, in the minds of those who crossed the ocean and brought Calvin's theology with them. Europe, after all, was a decadent, Catholic world that the reformers had convincingly proven to be wrong, corrupt, and satanically inspired. John Winthrop's famed "City on a Hill" sermon aimed to put all such notions and ways of living in the far distant past and begin a new world in Colonial America.

Finally, Calvin's eucharistic theology was yet another departure from his Catholic forbearers, and deviated further from Luther's.

> Calvin made a firm distinction between reality and sign.... The old church betrayed this principle by confusing reality and sign, attributing to the signs of bread and wine worship which was only due to the reality behind them. Luther, he felt, had also wrongly attributed to the signs that which was only true of the reality: in particular when he asserted that the physical body and blood of Christ were capable of being everywhere wherever the Eucharist was being celebrated in the world: a Lutheran doctrine called ubiquity, which

> Calvin devoted a substantial section in the final version of the *Institutes* to ridiculing. He thought on the other hand that Zwingli had separated sign and reality too much. Calvin was firm against Zwingli by stating his conviction that "in the sacraments the reality is given to us along with the sign." ... To Calvin, then, the signs of bread and wine become an instrument of God's grace in uniting the believer to Christ.[9]

Calvin's determination to let nothing stand in the way of the believer's worship of God accounts for his deep suspicion, even among the Reformers, of giving honor to Our Blessed Mother. Both Luther and Zwingli had written movingly about her and, in their individual lives, held a personal devotion to her as the human source of the Incarnation.

Through most of his active years in Geneva, Calvin housed and befriended the "Marian exiles" from England, those who were forced to flee their native land during the reign of the Catholic Queen Mary Tudor. Under the protection of the city of Geneva, they were able to establish their own reformed church in which to worship, and when political circumstances permitted, the congregants returned to England and brought with them Calvin's reformed theology, which also quickly diffused throughout Scotland. In this way, a path was paved for reformed theology to come to Colonial America and to exist side by side with Anglicanism.

Calvinism was to have enormous success spreading its message due to events in Europe. Luther died in 1546, and quickly division spread among his followers. A temporary truce between Catholics and Lutherans in Germany, the "Interim" of Augsburg, produced a lessening of tensions by giving considerable leeway to the Lutheran ministry within their own church, while seven years later, in 1555,

[9] Ibid., 250.

the Peace of Augsburg divided Germany according to the principle of *cuius regio eius religio*: The religion of the local prince monarch would be the religion of the people in that area. Calvinism was also intensely missionary, with adherents spreading the new theology throughout France, the Low Countries and England. Lutheranism, on the contrary, was less missionary in scope.

In addition, Protestant exiles, wherever they might study, were attracted to the model and organization of the church in Geneva. It was a coherent model, and more radical and less open to compromise than Luther's. It was presented as both doctrine and method—an alternative that could develop into a political force strong enough to take control of governments.

The daily living of Christian social and moral responsibilities was seen by Calvin as the establishment of God's sovereignty over humanity; hence his ecclesiology involved strict and far-reaching discipline. In Luther's mind, the law was the judgment of God, which revealed the sin of the human person; Calvin, on the other hand, saw the law in far more positive terms, stressing its importance in fostering discipline and norms for the Christian life.

To many of the more radical reformers, it seemed that Luther had only pretended to reform the Church. Calvin presented a compelling alternative: the model of a community reformed according to the word of God. That community in Geneva was very highly spirited (even to the point of being militant) and easily assumed an evangelical fervor. There was an active effort to spread their reform as far as possible.

In this brief synopsis of Continental Reform we can see many of the strains that contributed to early American religious thought. These ideas would make their way to the American colonies through England, and later Germany, and fashion a religious impulse starkly different from the Catholic Faith—and throughout most of the colonial period, openly hostile to it.

Chapter 2

The English Heritage

Cardinal Reginald Pole, the last Catholic archbishop of Canterbury, one of the papal legates to preside at the Council of Trent,[10] and one of the clerics who eventually broke with Henry VIII, had a friend in Thomas Starkey, the English political theorist and humanist whose commentaries on contemporary England were much read. He described his country in 1517, at the beginning of the Reformation, as being in extreme social crisis. It was underpopulated; its towns were filled with ruined houses; and the countryside, with deserted villages and untilled land, was a shambles. He felt the English were, on the whole, idle, and no country in Europe had such a high proportion of beggars. Money and food were both scarce, and much of the nobility were uneducated, with no appreciation for the concept of public service except when it might offer some sort of personal profit. Having painted such a

[10] The Council of Trent met between 1545 and 1563 in the Northern Italian city of the same name and is considered one of the Church's most important councils. It was convoked by Pope Paul III in response to the Protestant Reformation and has been called the embodiment of the Counter-Reformation. It condemned what it defined to be the heresies of Protestantism and issued clarifications of the Church's doctrines on such issues as Scripture, the biblical canon, Sacred Tradition, original sin, justification, salvation, the sacraments, the Mass, and the veneration of saints.

gloomy picture, Starkey observed that it was simply good fortune that a monarch like Henry VIII possessed so many virtues in rare combination, enabling him to save England from the catastrophic ruin. Amid such confidence, however, Starkey was quick to add: "What will happen when Henry goes?"[11]

Henry and Catherine and Anne

Such was the positive view that, undoubtedly, many took of their monarch and his reign, now eight years into its course. Starkey, a contemporary and a priest, expressed thoughts that secular historians centuries later were to echo in similar, if not more glowing terms:

> Henry VIII seemed to be a gracious Renaissance prince, generous and friendly, possessed of unusual gifts of personality and brains. He was a magnificent athlete, a musician, a poet, the living example of the Renaissance ideal of the versatile man. To his court came scholars from all over Europe to nourish and spread the spirit of the Renaissance. "The world is waking out of a long, deep sleep." Wrote Erasmus, "The old ignorance is still defended with tooth and claw, but we have kings and nobles on our side.... Where in school or monastery will you find so many distinguished and accomplished men as form your English court? Shame on us all! The tables of priests and divines run with wine and echo with drunken noise and scurrilous jest, while in princes' halls is heard only grave and modest conversation on points of morals and knowledge."[12]

[11] Philip Hughes, *The Reformation in England* (New York: Macmillan, 1956), 1:29–30.

[12] Goldwin Smith, *A History of England* (New York: Charles Scribner's Sons, 1966), 207.

In a real sense, though, the beginnings of the English Reformation were not the ferment caused by dissenting theologians, but rather the problems surrounding the marriage of Henry and Catherine of Aragon. Catherine had been born in Castile, Spain, and was the daughter of Isabella I of Castile and Ferdinand II of Aragon. She had been married to Henry's older brother Arthur, who died in 1501. Five months later, Catherine was betrothed to Henry, who was then twelve years old. Over the years, Catherine had borne Henry four sons and a daughter, all of whom died at birth or shortly after. One daughter, Mary, born in 1516, survived. But Henry felt that if he left only a daughter to succeed him, it would be the end of the Tudor dynasty. It didn't help matters that Queen Catherine was passionately loyal to her native land—and was sometimes a bit indiscreet in expressing her feelings at wrong moments. These surface issues were used by Henry in his selfish, lustful pursuit of Anne Boleyn, and in his campaign to have his marriage annulled.

In trying to convince the ecclesial authorities in Rome, he advanced the argument called the "curse of Leviticus"—that if a man marries his brother's widow, they shall be childless. Because of Henry's youth at the time of his marriage to Catherine, a dispensation had been issued; now he questioned the validity of the dispensation in light of his convenient scriptural findings. Pope Clement VII instructed the English Cardinal Wolsey and the Italian Cardinal Campeggio to set up an ecclesiastical court and try the case in England; at the same time Campeggio was given instructions to delay proceedings and a verdict for an indeterminate time.[13]

[13] Cardinal Thomas Wolsey was archbishop of York and Henry's chancellor; Cardinal Lorenzo Campeggio had served as bishop of Bologna, and legate to the Diet of Nuremberg. He was the last Cardinal Protector of England and served on the commission that excommunicated Henry in 1535.

Wolsey tried every feat of diplomacy possible to persuade Clement VII to grant the annulment. It was Campeggio's opinion, on the other hand, that the marriage was valid and that no grounds for an annulment could be found. Wolsey had been fiercely loyal to his king, and when relations between London and Rome were favorable, there was no time for heresy of any sort in the realm; Wolsey had ordered the burning of a questionable translation of the Bible, and those who spoke at any variance from orthodoxy were highly suspect and closely scrutinized. For all his loyalty to the monarch, however, his inability to secure Henry's desired results led to his undoing. Anne Boleyn and several of the nobility led an attack against him, and he was accused of traitorously corresponding with France and Rome and violating the statute of *praemunire*.[14] Wolsey was ordered north to London, where he received a royal pardon and several thousand pounds in compensation. Resigning his current See of Winchester, he was restored to his former Bishopric of York. Despite such favorable treatment, he knew he was no longer in the favor of the monarchy. He was eventually summoned back to London for what he knew would be the last time, but died on the southward journey, still bitter over his fate.

England Rethinks Church and State

The importance of Wolsey's fall was related to Henry's role as the leader of a growing political faction insisting that the power of the papacy in England be diminished and that royal prerogatives be strengthened. This growing English nationalism stood in

[14] The Statute of Praemunire was an Act of Parliament enacted in 1323 during the reign of Richard II. Its intention was to limit the powers of the papacy in England.

sharp contrast to the Church's internationalism, and reaffirmed a centuries-old conflict between church and state, which, in the past, had taken many forms. "I only wish to command my own subjects," Henry declared, "but on the other hand, I do not choose anyone to have in his power to command me, nor will I ever suffer it."[15]

Some fourteen years before his excommunication, Henry had written a theological work with the help of Sir Thomas More, explaining the sacraments and refuting many of the positions of Martin Luther. He presented a copy to Pope Leo X and was rewarded with the title Defender of the Faith. Despite this apparent commitment to orthodoxy, the Renaissance had brought a critical spirit and, with it, antipapal sentiments. There was a growing distrust of and disagreement with Catholic teachings, and, by the time of Henry's final break with Rome, the English mind-set was quite fixed:

> If the average Englishman of the sixteenth ... century were asked to sum up the policy of the Catholic Church on educational or intellectual matters in general, he had at his fingers' tips a formula, clear, terse, and, to his mind, comprehensive: "Ignorance is the mother of devotion". By that he meant that Rome deliberately kept her children in the grossest ignorance that she might the more easily exact from them a blind adherence to her teachings.[16]

The political and religious climates seemed to be merging in such a way that tumult was inevitable. Still, the Reformation's beginnings in England were unique:

[15] Smith, *A History of England*, 218.

[16] Sister Mary Augustina Ray, B.V.M., *American Opinion of Roman Catholicism in the Eighteenth Century* (New York: Octagon Books, 1974), 13.

> Leaders of the European Reformation were mainly concerned with a revision of dogmas and the practices associated with them; but there were important political and economic consequences. On the other hand, the leaders of the early English Reformation were particularly occupied with the revisions of the relations between church and state. What should be the position of a clerical organization as part of a body politic? The English Reformation was thus at first primarily a political reconstruction; the reformed religion came later. Englishmen, in this age of rising nation states, were increasingly aware of their separateness from other nations. Their emotions were becoming more and more attached to the king and to England. Thus they turned less and less to Rome. The emotions that linked them to Rome or to the Christendom of the Holy Roman Empire had never been national ones, and the fires of nationalism were now burning brightly.[17]

Even so, it is still important, before returning to the events of Henry's colorful reign, to look at the theological undercurrents that had been brewing in England for years and those who popularized them; they were the forerunners of the "reformed religion," and events would eventually unfold in their favor.

New English Theology

In the fourteenth century, John Wycliffe became the earliest spokesman of dissent. He was an English Scholastic philosopher, theologian, biblical translator, Reformer, and seminary professor at Oxford. He became resentful of the privileged position of the clergy in society

[17] Smith, *A History of England*, 218.

and was equally critical of pomp and ceremony, as well as the luxury in which so many Christians lived. He was an early advocate of translating the Bible into the vernacular, and the famous Wycliffe Bible may have included his translation of the New Testament, with the Old Testament translation left to his associates. There is no doubt that some of his objections, especially those based on the radical poverty of St. Francis of Assisi, were prompted by the opulence one often found in monasteries and religious houses of the time, not to mention their vast land holdings. His words attracted many of the peasant class, who became his faithful followers. Though he cannot be held responsible for the bloodshed of the Peasants' Revolt of 1381, his words had a powerful effect on much of the masses.

As his career unfolded, he began to write and preach on the sacraments in a somewhat questionable way, and, in the end, denied the doctrine of transubstantiation. Church authorities forbade him to preach and summoned him to Rome to explain his views, though he was too infirm to travel. His legacy has been well captured by modern writers:

> While it is difficult to find a direct link between Wycliffe and the first English Protestants at the time of Henry VIII 150 years later, his insistence on the Bible as the only rule of faith, his rejection of Catholic teaching on the Eucharist, and his opposition to ecclesiastical authority have caused him to be seen by friend and foe as the first Protestant.[18]

Wycliffe had much learning and great skill as a publicist and was very effective in building up what would soon be known as anti-Catholicism. His followers were called Lollards, a popular

[18] Father Benedict Groeschel, C.F.R., *I Am with You Always: A Study of the History and Meaning of Personal Devotion to Jesus Christ* (San Francisco: Ignatius Press, 2010), 191.

derogatory nickname given to those without a serious academic background who were knowledgeable only in English. The more educated among them came to be known as Wycliffites, but by the mid-fifteenth century, the term "Lollard" had come to denote any form of heresy. In the pages of the martyrologist John Foxe, Lollards, and heretics in general, are described in no uncertain terms:

> The pope's church, it was declared, was not the church of God; the pope has not the powers given to St. Peter; the pope is antichrist. In defiance of the laws enacted during the great crisis of Lollardry these groups possess and use, unauthorized English translations of the Scriptures; they meet in secret to read and discuss their English Bible; they teach those who cannot read to get it by heart. They use English prayers, saying, and teaching their children to say, Our Father, Creed and Ten Commandments in their own language. They organize collections of money to buy heretical books they need; and, in defiance that awaits such a crime, they circulate the literature from one group to another. They condemn the Catholic practice of praying to the saints as idolatry, and the whole business of pictures and veneration of images of the saints. They never, of course, go on pilgrimages, but mock at them and openly suggest that those who make these pious journeys do so for reasons that are anything but spiritual. They repudiate the Catholic sacraments of Penance and Extreme Unction, Confirmation and Holy Orders; they do not admit that matrimony is a sacrament, and they only marry from within their own sect. Christian burial they repudiate too, alleging that it is as good to be buried in the nearest field as in the churchyard. They do not believe in Purgatory and they deny the pope's power to grant indulgences. They have no belief in the value of such

> good works as fasting; and finally, they revolt utterly and completely against the Catholic teaching about the Holy Eucharist. For they utterly deny that Our Lord is present in the sacrament, and denounce the priests as idolaters for "making people believe it was the Lord's body."[19]

That such views existed as early as they did makes the events of the sixteenth century far more understandable. They were reinforced in the early sixteenth century by the writings of William Tyndale. Described as "the greatest English light in the heretical firmament in these first years, and the most powerful solvent of Catholicism since Wycliffe,"[20] Tyndale was much influenced by Erasmus and Luther and was well known for his translation of the Scriptures into English. It was the first translation to draw directly from Hebrew and Greek texts and the first to benefit from the printing press.

In 1530 Tyndale wrote *The Practyse of Prelates*, opposing Henry VIII's divorce from Catherine of Aragon on the grounds that it contravened Scripture. But the theologian was no partisan of Rome: he had also written *The Obedience of a Christian Man*, which was given to Henry and which provided the king with a rationale to break the Church in England from Rome. For his defiance of Henry's marriage plans, however, he was arrested, imprisoned for a year at a castle in Belgium, and executed by strangulation, after which his body was burned at the stake. Two years later, Henry gave authorization for a "Great Bible" for the Church of England, which was largely Tyndale's own work; hence, his influence continued to spread after his death, and much of his translation ultimately found its way into the King James Version, the standard Protestant rendition of Scripture.

[19] Cited in Hughes, *The Reformation in England*, 1:127.

[20] Ibid., 133.

Tyndale had fled England at one point, after the publication of his translation of Scripture, and influenced others to do the same:

> Other refugees followed Tyndale, ex priests, ex religious. They too made use of the new opportunity to print their case against Catholicism; and soon, through little ports and creeks all along the eastern coast, and across the heaths of Norfolk and the marshes of Essex, carried by pedlars and in the baggage of foreign merchants, the heretical book steadily steeped into English life.[21]

Following the lead of popularizers such as Wycliffe and Tyndale, it became easier for people to meet collectively to discuss the new theological ideas spreading to England from the Continent. Best known were a group of scholars who met frequently at the White Horse Inn at Cambridge, who actively sought means of propaganda to circulate heresy; on the university campus the Inn became known as "Germany." At Oxford the discussions became so popular and so intense that the archbishop of Canterbury was fearful where they would lead, so he appointed a committee headed by Rochester's John Fisher to investigate and report their findings.

England Breaks from Rome

With this background, we can return to Henry VIII's major scheme. He convoked a special session of Parliament, hoping to gain sympathy for his annulment and forthcoming marriage to Anne. He recognized the growing spirit of English nationalism and the popular resentment of papal supremacy. He also knew the propertied classes would not object to a general plundering of the churchmen, who were a wealthy and unpopular minority. Rochester's Fisher was the

[21] Ibid.

only man who stood up in this session and loudly protested what he foresaw to be the ultimate fate of the Church.

In 1531 Henry accused the clergy of the country of violating the acts of *praemunire* on largely trumped-up charges. They were told to pay one hundred thousand pounds, and to acknowledge Henry as their "special protector." The following year, Parliament passed several pieces of legislation giving the king effective control of the clergy and ecclesiastical law. At the same time, it became apparent that the Pope was not going to yield on the question of the king's marriage. By officially breaking with Rome, Henry failed to realize that "shattering the universal church would open the floodgates to the waves of Reformation doctrines that were dashing over Europe."[22]

In January 1533, Henry married Anne Boleyn, and the following month an Act of Parliament forbade all appeals to Rome. The civil government officially declared that the King's marriage to Catherine of Aragon had never been valid. Some months later the princess Elizabeth was born, and the English ambassador to Rome was recalled. The next year came several laws that asserted the crown's authority over the Church, culminating with the Act of Supremacy of 1534, which declared that "our sovereign lord, his heirs and successors, kings of this realm, shall be taken, accepted and reputed the only supreme head in earth of the Church of England to the pleasure of Almighty God, the increase of virtue in Christ's religion, and for the conservation of the peace, unity and tranquility of this realm."[23] The break from the Apostolic See of Rome was now complete.

Sts. Thomas More and John Fisher, the two most prominent men to refuse to take the Oath of Supremacy, were both executed

[22] Smith, *A History of England*, 221.

[23] Ibid., 222.

in the Tower of London in 1535, demonstrating that Henry would tolerate no opposition. His next step was the dissolution of the monasteries, in which he was aided by his chief minister, Thomas Cromwell, Earl of Essex. It was Cromwell who suggested that Henry declare himself head of the Church of England and who orchestrated the suit against Thomas More. Described as "vicious, coarse, ruthless and efficient,"[24] he began a visitation of the monasteries and greatly exaggerated reports of corruption and lack of discipline. Monasteries had changed much since the Middle Ages, and in their spiritually deteriorated condition many greedy men sought to own them. Some 645 religious houses were dissolved on Cromwell's personal recommendation and smaller monasteries were closed by an act of Parliament; by 1539, the process was just about complete.

These actions sparked a rebellion in the northern English counties, leading to the Pilgrimage of Grace, an event that paralyzed Henry's government for several months. The demands of the march's leaders were that "the monasteries should be restored, England should return to the papal fold, that the realm should be purged of heresy, and such men as ... Cromwell should be dismissed and punished, and that all who took part in the insurrection should be pardoned."[25] Most of the "pilgrim rebels" were peasants, however, and the movement was too separated geographically to be effective. Monks remaining in monasteries or scattered elsewhere could not decide whether to support it, and in the end Henry was able to crush it rather easily.

One of the leading protagonists in this story was Thomas Cranmer, appointed archbishop of Canterbury by Henry and confirmed by Pope Clement VII in 1533. He had been a public supporter of Henry's pursuit of an annulment and has often been called

[24] Ibid., 223.
[25] Ibid.

the theological and liturgical founder of the Church of England. He would eventually be burned at the stake by Henry's Catholic daughter, Queen Mary, though Anglicans have never considered him a hero; he vacillated at the end, recanting his apostasy from Rome—and then recanting his recantation. He is remembered for his authorship of two prayer books; his second work in 1532 was written without any restrictions from Henry, who even then wanted to retain the entire Catholic Tradition, and truly reflected his Protestant mind. This, coupled with a devout and eloquent revision of the Divine Office, the official daily prayer of the Church, has given him a place in history. Cranmer seemed to want to strike a balance between the old Catholic liturgical prayers and a newfound Protestant piety. He was not conspicuously devout or pious, and he labored in the Church for conflicting ends:

> This ambiguity began with the very personality of Cranmer. He managed to be a married man while a Catholic Archbishop. He served a monarch who, despite his rejection of the papacy, demanded the continuation of medieval Catholic customs. Although Cranmer has a bad reputation among Catholics, he apparently tried to save both Thomas More and Bishop John Fisher by keeping them out of harm's way in the Tower of London. When Cranmer went to the stake, he was still ambiguous, or perhaps conflicted.[26]

As the years went on, Henry's personal life became more and more complicated and tragic. Queen Anne had given him a daughter, Elizabeth, but the thought of no male heir made the monarch cringe. On the day of Catherine of Aragon's death, Anne miscarried—and Henry very shortly made plans for her demise. She was convicted of incest and adultery and immediately executed.

[26] Groeschel, *I Am with You Always*, 195.

The next day, the King was formally betrothed to Jane Seymour, who, one year later, died in childbirth; the young son, Edward VI, survived, and later reigned briefly after his father's death. Henry remained unmarried for two years until he was joined with another Anne, the Lutheran sister of the German Duke of Cleves. This was a purely political arrangement, hastily arranged by Thomas Cromwell to secure an alliance. But Henry eventually began to resent Cromwell's meddling and subsequently charged him with favoring heresy and its proponents, ordering him to be taken to the Tower. Prior to his execution, Cranmer, on Cromwell's behalf, asked the King, "Who shall your grace trust hereafter if you might not trust him"?[27] In 1540, Cromwell was executed, Anne of Cleves was quietly dismissed and given a generous alimony, and Henry next married Catherine Howard, a niece of the Duke of Norfolk and a cousin of Anne Boleyn. By contemporary accounts, Catherine was justly accused of adultery; she too was executed, and one year later Henry took his sixth and final wife, Catherine Parr. She had been twice widowed and retained the affection of her husband and his two daughters. Henry died in 1547, with Catherine surviving him.

Reformation England was an accomplished fact by the time of Henry's death, and, after the death of his young son, Edward VI, the Tudor legacy fell to Queen Mary, Henry's daughter with Catherine of Aragon; after a brief reign in which Catholics fared rather well and numerous Protestant heretics were killed in one fashion or other, Mary died and was succeeded by her half sister Elizabeth, Henry's daughter with Anne Boleyn. Her reign would last several decades and would witness the culmination of the Protestant ascendancy, one that would be challenged only briefly, and with no lasting success—and one in which so many true martyrs for the Faith gave the final testimony of their lives.

[27] Smith, *A History of England*, 226.

Chapter 3

The English Catholic Heritage

The men and women adventurers who heeded the call of George Calvert, First Lord Baltimore, to venture to the new world, where he had been given a title to what was designated the Palatinate of Maryland, were, for the most part, people of means. Largely, though by no means exclusively, Catholics, they were people who were accustomed to a comfortable way of life in England and intended to transplant that lifestyle to Maryland. Those who were of the household of faith had in some cases come to it through conversion—or reversion, after a temporary lapse into the state religion for fear of their lives.

But more often these Catholics had possessed the Faith and fervently practiced it throughout their lives. Those devout souls who ventured across the Atlantic were well prepared not only for a long, strenuous journey, but for living the Faith freely and openly.

Whether it was Maryland, Pennsylvania, New York, or other colonies where a smattering of Catholics were to be found, the mentality was the same. These people knew only too well the ravages of persecution and had paid a great price for their Roman loyalty. No story of their life in Colonial America would be complete without an appreciation of their heritage as Catholics in Reformation England.

Pioneer Priests and Makeshift Altars

A Secret Faith

A late eighteenth-century account of their travails might well have been written two centuries earlier:

> We started from our lodgings about five in the morning, to be present for the first time at a Catholic religious service, or at prayers, as it was generally called, for the word Mass was scarcely ever used in conversation. We arrived at a public house in some back street near the house in which Mr. Horne (the priest) resided. I felt rather frightened seeing some very rough looking people as we passed through the entrance, tho all were very quiet. We hurried past them, but I could not help clinging to Marlow, having an undefined fear of what was going to happen. We mounted higher and higher. At the top the door of a garret was unlocked and we saw at the far end what seemed a high table or a long chest of drawers with the back turned toward us. A piece of carpet was spread before it by a young man, who pointed us to our seats. In a few moments the door opened, and the Venerable Dr. Challoner, accompanied by Mr. Horne and another priest entered the garret, the door of which was secured inside by an assistant, who then unlocked some drawers behind what, I found, was to be used as an altar, and take out the vestments and other things for the service.
>
> Soon after we heard the door-key turned and several rough foot steps enter the garret, some gentle taps and words were exchanged between a powerful looking Irishman who kept his post close to it, and those outside, which were pass-words of admission. The key was again turned each time anyone entered, and just before the Bishop vested himself to say Mass, bolts were drawn also, and no one else could pass into the garret. In the mean time the young man had

> prepared all that was needed at Mass, taken from behind what was used for an altar, which was covered with a white linen cloth. A crucifix and two lighted candles were placed on it and in the front was suspended a piece of satin damask, in the centre of which was a cross of gold lace.
>
> When all was over, I heard the door key turn once more, and all the rough footsteps leaving the garret. The Bishop having un-vested, remained kneeling before us while the people departed. The two priests assisted by the young man replaced the vestments, candlesticks, and all that was used at Mass, behind the altar, locking all up carefully, and leaving the garret an ordinary one in appearance as before.[28]

This description would have been valid almost any time from Henry VIII's death in 1547 until at least the reign of George II, the first in which no further penal enactments were directed against those of the old Faith. Henry's son, Edward VI, was a mere nine years of age at his father's death and died at fifteen. Because of the monarch's youth, his official protector—and therefore the power behind the throne—was the Duke of Somerset, a skilled politician who had carefully maneuvered himself into his position. This description of him is telling:

> Somerset was committed to the Protestant cause and under his protectorate strict religious reforms were put in place. The 1549 Act of Uniformity outlawed the traditional Catholic

[28] Paul Kennedy, ed., *The Catholic Church in England and Wales: 1500–2000* (London: PBK Publishing, 2001), 70–71. The account was written by a Mrs. Marlow, and appeared, according to the editor, in Dr. Burton's pamphlet on Bishop Talbot, CTS Tract No. 49. The Dr. Challoner referred to was Bishop Richard Challoner, vicar apostolic of the London District, and the prelate responsible for all Catholics living in Colonial America.

Mass and made the use of the Book of Common Prayer compulsory.[29]

Somerset's hold on power, though, was very precarious as time passed: A Catholic uprising in the West Country and the young king's quickly deteriorating health all conspired against him. Further, Henry's will was clear: If Edward died childless, the throne would pass to Henry's daughters, first Mary and then Elizabeth. With Mary's ascendance, Catholics were to have a brief respite and a short-lived flowering of the Faith.

A Respite under Queen Mary

Within two months of her accession to the throne Mary had arrested some of the most important Protestant clerics, including Thomas Cranmer. Because of his authorship of the Book of Common Prayer, and his implementation of many of the anti-Catholic policies promulgated during the reign of Edward VI, he was a particular target. In addition, several Acts of Parliament repealed the anti-Catholic legislation of previous years. The queen announced her intention to marry Prince Philip of Spain; he was eleven years her younger, but the wedding went ahead in the summer of 1554. Through this union, Mary hoped to reunite her country to the Apostolic See of Rome and to eliminate any and all vocal Protestant opposition. Philip, for his part, became only king-consort and could not succeed to the throne if the marriage were to be childless.

In the fall of 1554, Cardinal Reginald Pole, exiled for more than two decades because of his protest of Henry's religious reforms, returned to his native land. An Oxford-educated native of Staffordshire, he was one of the earliest to object to Henry's divorce

[29] Charles Phillips, *The Illustrated Encyclopedia of Royal Britain* (London: Anness Press, 2013), 112.

and remarriage. He castigated Henry for his behavior, and was particularly vocal in his protest of the executions of Cardinal John Fisher and Sir Thomas More. Once back in England, he committed himself to the reunification of his country with Rome. Pope Paul III appointed Pole *legate a latere*—a personal representative of the Holy Father—to England to effect such a reunion, but Queen Mary, sensing the danger to him, advised that for the present he come no nearer to England than Brussels. One difficulty that had plagued him for years was the theological position he had taken on the subject of salvation—a position not terribly dissimilar from Luther's *sola fide* doctrine—justification by faith alone. Though he always supported the reunification of the church under the Pope and the indispensable call for obedience, he also always remained under suspicion of heresy in certain quarters.

A character study of Pole upon his return indicates that his impressiveness had diminished during his exile:

> When he arrived ... after twenty years abroad he was a changed man. He had lost the wit and urbane style, and the decisive mind that made him such a favorite of Henry VIII. He was now sadder and grave in appearance, his drawn features and solemn eyes were more in tune with the ascetic churchman.[30]

At the beginning of 1555, the Act of Repeal, finally reuniting England and Rome, was passed, and the day after, Pole formally absolved the entire realm "from all heresy and schism and all judgements, censures and penalties for that cause incurred, and restored them to Communion of Holy Church, in the name of the Father, Son and Holy Ghost."[31]

[30] Kennedy, *The Catholic Church in England and Wales*, 14.
[31] Ibid.

Straightaway, trials of prominent Protestants began; of these, the executions of Bishops Hugh Latimer and Nicholas Ridley were the most famous. Thomas Cranmer witnessed these from his prison cell and was himself eventually dragged through the streets of Oxford to be burned at the stake. In the end 287 Protestants lost their lives during Mary's reign.

As for the queen, her marriage to Philip was short lived and unhappy. She deeply loved her husband, but he did not reciprocate; he fled to the Netherlands and did not return to England until 1557, despite the queen's constant entreaties. Even then, his chief motivation to return was to persuade Mary to join with Spain in a military effort against France.

Reginald Pole, who advanced to the rank of cardinal *before* his reception of Holy Orders, was finally ordained and consecrated archbishop of Canterbury. The ceremony took place in the presence of the queen and appeared to be a hopeful sign for Catholics. Pole was intent on the invigoration of the Catholic clergy; a well-disciplined life coupled with an intense spirituality, he thought, would best enable them to serve the people. He was a strong proponent of the establishment of seminaries, attached to cathedrals, for the training of priests, and directed bishops to reside in their dioceses to oversee the religious life of their parishes. St. Ignatius Loyola offered the services of his new Society of Jesus for such work, as well as for apostolic activity in England, but Pole felt that the intensity of preaching, for which the Jesuits had become known throughout Europe, might be too inflammatory in England. The Jesuit mission would have to wait some time.

In 1555, Cardinal Gian Pietro Carafa was elected to the See of Peter and took the name Paul IV. He had always been suspicious of Pole and within two years deprived him of his legislative authority in England and summoned him to Rome to stand trial for views that were considered too friendly to the new theology that had spread through Europe. This was a grave disappointment to the queen, who was the first to recognize Pole's loyalty to Rome and his efforts at reunification. Her five-year reign ended with her peaceful death at St. James Palace in London, in November 1558. At seven o'clock the same evening, Pole died.

Protestantism Reestablished with a Vengeance

Mary's half sister Elizabeth and those who supported her had contrived a plot that was to take effect as soon as power was theirs. Outwardly, they professed Catholicism; but as soon as the reins of government were theirs in 1558, England saw the publication of *The Device for the Alteration of Religion in the First Year of Queen Elizabeth*. It was a well-thought-out plan for the destruction of the Catholic Faith in England. Upon the death of Cardinal Pole, leadership fell to Archbishop Heath of York, a somewhat meek and humble man, but very principled in matters that counted. Despite his deep loyalty to Rome, Heath was forced, as lord chancellor, to proclaim Mary's successor in a session of Parliament the day following the queen's death. At the end of the year, a proclamation was issued to all of Elizabeth's subjects to abandon preaching or teaching any religious doctrine at variance with that of the existing monarchy. Despite this, Archbishop Heath did all he could to persuade the young queen to reconsider her positions and reconcile with the See of Rome—all to no avail.

A practical example of the queen's determination to enforce her thinking occurred on Christmas Day, 1558:

> The Queen made an attempt to interfere with the High Mass sung in her chapel by Bishop Oglethorpe of Carlisle. The Queen sent to tell him that he was not to elevate the Host. The Bishop replied that he had thus learnt the Mass

> and she must pardon him, as he could not do otherwise. So when the Gospel was read and completed, Her Majesty rose and departed.[32]

Her specific liturgical instructions for her coronation Mass left the bishops in such disarray that none of them attended the subsequent banquet in Westminster Abbey. In January 1559, Elizabeth opened the first Parliament since her accession, in which she formally severed ties with Rome. Archbishop Heath reminded the same body that in breaking ties with the Holy See, they were abandoning all the general councils of the Church, all canonical and ecclesiastical laws of the Church, the judgment of all other Christian princes, and, most important of all, the unity of Christ's Church.

An Act of Uniformity soon followed, passed by the same Parliament. The Holy Sacrifice of the Mass was abolished throughout the realm, and all liturgical forms not in accord with what was now the established church were forbidden; in addition, only the Book of Common Prayer was to be used. Nonetheless, the archbishops, bishops, and other clergy present in Parliament felt it their duty to go on record: They expressed full and total belief in the Real Presence of the Body and Blood of Christ made present through transubstantiation; they believed the Mass to be a propitiatory sacrifice for the living and the dead; they believed the Roman Pontiff to be the Head of the Church and the Vicar of Christ; and finally they affirmed that laymen had no right to make laws or to express opinions to the contrary. The Keeper of the Great Seal, who presided over Parliamentary sessions, allowed the formal presentation of these resolutions, but quickly saw to it that they were not published.

As radical religious changes were taking place throughout the country, Pope Pius IV was elected and tried desperately to get

[32] Ibid., 24.

Elizabeth to return to the Catholic Faith. He sent an apostolic nuncio to Britain in 1560 with written pleas to her, but he was denied entry. In 1563, Elizabeth summoned her second Parliament, increased penalties for failure to comply with the Act of Supremacy, and declared violations of the act to be high treason meriting death. Many, especially bishops, were imprisoned and beheaded rather than accept the new religion. Pius V, elected to the See of Peter in 1566, still in the early years of Elizabeth's reign, made it very clear to English Catholics that, despite the persecution that would follow, it was gravely sinful to participate in the new schismatic form of worship. This was a truly inspiring witness, as a later writer would observe:

> We must not think of these intruders into the Catholic Sees of England as if they were modern Anglican Bishops, gentlemen of refinement and of enlarged and liberal minds, who, if we could imagine them in the position of unwilling jailers to Catholic Bishops, would seek by every means to alleviate their lot. The first Protestant Bishops were, almost without exception, the bitterest of Puritan fanatics, and they were under express orders ... to seek by every means to bring their prisoners to conformity.[33]

By 1570, Pius V had no choice but to issue the papal bull *Regnans in excelsis*, formally excommunicating the British monarch. She had, in the words of the Holy Father, "forbidden the observance of the true religion, and embraced the errors of heretics, oppressing the observers of the Catholic faith."[34]

[33] Cited in ibid., 33. The thought is that of G. E. Phillips, professor of history at St. Cuthbert's College, Ushaw, in 1905.

[34] Ibid., 34.

Dismal as all of this was, there appeared in this story one prelate whose life and work cast great light and hope on an otherwise frightening period. He was Cardinal William Allen, a native of Lancashire, in the North, who determined that the light of faith would not be extinguished.

The Church in Exile on the Continent

Even living in "Old Catholic Lancashire" a young William Allen witnessed the stripping of altars, the ransacking of churches, and the burning of thousands of books in libraries throughout the land that contained "superstition" and "Romish errors." A staunch Catholic throughout, he managed to live at Oxford for two years before he was forced to resign and leave the country. He took refuge at the University of Louvain in Belgium and found there a significant colony of refugee English Catholics. Over the years his desire to become a priest increased, and he was finally ordained at Malines in 1565. Soon thereafter he made a pilgrimage to Rome in company with a certain Dr. Vendeville, a professor of canon law at the University of Douai in Flanders and a friend of Sts. Charles Borromeo and Philip Neri.

Allen outlined to Vendeville a plan he had been forming for the establishment of a Catholic university where young English Catholic men might come to study the great truths of faith as well as the arts and sciences. Vendeville was immediately receptive and welcomed Allen to begin his enterprise at Douai. The new college opened in 1568 and was the first institution to respond to the dictate of the Council of Trent that such schools be opened in dioceses throughout Europe. New students began to flock to Douai from all parts of England—not the least famous of whom was Cuthbert Mayne, who was to return to his native soil to become the first martyr for the Faith from any of the seminaries.

The college was put on a secure financial footing in 1575 by Pope Gregory XIII, who donated a monthly pension of one hundred gold crowns. Eventually, in 1578, European military conflicts forced the students to leave Douai for some fifteen years. In this period, they were warmly welcomed at the town of Rheims. In time they returned to Douai—though both cities played integral parts in the creation of the famed Douai-Rheims translation of the Scriptures.

During these years, Allen was summoned to Rome by Pope Gregory XIII to ask about the possibility of establishing a second seminary in the Eternal City. Two centuries earlier, a wealthy London merchant had opened a hospital on the Via Monserrat for those traveling to Rome on pilgrimage, who were allowed to stay a certain number of days free of charge. A plan was presented to Allen to enlarge the facility and, while not changing its original purpose, to add a seminary for the training of young English priests. Such was the origin of the famous English College in Rome, more popularly called the Venerable English College. Cardinal Allen is buried within its walls, as is Gregory XIII, both considered its founders.

While opportunities were now available for the training of young Englishmen in two locales, the fact was that the older Marian priests—those ordained during Queen Mary's reign—were getting older, and thus other sources of personnel were still needed. It seemed to be an opportune time to begin the Jesuit mission to England, and Allen was receptive to their fervor and their help. Fathers Robert Persons and Ralph Sherwin were to be the first, and soon the influx of Jesuits who followed provoked a proclamation from Elizabeth calling for the recall of all students from seminaries and the banishment of all Jesuits from England. Parents with sons in the seminary were to withdraw them within four months and present them to the local Protestant Bishop; failure to do so would result in severe penalties.

In response to the Queen's proclamation, Cardinal Allen wrote his famous *Apologie of the English Seminaries*. In it, he strongly presented the case for loyalty to the Crown and the faithfulness of all Her Majesty's Catholic followers. He argued convincingly that Elizabeth had been unduly influenced by enemies of the Church and asserted that if the government would allow Catholics to practice their faith freely, most living abroad would soon return home. Catholics were being deprived of the sacraments necessary for their salvation and were not guilty of any crime of disloyalty. Though Allen's arguments were cogent and charitable, they made little or no impact on those at court—but they did give much consolation to those exiled and suffering for the profession of their Faith.

Pope Gregory XIV later appointed Cardinal Allen papal librarian, a post in which he would serve for some years. He took part in four successive conclaves and was given the greatest possible authority over priests working in England: He was their Ordinary, their adviser, and very much a father figure. His death in 1594 brought an illustrious career to a close and surely caused the poignant realization that a powerful voice in defense of Catholicism had been silenced.

Catholic Life in England During and After Elizabeth's Reign

When Elizabeth's reign began, Catholics had entered Penal Times in the truest sense of the word. No public chapels were allowed in any of England's cities; many of the faithful gathered in the large Catholic Manor Houses that dotted the nation and where, for the most part, there was no government interference. It became necessary for priests to conceal their real identity and to dress in lay clothes. Even when tensions lowered a bit and chapels were allowed to be constructed, they generally were built in back streets with no exterior furnishings to indicate their purpose. To be even safer, neither statuary nor confessionals were to be found; confessions were heard in the priest's lodgings. Any Catholic liturgical devotions, such as Benediction of the Blessed Sacrament, were considered far too hazardous, and there were no Stations of the Cross or side altars, since daily Mass was too dangerous to hold. One prelate, the vicar apostolic of the London District (a bishop, though forbidden by law to use the title), had a particularly interesting experience:

> Bishop Challoner used to preach in an Inn with an unsavoury reputation in Holborn, for he had no chapel, and the congregation sat around him at table, each member being supplied with a pipe and a mug of beer, in order to disguise what was really going on.[35]

Difficult as things were, they could have been far worse:

> Had the Elizabethan penal code been rigorously enforced the practice of Catholicism in England could not, perhaps, have survived. In reality, the laws were only intermittently activated, and even then there was great local and regional variation in the extent to which officers of the Crown were prepared or were able to take action against Catholic gentry. The distinction between Catholics and non-Catholics was still in many cases unclear. Enormous numbers of people who retained Catholic inclinations conformed to the law by attendance on Sundays at parish churches in order to avoid the fine; there is evidence that some Catholic priests, too, felt able to say the new Protestant services in

[35] Ibid., 69.

> church and to continue the celebration of Mass in private houses. [36]

During the forty-five years of her reign, Elizabeth faced several challenges whose purpose was the restoration of the ancient Faith in England. Perhaps the best remembered was the ill-fated offensive of the Spanish Armada in 1588, in which fifteen thousand Spaniards lost their lives. Despite this, by the end of her rule, nearly eight hundred priests had returned to England, over half of whom had been trained at the English Seminary at Douai.

One of the constant difficulties encountered by both the Tudor and Stuart dynasties was a very vocal minority of English Catholics, mostly residing on the Continent, who continually advocated armed force to change the religious map of their country.

> It was awareness of this tradition which enabled successive governments to renew the penal legislation and to keep alive popular suspicion of Catholic disloyalty. There can be little doubt that most Catholics preferred the civil disabilities and physical deprivations of the Protestant administration to the conquest of their land by the Spanish or the French. St. Henry Walpole declared his love of England from his prison cell in 1595: for "peace, moral virtue and good government" his own land was beyond comparison.[37]

King James VI of Scotland, a cousin of Elizabeth's, received word of her death two days after the fact. After an emotional farewell to his people, he began a slow procession to London, reaching the city in May 1603, when he initiated the Stuart Monarchy as

[36] Edward Norman, *Roman Catholicism in England from the Elizabethan Settlement to the Second Vatican Council* (Oxford: Oxford University Press, 1986), 14.

[37] Ibid., 29.

James I of England. His wife, Anne of Denmark, had been secretly reconciled to the Church, and the king himself seemed anxious to avoid further conflict with Rome. From this, one might expect that there was a relaxation in Catholic persecution. Nevertheless, in 1606 two pieces of legislation passed Parliament: the first imposing an "annual sacramental test" for public office, including a revised Oath of Allegiance, and the second severely restricting the movement of recusants[38] and closing many of the public professions to Catholics.

Within one year of his assuming power, James was significantly challenged by two open rebellions. Of the two, the second was far more serious, involving a plot to depose the king and to restore Catholicism to the land. The particulars have often been recounted, and the event, celebrated as it was for years thereafter, had significant repercussions in the American colonies:

> The plot centered on the opening of James's second session of Parliament, scheduled for 5 November, 1605. Catholic Lords led by Robert Catesby and Guy Fawkes planned to blow up the palace of Westminster with gunpowder and then foment a Catholic rebellion in the Midlands. Details of the plan came out when one of the gang, Francis Tresham, warned his brother-in-law Lord Mounteagle, who would have been killed in the Lords by the explosion. Lord Mounteagle passed on the information to those in authority and the plot was foiled at the last moment.[39]

More significantly, it was during the reign of James I that exploration to the New World began. The settlement of Jamestown,

[38] "Recusants" comes from the Latin verb *recuso*, "to refuse." In this case, to refuse either to pay tithes to or to attend services in the Church of England.

[39] Phillips, *The Illustrated Encyclopedia of Royal Britain*, 139.

Virginia, begun in 1607, was followed by a royal charter two years later, offering opportunity to invest in the Virginia Company. Later, in 1620, one of the more celebrated trans-Atlantic journeys left from London with royal blessing; it included 101 Puritans sailing on the *Mayflower*, seeking the religious freedom denied them by the established church. Thus, the beginnings of the Massachusetts Bay and Virginia colonies owe their origins to the first Stuart monarch, whose life would end in 1625. James died after suffering a stroke in relatively old age; his death would be followed by the accession of his son, Charles I, who, more than two decades later, would die far more tragically than his father.

Penal laws against Catholics were even less systematically enacted during Charles's reign, and the Catholic cause was aided by his devoutly Catholic wife, Henrietta Maria, for whom the Palatinate of Maryland would eventually be named. Though Charles remained loyal to Anglicanism, his wife's faith was expressed "with an exuberance which not only enhanced Catholic morale, but provided protection for the public reappearance of Catholic worship."[40] The Chapel Royal in St. James Palace became a Catholic center, and the new respectability brought to Catholicism alleviated the temptation, especially among noble families, to defect to the established religion.

With the growing Catholic presence and ambiance at court, however, came corresponding public disapproval. And this, in turn, led to rising antipathy between king and Parliament. This reached a fever pitch in 1626, when Henrietta Maria offered public prayers at Tyburn in honor of so many Catholic martyrs who had died at that place of execution.

These details of the Stuart years confirm one commentator's observation that

[40] Edward Norman, *Roman Catholicism in England*, 34.

> with the ebb and flow of the tide of religious persecution, whether of Anglican against dissenter, of Independent against Churchman, or of both against the "Papist," the cause of toleration was slowly, if at times obscurely, making headway.[41]

No doubt the one event in the reign of Charles I most directly related to our story is the friendship between the king and one of his closest advisers, George Calvert—for in that story lies the beginning of the Catholic Church in the thirteen British colonies.

[41] Ray, *American Opinion of Roman Catholicism*, 46.

Chapter 4

Lord Baltimore Establishes a Colony

As early as 1578, Queen Elizabeth had granted a patent to Sir Humphrey Gilbert for an ill-fated colonial establishment in Newfoundland. England was becoming interested in overseas enterprise for commercial reasons; a strong contributing factor in this was the 1584 publication of Richard Hakluyt's *Discourse Concerning Western Planting*, presenting a strong argument for colonization in the new world, especially to combat Spanish Catholicism and its perceived superstitions. Hakluyt's arguments were used over and over, and while his political and economic reasoning was strong, nothing seemed to resonate with the English establishment as his "exhortations for the conversion of the native peoples to the Protestant faith, so that they might be saved from the superstitious beliefs of the Spaniards and Portuguese."[42] This laid the foundation for a mode of thought never far from England's enterprise:

> Thus from the beginning of the agitation for English colonization of America to the very outbreak of the War for Independence the Protestant crusade against Roman Catholicism

[42] John Tracy Ellis, *Catholics in Colonial America* (Baltimore: Helicon Press, 1965), 319.

> was a major motive in projecting, in planting, and in extending the English colonies in America.[43]

The reason for this was domestic: A substantial number of English Catholics did not share a religious commitment with their monarch. For the sake of stability and order, religious leaders of the established church had assigned the dominant role to civil government. All citizens were thus to accept a common doctrinal way of thinking and liturgical form of worship. The fear was those who could not do so might be not just religious dissidents, but disloyal citizens.

George Calvert's Establishment Roots

One interpretation long held in Maryland historiography was that the Lords Baltimore, beginning with George Calvert, the first to hold that title, sought to establish a religious haven for their coreligionists in North America. More recently, however, historians have identified other motives for his transatlantic enterprise. George Calvert was formed by many years in the established church, following the lead of his father, who had embraced Anglicanism; the son's ultimate reversion to the faith of his Baptism was a more complicated and personal story. Calvert had also had a very successful secular career at court in which he sought and achieved significant advancement, and so political and economic motives—expansion of the empire and of his own personal fortune—also influenced his course. All of this must be considered when examining his family's voyage to America.

To be sure, that voyage and his family situation were unique:

> The continued existence of Catholicism was not so much corporate as it was familial. Each family had to cut its own

[43] William Warren Sweet, *Religion in Colonial America* (New York: 1942), 12, cited in ibid., 320.

> path. The Calverts demonstrated that some English Catholics could function within a culture that all too frequently proclaimed its hostility to their religion. They accepted their situation for what it was and made the most of it. The founding of Maryland, the only successful overseas plantation by English Catholics in the seventeenth century, was a singular experience in English colonization. As English Catholics, Calvert and his family brought a unique perspective to colonization and encountered a unique set of problems that complicated their efforts.... Their Catholic connection led them to build a community on a vision of religious and political allegiance that was radically different from that of other English entrepreneurs. In their effort to succeed, they offered religious liberty to the religiously diverse planters who ventured to their colony. In return, they expected loyalty to themselves as proprietors.[44]

George Calvert was born in Yorkshire, where his family had lived for generations, in 1579 or 1580. His father, Leonard (for whom George's son Leonard was named), as well as his mother, Alicia Crosland, were rather pointedly told of the expectation of conformity with the established church. Leonard replied that he and his wife would indeed conform, and by 1592, when young George was no more than thirteen, secular authorities compelled him to conform as well. The point is significant: It underscores that George was a practicing member of the Anglican church for more than three decades.

After graduation from Oxford (where he may well have taken the oath to support the Protestant Thirty-Nine Articles of faith as

[44] John D. Krugler, *English and Catholic: The Lords Baltimore in the Seventeenth Century* (Baltimore: Johns Hopkins University Press, 2004), 10.

well as the Book of Common Prayer), he studied law at Lincoln's Inn. After an extended stay on the Continent, he returned to place himself under the political mentorship of Sir Robert Cecil, the "principal manipulator of the dynastic change in 1603."[45] This was not uncommon among politically ambitious young men; as one of Cecil's principal secretaries, Calvert was introduced to court politics and to many of the political luminaries of the age. He also married in the Anglican church and purchased a small house in Charing Cross. He further advanced to clerk of the Privy Council, and then to the position of courtier in the service of King James. One of the occupational hazards of his loyalty was Calvert's staunch support for the policy of reconciliation with Spain that King James favored, exemplified by his plan to wed his son Charles to the "Spanish infant," Maria Anna. While this never came to pass, it caused Calvert to be labeled, like his monarch, as worryingly pro-Catholic.

Opinions varied among contemporary commentators about if and when Calvert had reverted to the faith of his Baptism. Observers figured that it was not difficult to be a Catholic and support James's Spanish policy, but just about impossible to be a zealous Protestant and do so.

Did Calvert's defense of the king's policies justify labeling Calvert a Catholic? Much depends on what is meant by "Catholic." Under the conditions prevailing in 1621, one could be labeled, or libeled, a Papist for no more than supporting the king's policies. In Calvert's case the available evidence suggests that this is what happened. Calvert both defended and attacked the Spanish during the 1621 Parliament in accordance with what he considered

[45] Ibid., 30.

to be the king's position.[46] Many years prior to this, Calvert had expressed much interest in overseas colonization. In 1609 he invested twenty-five pounds in the Virginia Company of London, and an even more substantial sum a few months later in the East India Company. As his income increased in 1619 with his appointment as one of James's principal secretaries of state, he became active in projects for colonial organization in New England, Ireland, and especially Newfoundland. In 1620 he purchased part of an earlier Newfoundland grant and began financing a small settlement called Ferryland located on the Avalon peninsula. Initially, he received encouraging reports about Avalon's climate, soil, and so on, so he moved his family there in 1627. One winter's stay convinced him that a colonial enterprise would be futile, and he wrote to England's new King, Charles I (who succeeded his father in 1625):

> I have found by to deare bought experience which other men for their private interests always concealed from me, that from the midst of October to the midst of May there is a sad face of winter upon all this land, both sea and land so frozen for the greatest part of the tyme as they are not penetrable, no plant or vegetable thing appearing out of the earth until it be about the beginning of May nor fish in the sea besides the ayre so intolerable cold as it is hardly to be endured. By means whereof . . . my house hath beene an hospital all this winter, of 100 persons 50 sick at a time, myself being one and nyne or ten of them dyed. . . . I am determined to committ this place to fishermen that are able to encounter stormes and hard weather, and to remove

[46] Ibid., 43. Calvert seemed to lose much political power after his support for a failed marriage alliance between his son Prince Charles and the Spanish House of Habsburg.

myselfe with some forty persons to yo'r ma'ty's dominion in Virginia.[47]

Coming Out Catholic

By the time of his Newfoundland experiment, Calvert had been publicly Catholic for nearly three years—though right up to his public declaration in late 1624 none in the highest offices of government suspected. The traditional historical interpretation has always been that Calvert resigned his position in English government because of the conversion. Today, the prevailing opinion is that it was more court intrigue, especially frustration with Calvert's support for James's Spanish policy, that forced him out. Religion, while surely an important factor, does not appear to have carried the full weight previously thought.

There has always been much speculation about Calvert's final decision to announce publicly his return to the Faith, but since he never put into writing the deepest sentiments of his heart, we are left with only conjecture. Surely the death of his young wife had an influence, as did his stay with Thomas Howard, the Earl of Arundel, following her death. Howard had conformed to the Church of England, but his wife and mother were devout in the true Faith, and his household at Highgate had the services of at least one resident Catholic priest. Could Calvert have approached him for spiritual guidance? Finally, because of many years engaged in negotiations with Spain and its diplomatic representatives, Calvert had much contact with many Catholics, any number of whom could have influenced his decision.

[47] A *Declaration of the Lord Baltemore's Plantation in Mary–land: February 10, 1633* (Annapolis: Maryland Hall of Records Commission Department of General Services, 1983), xi.

> Why did Calvert abandon his long standing conformity? No one individual ... was responsible for his decision. Rather, it was the culmination of many influences.... Contemporary descriptions indicate that the events that led to his resignation as secretary depressed him and led to a period of introspection and reassessment. He realized for the first time in more than two decades that he faced the prospect of exclusion from the nexus of power. He also came to see that the loss of office relieved him of a burden. It allowed him to resolve his conflicted religious loyalties.[48]

A somewhat more admiring commentator noted:

> The single fact of his public conversion to Catholicism in 1624 when every earthly inducement would prompt him to remain an Anglican, proves as nothing else could the depth of the man's sincerity and moral rectitude. In general historians have not been conspicuous in their praise and credit to Calvert for setting on foot what was for that time an altogether unprecedented experiment in religious freedom.[49]

Calvert's realization that Avalon was no place for the type of settlement he desired in no way diminished Charles I's desire to grant him whatever reasonable request he might make; conversion to Catholicism, while carrying a certain stigma, would not preclude recognition of his past loyalties to the Stuart dynasty. In fact, King James, in the final days of his reign, had bestowed on Calvert the title Lord Baltimore, an Irish peerage of some distinction. It was a

[48] Krugler, *English and Catholic*, 73–74. Calvert and his wife, Anne Mynne, were married in 1604 in an Anglican ceremony. Anne died in 1622 and had given him thirteen children. She was buried at St. Martin's in the Fields, London.

[49] Ellis, *Catholics in Colonial America*, 325.

large tract of land, traditionally thought to be in County Longford, in the Province of Leinster in the midlands of Ireland. However, "The Complete Peerage states: There was not and is not any place of that name [Baltimore] in County Longford, which is the county generally assigned to this creation [Barony of Baltimore]."[50] In fact, Baltimore is a village in western County Cork, in the Province of Munster; it is the main village in the parish of Rathmore and the southernmost parish in Ireland and was the scene of much military conflict in the seventeenth century. For its intense Catholicism, though, it was viewed by the crown as a peerage of distinction befitting Calvert's allegiance.

The Palatinate of Maryland

Charles I also granted Calvert a charter in the Chesapeake. The king's wife, Henrietta Maria, was a sister of the King of France and a devout Catholic who had great concern for her coreligionists in Britain, and so the Calverts continued to receive the favor of the crown. Before the geographical particulars of the charter were finalized, however, there were complications:

> King Charles granted Calvert territory ... extending from the James to the Roanoke and west to the mountains. When the members of the defunct Virginia Company learned of this gift, they raised such a clamor that the bill had to be withdrawn. A new warrant was prepared designating "Mari-land," the territory east of Chesapeake Bay from Delaware Bay to Cape Charles, as a patent for Baltimore, perhaps

[50] Cited in Harry Wright Newman, *The Flowering of the Maryland Palatinate* (Baltimore: Genealogical Publishing, 1961), 6. Newman lists the reference in the Maryland Historical Magazine of 1954 in which Kenny develops the theme in greater detail.

> in the hope of staving off the Dutch in New Netherland. Thus the original Maryland encompassed only the Eastern Shore. Again there were outcrys from the Virginia adherents, who objected to the southern boundary. Subsequently that boundary was altered to run from the mouth of the Potomac across the Chesapeake to Watkins Point, thence to the Atlantic Ocean, leaving part of the Eastern Shore for Virginia.... A fourth warrant was prepared that not only pushed the northern boundary to the fortieth parallel, where Philadelphia is now located, but extended it westward to the source of the Potomac. This was the last warrant in these drawn out proceedings, for on June 30, 1632, the government finally issued the charter.[51]

George Calvert died before his American grant could be settled, and so it passed to his son Cecil. The charter Cecil inherited was not for the "colony," but for the "Palatinate of Maryland." It was a document similar to that associated with the Palatinate of Durham, on the English-Scottish border, which included a clause giving the proprietor sweeping legal powers. Parliament didn't grant this special authority due to some urgent necessity, but out of deference to the Calvert name.

The powers granted in the charter were truly extraordinary. The proprietor was to maintain loyalty to the crown, but otherwise his powers were regal. To defend Maryland, he could "raise an army and prosecute war, build and maintain forts, and institute martial law in the face of rebellion"; to protect trade he could "incorporate towns, erect ports, and impose duties." He and his followers were exempt from British taxation, and he could "establish courts in his own name, issue pardons, and appoint magistrates and other

[51] John E. Pomfret, *Founding the American Colonies: 1583–1660* (New York: Harper and Row, 1970), 78.

officials necessary to maintain order and run a government, and his courts could pass the sentence of death." He had power to issue ordinances, provided they did not conflict with those of the Mother Country, and he could encourage persons of wealth and means to settle in his colony. Any doubts of any sort regarding the interpretation of the charter were to be settled in the proprietor's favor, so long as "the Christian religion and allegiance to the crown were not prejudiced."

Since Baltimore had in mind a Catholic refuge, he obtained further changes in the charter working to his benefit. To create spaces free from the smothering effects of English anti-Catholic laws, he received the power to "subgrant land to be held of the Proprietor, not the crown, with the privilege of erecting manorial courts—that is, courts held in the name of the landowner." He received an exemption from a thirteenth-century statute forbidding this arrangement except in Durham; in other words, Maryland was another Durham. Calvert also succeeded in substituting the conventional requirement of a heavy military commitment to England with a nominal token of dependence: "two Indian arrows a year to be delivered at Windsor Castle and one fifth of any precious metal mined." He also had the protection of "fully defined powers with minimal checks on proprietary authority and virtually no compensatory payments."[52]

Liberal as were the concessions of his charter, Baltimore knew that recruitment to Maryland would be a difficult task. In many ways things were far better for Catholics in England than in previous years; the presence of the Catholic Queen Henrietta Maria made it far easier for Catholics quietly to practice their Faith, and some even entertained the hope that Charles I might convert. The

[52] *Declaration of the Lord Baltemore's Plantation*, xiv–xvi. See also Pomfret, *Founding the American Colonies*, 78–79.

Catholic population was scattered, and those actively practicing the Faith tried to live as unobtrusively as possible. Many well-to-do Catholic families far distant from London experienced minimal obstacles to the fulfillment of their religious duties.

Furthermore, the penal laws were not always and everywhere strictly enforced, and, in many local areas, a lasting civility had existed between Protestants and Catholics. Those in the wealthier manor houses had resident chaplains and tutors who also taught the Faith to children, and their servants and tenants had easy access to Mass and the sacramental life of the Church in home chapels. In addition, Catholics of lesser means living near these large homes were always invited to come to Mass. In all this, no matter how attractive the Maryland enterprise might sound, there was a significant number of Catholics who would not part with the comforts of home to embark for the unknown.

The city of London, however, was a different story. In the capital the Catholic population was more concentrated and growing. There were several outcries from Anglican leaders about the number of Papists in the city—and the threat they would ultimately pose if their numbers grew any larger. Even here, though, the city offered many advantages that Maryland could not: Mass could be easily attended in the embassy chapels, and one could prosper economically and practice one's Faith at the same time. Jesuits were even increasingly apparent during the first two Stuart reigns: The English Province of the Society could boast 218 members by 1623; thirteen years later the number had risen to 374, with a large percentage of them working in London.

Baltimore had a formidable task, and apparently had some of his initial enthusiasm dampened:

> He and the missionary priests promoted the enterprise according to his vision. The later testimony of Catholic

Commissioner Thomas Cornwallis indicated that freedom of conscience ranked high among the inducements offered. But like nationalism and the opportunity to prosper under Baltimore's benevolent leadership, religious liberty failed to excite many Catholics. Ultimately, their reluctance, and for that matter Protestant reluctance, to emigrate to Baltimore's colony dampened his high hopes for an auspicious beginning. Even the Jesuits failed to recruit a significant number of Catholics willing to go to Maryland as their servants and had to rely on Protestants to fill their quota.[53]

His greatest success would come from those who saw the opportunity for political power and social status. Generally, these were the second and third sons of prosperous British families who knew they would not inherit the whole of the family fortune. Of these, the majority were Catholics of the gentry class—and usually had long ties to the Calvert family. Their religion generally stood in the way of any type of advancement in England, and their willingness to make the voyage to the New World became stronger the more they eyed their current reality.

Cecil Calvert tried his very best to attract potential settlers. He did not appeal to religious motives, though; instead he stressed the positives of life in Maryland:

> The situation of the country is excellent and very convenient and is in location not unlike Spain, Sicily, Jerusalem and the best parts of Arabia.... The climate is serene and mild, not oppressively hot like that of Florida and Old Virginia, nor bitter cold like that of New England, but preserves

[53] Krugler, *English and Catholic*, 148. Thomas Cornwallis was to become one of the leading Catholics and governmental figures in the Maryland Colony.

> so to speak a middle temperature between the two, and so enjoys the advantages and escapes the evils of each.... The tidal waters provide an abundance of cod-fish, herring, trout, mussels, to mention a few. The country is thickly wooded with many hickory trees, mulberry trees, alder, ash, chestnut, cedars, laurel, pine, sassafras, cypress trees 80 feet tall, and oak trees so tall and straight that beams 60 feet long and 2 and one half feet wide can be made of them.... On the east this land is washed by the ocean, on the west it borders upon an almost boundless continent, which extends into the Chinese Sea.... The woods are passable, not filled with thorns or undergrowth, but arranged by nature for the production of animals and for affording pleasure to man. There are vines of wonderful fruitfulness, from which wine can be made, and a grape as large as cherries, the juice of which is thick and oily.[54]

It has always been open to dispute how many colonists responded favorably to this and other promotional pamphlets encouraging settlement in Maryland. An early account estimated that the Oath of Supremacy was administered to 128 persons before they boarded ship, though the Catholics on board would have had great difficulty with it. In all likelihood, many did not board at the original point of departure, but further down the channel.[55] A Maryland

[54] Cited in Robert E. T. Pogue, *Yesterday in Old St. Mary's County* (New York: Carlton Press, 1968), 33.

[55] If not this, Catholics on board from the original destination would likely have concealed their identities from embarkation authorities. Harry Wright Newman notes that "it would have been difficult for any one or more persons to hide in such compact quarters on the *Ark* and the *Dove*. It is possible, and this author is of the opinion, that the few Catholics who were on board subscribed to the oath with their tongues in their cheeks as a means to an end, hoping for

governor more than a century later estimated to the Lower House of the Maryland Assembly that between two and three hundred were on board the two ships. This is based on established claims for land rights and recorded lists of indentured servants brought by the adventurers themselves; further historical investigations through the centuries, however, have placed it at a much lower number.[56]

The Ark and the Dove

The *Ark* was a 400-ton ship, the *Dove* a 40-ton pinnace. They sailed from Gravesend, England, on November 22, 1633, the day before the feast of the martyr St. Clement, and under the leadership of Cecil Calvert's brother Leonard, who would become the colony's first resident governor. Once launched, the ships first set anchor at the Isle of Wight the following day, where Jesuits and more Catholic adventurers joined them; this, no doubt, was to avoid taking the Oath of Allegiance to the monarch before leaving. Weather prevented the ships from clearing the harbor, but eventually they were able to sail; Jesuit Father White was convinced that St. Clement, who had been martyred by being tied to an anchor, was interceding for the colonists. In the comparatively brief seven-week crossing, they journeyed by way of Barbados and Guadeloupe, following Baltimore's instructions to land on Virginia's eastern

absolution in the next confessional." *The Flowering of the Maryland Palatinate*, 155.

[56] The original figures were taken from estimates by Cecil Calvert, hoping to attract yet more adventurers. The figure of two hundred was, for many years, considered far more accurate, but passenger lists from nonofficial sources placed the number lower yet. Today's guess would place the original party at between 120 and 130. Ibid., 157.

shore. From there they were to engage a pilot to direct them to the area granted to Calvert by his charter.

Maryland was to be a colony conspicuous for religious toleration, at least for a time. The beginnings of this were to be seen in Baltimore's instructions to his colonists before embarking on their journey. He requested them to be

> very carefull to preserve unity and peace amongst all the passengers on Ship-board, and that they suffer no scandal nor offence to be given to any of the Protestants, whereby any just complaint may hereafter be made, by them, in Virginea or in England, and that for that end, they cause all acts of Romane Catholique Religion to be done as privately as may be, and that they instruct all the Romane Catholiques to be silent upon all occasions of discourse concerning matters of religion; and that the said Governor and Commissioners treate the Protestants w(th) as much mildness and favor as Justice will permit. And this to be observed at Land as well as at Sea.[57]

Among the adventurers who first settled Calvert's claim, a handful would eventually distinguish themselves in the Maryland Colony. Some years before his death, while still involved in the Avalon venture, George Calvert was in contact with the Jesuits in the hope of recruiting missionaries—if not for the cold of Newfoundland, then perhaps for milder climates. He later made contact with Father Andrew White with the intent to provide a Catholic chaplain for the voyage—and then, eventually, to recruit several priests to minister to the spiritual needs of the Catholic settlers across the Atlantic.

[57] Baron Baltimore's Instructions to His Colonists, November 13, 1633, cited in John Tracy Ellis, *Documents of American Catholic History* (Milwaukee: Bruce, 1956), 100–101.

At the time Father White agreed, he was already quite an accomplished man. Born in London in 1579, he received his education at Douai, was ordained a secular priest about 1609, and returned to England to engage in the difficult and dangerous work of tending to his coreligionists. He violated the law by celebrating Mass publicly, was imprisoned, and, upon his release, sought refuge in the English Catholic community at Louvain in Belgium. While there, he entered the Society of Jesus and eventually returned to his native land for missionary work. He then spent a number of years teaching in Portugal, Spain, and Belgium. In 1632, he became secretary to George Calvert, who convinced him to be part of the Maryland expedition. It was Father White who wrote extensively of the voyage of the colonists to Maryland:

> His lengthy letters to Lord Baltimore which must have required hours to compose and [were] carefully preserved for many years in the Calvert family gave a remarkable insight into conditions during the first few years.[58]

Father White was joined by two fellow Jesuits: Father John Altham and Brother Thomas Gervase. Also making the voyage was Thomas Cornwallis, a devout Catholic and one of the principal advisers to the Calverts. In describing his adherence to the Catholic Faith, he wrote to Baltimore that he would "rather Sacrifice myself . . . then Consent toe anything that may not stand with the Good Consiens of A Real Catholick."[59] Cornwallis's secretary, Cuthbert Fenwick, joined them in America and was listed as a "servant." It is not known when he joined the group, though he does not appear to have been on the original departure list. Some have conjectured that the *Ark* and the *Dove*

[58] Newman, *The Flowering of the Maryland Palatinate*, 270.
[59] Ibid., 188.

may have met up with some ship along the way whose captain had on board a number of "redemptioners" (that is, people in indentured servitude) and that Cornwallis found it expedient to increase his entourage. In any case, Fenwick "possessed a keen sense of legal acumen and it is possible that he had some training in law at home, if not he must have read jurisprudence with one of the learned gentlemen during his service."[60] Finally, there was Jerome Hawley, who would become, with Cornwallis, one of the two co-commissioners in the new Maryland Colony—"one of the learned and fashionable Roman Catholic gentlemen on the voyage,"[61] and, by all accounts, a colorful and unpredictable character. One of his brothers was governor of Barbados, and another was deputy governor of the same island. The family, therefore, were well placed and interested in British colonization. Jerome himself, as was the case with the privileged, served as a "sewer"—one of those in charge of making preparations for royal banquets, receptions, and the like—to Queen Henrietta Maria. There were several passengers of similar prestige on both ships, but these were the men who attracted particular attention at the commencement of the journey.

Father White's Notes

In the course of the colonists' journey, Father White wrote much about the flora and the fauna they observed—but even more on the Native American tribes. He makes reference to the Piscataway, Yaocomico, and Patuxent, as well as the Pattawomecks on

[60] Ibid., 200. Fenwick, it has been noted, was present with the Catholic colonists on St. Clement's Island on March 25, 1634, when Father White offered the first Mass in the British Colonies.

[61] Ibid., 226.

the Virginia side of the Potomac River. They all belonged to the Algonquin-language family, which was dominant along much of the eastern seaboard during the period of European colonization. The most threatening enemies to the settlers were the Susquehannocks, who sided with William Claiborne of Virginia, a sworn enemy of Maryland—and of Catholicism.

More significant, however, were Father White's spiritual observations. At one point during the journey a very threatening storm arose, one that

> kindled the prayers and vows of the Catholics in honor of the Most Blessed Virgin Mother and of her Immaculate Conception, of St. Ignatius, the Patron St. of Maryland, of St. Michael and of all the guardian angels of that country. And everyone was hastening to purify his soul through the Sacrament of Penance; for when we had lost control over the rudder, the vessel, abandoned to the waves and winds, soon tossed about like a quoit, until God opened a path for her safety.

White's personal fear, however, was very short lived, as he considered:

> The purpose of this voyage was to honor the blood of our Redeemer through the salvation of the savages, to erect a kingdom for the Savior (if He considered our feeble efforts worthy of assistance), to consecrate another gift to the Immaculate Virgin Mother, and many similar things. After this, a great consolation shone inside my soul, and at the same time such a firm conviction arose that we were to be rescued not only from this, but from every other storm on this voyage, that there was no room for doubt with me. I had given myself to prayer when the

> sea raged most severely, and (may this be to the glory of God alone) I had barely finished when I perceived that the storm subsided.[62]

On the first of March 1634, the two ships entered Chesapeake Bay and sailed north toward the Potomac. At the mouth of the mighty Potomac they dedicated the southern promontory to St. Gregory and its northern counterpart to St. Michael, in honor of all the angels of Maryland. The English Jesuit claimed never to have seen a grander river: "compared to it the Thames seems a mere rivulet." Upon disembarking, Father White became the first Englishman to celebrate Mass in the New World:

> On the day of the Annunciation of the Most Holy Virgin Mary we celebrated Mass for the first time in this island: this had never been done before in this region of the world. When Mass was over, we took an enormous cross, which we had hewn out of a tree, on our shoulders, proceeded in rank to a designated place and, with the help of the governor, his associates, and the remaining Catholics, erected a monument to Christ, Our Savior, while we humbly recited the Litany of the Holy Cross on bended knee, with much emotion.

Events moved quickly, and Catholic life was soon to be established:

> We went from the coast inland on the right side, and about a thousand paces removed from the shore, we gave the name of St. Mary to the designated city, and in order to prevent

62 Barbara Lawatsch–Boomgaarden, ed. and trans., *Voyage to Maryland: Relatio Itineris In Marilandiam* (Wauconda, IL: Bolchazy–Carducci Publishers, 1995), 26.

> any pretext for energy or occasion for enmity, we bought thirty miles of that land from the chieftain in exchange for hatchets, axes, hoes and some amount of cloth.[63]

The Colony Grows

A steady stream of immigrants began pouring into the colony in the earliest years of settlement. Among the Catholics, the most prominent family were the Brents, converts to the Faith who originated in Gloucestershire and who arrived in 1638. Three of the Brent sisters entered a recusant convent on the Continent, and the two remaining, Margaret and Mary, accompanied their brother Giles, whom Baltimore had appointed treasurer, for a new beginning in Maryland. The family would make a considerable Catholic imprint on the New World.

In addition, a Catholic aristocracy of sorts was taking shape:

> The first grants were enormous: 12,000 acres each to Thomas Cornwaleys,[64] Richard Gerrard, Jerome Hawley, and John Saunders. Gerrard subsequently, perhaps by prearrangement, passed on to the Jesuits his grant, St. Inigoes, just south of St. Mary's. Others, such as Giles Brent and Thomas Gerrard, received smaller grants, ranging from 1,000 to 6,000 acres. By 1642 there were sixteen manors that had been laid out—some 31,000 acres that represented over four-fifths of the land that had been patented. These manorial lords also gained, under the same conditions of plantation, 10 acres of each town land, which

[63] Ibid., 35, 37.

[64] Depending on which historian is narrating, the name is spelled as above, or Cornwallis.

amounted to 90 percent of the property that constituted St. Mary's.[65]

St. Mary's City did not develop into the commercial center once expected, since the waterways provided for the construction of docks at individual plantations, making a central facility unnecessary. Early on, tobacco became the principal economic staple; within five years of its founding, colonial Maryland was exporting a hundred thousand pounds of tobacco from large plantations such as St. Clement's Manor, the home of Thomas Gerrard.

> As Baltimore intended, Gerrard established a manorial court that had jurisdiction over the inhabitants of the immediate area. As the possessor of a manor, Gerrard was among the elite eligible for appointment to the provincial council, which he eventually received.... Gerrard was planter, judge, provincial ruler, and lord of his manor.[66]

Catholics such as Gerrard quickly assumed leadership roles in the colony, yet they did not constitute a numerical majority. There was no way Calvert could have established the Anglican church in Maryland, so he settled for a rudimentary separation of church and state. He knew from the outset that he would have religious pluralism in his colony, so neither could he adopt the European concept of *cuius regio eius religio*—that is, the religious faith of the ruler being normative in his state. If, therefore, the concept of religious liberty was implicit in Calvert's planning for his colony, this was a concession to pragmatism. One secular view stresses:

[65] Robert Emmett Curran, *Papist Devils: Catholics in British America, 1574–1783* (Washington: Catholic University of America Press, 2014), 37.

[66] Ibid., 39.

> Maryland is unique in early English colonization, because it was the only plantation whose stated goal was to enable Catholics and Protestants to live together in equality, amity and forbearance. This effort had to be made since there were too few Catholics to support a colony by themselves. The first Lord Baltimore was constrained, in order to attract settlers to Maryland, to promise full religious toleration.[67]

It was apparent to the colonists, and those nearby observers, and especially to the Mother Country, that the colonial experiment would be a successful one because of geography and natural resources. The relationship between England and her transatlantic settlers would be, it seemed, mutually profitable.

> Maryland's steady increase was due in some measure to good climate and soil, excellent water transportation, and a liberal land policy. Its agricultural system paralleled that of Virginia to some degree. Most of the plantations and farms were on or near waterways, and the ships that carried the colony's tobacco to England brought back clothing, shoes, farm equipment, and assorted wares. As a matter of fact, Maryland's agriculture was somewhat more diversified during the early years than Virginia's, for there were substantial crops of wheat, corn, vegetables, and fruit. [68]

The first major colonial difficulty was the Kent Island boundary dispute, initiated by William Claiborne of Virginia. A number of secular historians have viewed Claiborne simply as prideful and unyielding, but given the temper of the times—the common fear of Roman Catholicism and the bigotry openly displayed over and

[67] Pomfret, *Founding the American Colonies*, 82.
[68] Ibid., 85.

over—it is not unfair to assume that anti-Catholicism also motivated this particular Virginian.

Kent Island is on Maryland's eastern shore. Claiborne had established a fur trading post there three years before the arrival of the Maryland colonists. He also had a smaller enterprise at Palmer's Creek, a bit further up the Chesapeake. He was informed that, to continue engaging in trade, he would have to obtain a license from the Maryland colony, and had he done so, it would have been very easy to continue in business. King Charles I had given to Calvert nearly monarchical power; all who were loyal to the crown should have accepted the legitimacy of these powers.

> Claiborne could have avoided much trouble for himself had he acknowledged this great authority of Leonard Calvert. It is almost certain that Lord Baltimore would have given Kent Island to him as a Manor grant, and he could have lived there and conducted his trade in peace, under Maryland laws. Cecil Calvert welcomed such settlements as Claiborne's, and would have gladly welcomed him as a loyal colonist. However, Claiborne chose to be defiant, and thereby caused the first serious trouble and bloodshed in Maryland.[69]

Leonard Calvert was at first patient with Claiborne, though he realized that if he allowed such a challenge to his authority to go unchecked in one situation, such challenges could become the norm. If persuasion would not work, force was the next step. Kent Islanders soon engaged in open rebellion against Marylanders; the first episode was an attack on a Maryland pinnace commanded by one Robert Vaughan. Claiborne's strongest supporters, John Butler and Captain Thomas Smith, led this attack; when Vaughan landed

[69] Pogue, *Yesterday in Old St. Mary's County*, 59.

at Palmer's Creek to trade with the Indians, he was immediately set upon and quickly surrendered. Shortly thereafter, one of Claiborne's pinnaces, the *Long Tayle*, was engaged in similar Indian trade at Mattapany, near St. Clement's Manor, when a company of Marylanders captured the ship and brought Captain Smith before Governor Calvert, who confiscated Claiborne's ship but sent Claiborne's men back to Kent Island.

Not long after, the first naval battle occurred when two Maryland pinnaces were sailing in the Pocomoke River near Claiborne's plantation. When Claiborne heard of it, he sent thirteen men to seize the boats. When they were sighted, they were ordered to change course or face the consequences; they refused, and Thomas Cornwallis, the commander, ordered his men to open fire. Three of Claiborne's crew and one Marylander were killed. At this point, Leonard Calvert went himself to Kent Island, intent on capturing the leaders. Claiborne was in England, but his chief advisers were captured, charged with a number of crimes, and imprisoned. Calvert remained some time on Kent Island to make sure that none of Claiborne's followers, about 120 in number, made any further attempt at violence.

Calvert's court tried Captain Smith, convicted him, and sentenced him to be executed. After his hanging the Kent Islanders again revolted, and Calvert had to return to the island to put down the insurrection; he later reported that the entire island was "wholly reduced . . . without any tryall of Law."[70] All of Claiborne's supplies, cattle, and servants were confiscated and brought to St. Mary's City, and so for a time Claiborne ceased to present difficulties for the Catholic colonists. The significance of this episode, though, was that it was the first of numerous displays of anti-Catholic bigotry

[70] Ibid., 65.

whose purpose was to rid the British Colonies of all vestiges of Popery.

Tension with the Jesuits

The colonists had been in Maryland only four years when an official report was sent to the English Jesuit Province concerning the spiritual life of the Catholics. The report was brief, and the author unknown; either the English Jesuits removed his name before they sent it on to Rome, or the document was simply not signed at all. In 1638 there were three Jesuits in the colony: Fathers White, Altham, and Thomas Copley; Brother Thomas Gervase had died shortly after their arrival. Until then colonial officials had not permitted any of the missionaries to evangelize among the Indian tribes, largely for safety reasons. Converts had been made, though: Nearly all the Protestants who had arrived in the calendar year 1638 had been received into the Church. As to the Catholics themselves:

> the attendance on the sacraments here is so large, that it is not greater among the Europeans, in proportion to the number of Catholics. The more ignorant have been catechized, and Catechetical Lectures have been delivered for the more advanced every Sunday; but, on Feast days sermons have been rarely neglected. The sick and the dying, who have been very numerous this year, and who dwelt far apart, we have assisted in every way, so that not even a single one has died without the sacraments. We have buried very many, and baptized various persons.[71]

[71] *The State of Catholicism in Maryland*, 1638, cited in Ellis, *Documents*, 112.

Encouraging as this may have sounded, there were difficulties between Lord Baltimore and the Society of Jesus that threatened the spiritual growth of the colony. Calvert opposed the Jesuits' accepting lands from the Indians without his approval; likewise, he felt he should be the first to give permission for any evangelizing efforts among the tribes. To counter the Jesuits' independence, Calvert secured the assistance of several secular clergy to take over some of the responsibilities of the Society in the colony. The Jesuits naturally felt this was an unwarranted intrusion into the work. (In any event, the first secular priests who arrived in Maryland in the early 1640s quickly sided with the Jesuits.) What the Society didn't appreciate, however, was just how little support Calvert would be able to procure for them from the Protestant government in London. Even across the ocean, they couldn't have complete liberty of action and were never far removed from hostile eyes.

> They objected to the introduction of the secular clergy into Maryland; to the payment of quit-rents in corn; to the obligation of military service on the part of their servants; and to being assessed for the building of a fort; to the rule that their adherents should have been considered amenable to the civil laws in temporal affairs in common with the rest of the settlers of the colony; and finally, they protested against the determination of the Proprietary that they should not receive lands from the Indians except according to the terms of his charter.[72]

Further exacerbating the division, the Jesuit superior, Father Thomas Copley, and his secular counterpart, John Lewger, a convert to Catholicism whom Calvert had entrusted with several

[72] William T. Russell, *Maryland: The Land of Sanctuary* (Baltimore, 1907), 149, cited in Ellis, *Catholics in Colonial America*, 330–331.

important colonial positions, had wills of iron and were only too happy to keep arguments alive. Despite all this, the Jesuits focused intensely on their missionary activity. Father White went to live among the Patuxent tribe in 1639; later, for fear that the Indians' goodwill to the English might not last, he was persuaded to move to the Piscataways, where, in time, he succeeded in catechizing and receiving the emperor of the tribe, along with his family, into the Faith. About the same time, a Father John Brock, S.J., was working with the Indians at Mattapany and Father John Altham was on Kent Island. Father Copley, meanwhile, remained in charge of the chapel at St. Mary's City. Between 1634 and 1641, in all, nine Jesuit priests and two Brothers arrived in Maryland; they made great strides among both the white settlers and the Indians.

> By the early 1640's, Protestants were clearly in the majority, and that majority was growing stronger each year. Government positions, though, continued to be retained by Catholics, who made every effort to avoid any action which might be construed as an interference in the religious liberty upon which the colony had been built. One case in point involved a man named William Lewis, an overseer for Father Copley on St. Inigoes Manor. He caught two of his Protestant servants reading anti-Catholic literature, for which he reprimanded them strongly. When these men reported Lewis, he was taken to court and heavily fined for having violated the ban on public disputes on religion. Yet another case was Thomas Gerrard, who was also heavily fined for confiscating the key to the Protestant Chapel, as well as certain books from within. He was ordered to return the contents, and pay five hundred pounds in restitution—not a small sum in colonial days.

What was even more remarkable, perhaps, and certainly in the end more harmful to Catholic interests, was the benevolent attitude of the proprietor and his deputies toward those who were harassed for their religious beliefs in other colonies. Thus in 1643 Samuel Gorton and his followers who had suffered much at the hands of the Puritan majority in Massachusetts were offered a haven in Maryland, and a similar invitation was extended to a group of Puritans in Virginia who had come from New England some years before. The latter had run afoul of the Anglicans when they brought three Puritan ministers into the colony and thus occasioned an act of the Virginia Assembly in March, 1643, against any minister who did not conform to the doctrines of the Church of England. Calvert did not abandon his friendly attitude towards the Puritans, and in 1649, about three hundred of them migrated from Virginia and settled along the Severn River near present day Annapolis.[73]

Puritan Crisis

The dispute between Calvert and the Jesuits, though, soon took a permanent backseat to other events. Calvert's invitation to the Puritans to settle in his colony had serious repercussions. The story of Robert Ingle is a good example of the problems that came with Puritan settlement. Accused of treasonous comments against King Charles I by Giles Brent, who was briefly serving as acting governor of the colony in Calvert's absence, Ingle was arrested and strictly forbidden to board his ship, the *Reformation*. But Captain Thomas Cornwallis and James Neale, both prominent in government, persuaded the local sheriff to permit Ingle to board his ship

[73] Ellis, *Catholics in Colonial America*, 334.

in their company. Brent was furious when the news reached him, and Cornwallis, Neale, and the sheriff were convicted and heavily fined.

Leonard Calvert must have sensed difficulty ahead, because no sooner had he returned from abroad than he sailed to Virginia to enlist the help of that colony's governor in case trouble arose. But it already had. In his absence, on February 24, 1645, Ingle suddenly arrived in the St. Mary's River with his heavily armed ship carrying twelve cannon and several armed vessels. Giles Brent, by coincidence, was on board a Dutch ship anchored in the harbor, and when Ingle spotted him, he immediately had Brent put in chains.

> Ingle's men pillaged, burned houses, killed cattle, and destroyed or stole the personal property of prominent Catholics, including Thomas Gerrard, the Brents, Cornwallis and Lewger. They struck especially hard at the Jesuits, who collectively owned the most substantial estate in Maryland. (Father) Copely claimed that Ingle destroyed or stole property valued at eighteen hundred pounds. That priest, who described himself as "a sober honest and peaceable man not given to contention or sedition nor any way opposing or in hostility to the King and Parliament", fell victim, as did his colleague, the ancient priest Andrew White. Ingle took a number of Catholic prisoners and transported them to England, where he justified his behavior by claiming that the people of Maryland were "Papists and of the Popish and Romish religion" and that most of them had assisted the governor in putting his commission from the king in force. He claimed that only Papists held office and that it was generally held in Maryland that if he had not come, the Papists would have disarmed the Protestants. Finally,

he rationalized his seizure of property by stating that all he took or destroyed had belonged to Catholics.[74]

Ingle, aided by his fellow Protestant William Claiborne, who had used this opportunity to return to Kent Island, seems to have had no plan to take over the government; his objective was simply to rob, pillage, and destroy—not only in St. Mary's City but across much of the province. So Ingle and Claiborne both left the colony without further bloodshed, and Leonard Calvert reclaimed Maryland in the name of the king in 1646.

One of the long-term effects of Ingle's raid was the loss of Fathers White and Copley, whom Ingle had sent to London in chains for their Catholic preaching. Once back in the capital, Father White was tried for the crime of returning to London after having been banished in 1606. This charge carried a death sentence, but he escaped his fate by arguing that his return was against his will. His petitions to return to Maryland were denied, however, and he spent the final decade of his life living quietly in London, where he died in 1656 at the age of seventy-seven, a little more than two decades after he had offered the first Mass on St. Clement's Island. Meanwhile, Ingle's disruption foreshadowed future events:

> Ingle's behavior was no more than an extension of the turmoil then developing in England between the Royalist and Parliamentary Parties, and Maryland would have been wise to have steered clear of it.[75]

[74] Krugler, *English and Catholic*, 180–181. A more thorough rendering of this story is to be found in Timothy B. Riordan, *The Plundering Time: Maryland and the English Civil War: 1645–1646* (Baltimore: Maryland Historical Society, 2004), 199–218. The title of this particular chapter of Riordan's work is telling: "Burn Them Papist Divells."

[75] Pogue, *Yesterday in Old St. Mary's County*, 71.

Leonard Calvert realized his health was deteriorating from the time he returned from Virginia in search of aid to put down Ingle's rebellion. Death came to him in June 1647, and he was buried sometime between June 10 and 15. He had named Margaret Brent—an attorney, businesswoman, and sister of Giles Brent—his executrix, and further specified that Thomas Greene be named temporary governor. Calvert's funeral was, by all reckoning, very elaborate, befitting his office and social pedigree both in England and Maryland. Margaret Brent tried to ensure a traditional Catholic funeral for the governor, but curiously

> there is no evidence of a Catholic priest in Maryland to oversee the burial. All of the Jesuits and secular priests had been scattered or had died during the rebellion. Father Copley would not return to Maryland until the next year. In addition to the lack of a priest, there may not have been a church in which to hold the funeral. The chapel at St. Mary's had been plundered during the rebellion and may have been burned down. The lack of such services and facilities must have made Calvert's burial even more poignant for his mourners.[76]

Toward Religious Toleration—and Back Again

On the eve of the Civil War in England, the murder of King Charles I, and the coming to power of Oliver Cromwell and the Rump Parliament, and all of the consequences this would have in Maryland, it is quite remarkable that an act of religious toleration could have become a reality in the colony in 1649. Cecil Calvert saw

[76] Riordan, *The Plundering Time*, 299. Father Copley was also taken to London as a prisoner with Father White. To this day, the exact locale of Leonard Calvert's grave is unknown.

that the influx of Puritans into Maryland could have dire results. Baltimore—Cecil had inherited the title—thus sought to ensure religious freedom just as much out of expediency as religious conviction, though credit may still be given him for his broadmindedness, as well as that of the Protestants in the colonial legislature who voted in favor of the measure.[77]

The policy was unique—and short-lived. After King Charles I was executed, the Rump Parliament lost no time passing a bill abolishing the monarchy. The House of Lords was also abolished, and Parliament proclaimed itself the highest authority in the land. On two occasions Oliver Cromwell turned down offers to be named king, preferring to hold the title Lord Protector; hence, much of this decade in British history has become known as the period of the Protectorate and Commonwealth. Several Parliaments were called in the brief years of Cromwell's command, but they either self-dissolved or were dissolved by him. Cromwell won decisive military victories against rebels in Scotland and especially in Ireland, where he was determined to wipe out the ancient Faith. It seemed like a decade-long aberration in British history, with the only similarity to monarchial years being Cromwell's attempts to limit religious toleration throughout the realm. The Catholic apologist G.K. Chesterton has summarized the mentality of these years in characteristically elegant fashion:

> The honest Puritan, growing up in youth in a world swept by the great pillage, possessed himself of a first principle which is one of the three or four alternative first principles which are possible to the mind of man. It was the principle that the mind of man can alone directly deal with the mind of God. It may shortly be called the anti-sacramental principle;

[77] See Maryland's Act of Religious Toleration, April 21, 1647, cited in Ellis, *Documents*, 115–117.

> but it really applies, and he really applied it, to many things besides the sacraments of the Church. It equally applies, and he equally applied it, to art, to letters, to the love of locality, to music, and even to good manners. The phrase about no priest coming between a man and his Creator is but an impoverished fragment of the full philosophic doctrine; the true Puritan was equally clear that no singer or story teller or fiddler must translate the voice of God to him into the tongues of terrestrial beauty.[78]

In 1650, Maryland's Catholics and Protestants seemed to enjoy equality; the proprietor still controlled the province; and the oath of fidelity required of Marylanders upheld his prerogatives. Although Catholics were now in a distinct minority, they enjoyed full religious liberty by terms of the act passed the previous year. There was very soon to be a complete shift in political control, however, largely due to Calvert's previous generosity in admitting so many persecuted Puritans. One leading Maryland historian has observed:

> The Toleration Act ... represented a high achievement in provincial government, the result of a balance of forces that worked for the general good. It was a precarious balance, as became evident a short time later. Congregationalists on the Severn began to doubt that they could submit in conscience to the Oath of Allegiance to Lord Baltimore—it seemed to contain royalist implications and required sworn commitment to officials whose spiritual head was the "Antichrist", the Pope himself. While the Puritans entertained these scruples, word reached the Chesapeake of Charles'

[78] G. K. Chesterton, *A Short History of England* (Sevenoaks, Kent: Fisher Press, 1994), 120–121.

> execution and of a parliament act declaring it treasonous to speak of an heir to the throne, to support the claims of Charles' exiled son. Like Virginia under William Berkley, Maryland in November, 1649 ... pronounced Prince Charles rightful King of England.... Baltimore's enemies in England plotted to lump Virginia and Maryland together as mainland governments in need of chastisement. Parliament named commissioners to obtain the submission of ... Virginia, and two of them, Richard Bennett and William Claiborne, sailed to St. Mary's to obtain the submission of Maryland.... Bennett and Claiborne vied with the proprietary governor for authority, the Puritans finally succeeded in portraying [Governor] Stone as rebellious to Cromwell and persuading Bennett and Claiborne—who were serving as governor and secretary of Virginia—to place Maryland government in the hands of a ten-man Puritan council.[79]

The act granting religious toleration was the first victim of the Puritan ascendancy in Maryland. The new leaders struck the law and forbade Catholics to practice their Faith openly. Interestingly, *all others* who differed from the now-established Calvinist faith were not to be interfered with in the exercise of their religious beliefs and worship, provided they did not disturb the peace and order of the colony; but at the same time, such liberty would not be extended to "popery or prelacy nor to such as under the profession of Christ hold forth and practice Licentiousness."[80] By enacting

[79] Robert J. Brugger, *Maryland: A Middle Temperament: 1634–1980* (Baltimore: Johns Hopkins University Press, 1988), 21.

[80] *Disfranchisement of Catholics in Maryland*, October 20, 1654, in Ellis, *Documents*, 117–118.

such, "the Maryland Puritans had now emulated the intolerant example of their coreligionists in England."[81]

No longer did Marylanders have to take the oath of loyalty to the proprietor when purchasing land grants. The Puritans also passed laws against sin, vice, and Sabbath-breaking. Governor Stone tried to claim that Cromwell had supported the restoration of Lord Baltimore's charter, though the new Puritan leader dismissed and scoffed at this idea. Stone went on to gather some faithful troops and mount a military attack on the Severn River, but he was badly defeated by a fleet of ships sympathetic to Puritan rule. Baltimore's enemies, now on the ascendancy in England, published such scurrilous pamphlets as *Babylon's Fall in Maryland* and *Lord Baltimore's Printed Case, Uncased and Answered.* For some years, Catholic life would be extremely restricted, though loosening would come in 1660 with the Stuart Restoration in England and the ascendance of King Charles II.

A Turning Point

After 1650, and particularly after the debacle of Ingle's plunder, the general Maryland population began to decrease. During the Civil War that brought Cromwell and the Puritans to power, however, many young Britons sought to flee the mother country and come to the colony. By the time of the Stuart Restoration in 1660, the population had reached 2,500, only about ten times the size at inception in 1634. Two decades later, that number had risen to 20,000. Planters, farmers, and traders began to fill up the areas of Kent Island and the Eastern Shore. In addition, for the first thirty-five years of colonial life, numerous indentured servants continued

[81] Pomfret, *Founding the American Colonies*, 98.

to emigrate, to serve their period of indenture (usually seven years), and to go on to become landowners themselves.

Lord Baltimore appointed Josiah Fendall governor following Stone's defeat at the Battle of the Severn and the ultimate failure of Puritan rule in the colony. It was Fendall who issued writs for an assembly session to be held in what is now Calvert County, about halfway between St. Mary's City and the Puritan settlements, in what had by now become Anne Arundel County. By the time of the Restoration of the Stuarts, two new counties had been created: Baltimore, on the northwestern edge of the original land grant, and Charles in the colony's southern extremity. This expansion presented much opportunity for the growth and development of Catholicism; the few resident priests present in the colony during these decades would find themselves becoming true Maryland missionaries—the real planters of the Catholic Faith.

Chapter 5

Catholic Life Begins in Maryland

The Catholic presence in Maryland, as we have seen, begins with the beginning of British settlement in 1634. After a few decades, a Protestant divine could write: "We have Popish Priests daily flocking in among us, and the whole province smells of Popish superstition, & I wish these Caterpillars were destroyed; they poison apace our young Plants that are growing up."[82] This anti-Catholic rhetoric deserves a closer look: How did this situation develop so decisively? One answer is the granting of land by the Calvert family to prominent English Catholic Gentry, who, in turn, subdivided it liberally. From such land development there evolved manor houses, chapels, and significant numbers of homes in which a Catholic culture developed. Here is a list of Catholic manors in the colony from the mid-1660s:[83]

[82] Ray, *American Opinion of Roman Catholicism*, 71.

[83] Regina Combs Hammett, *History of St. Mary's County, Maryland: 1634–1990* (Ridge, Maryland: Regina Combs Hammett, 1991), 25–26. Ms. Hammett also cites Harry Wright Newman as including Evelynton to Capt. George Evelyn, 1,000 acres in 1638; Little Brittaine to Capt. William Bretton, 850 acres in 1640 in Newtowne Hundred; St. Anne's to John Lewger, 1,000 acres in Patuxent Hundred in 1640; St. Helen's, for Jerome Hawley, before 1636; St. Jerome's, also for Jerome Hawley, 6,000 acres, before 1636; and West St. Mary's, granted in 1634 to Capt. Henry Fleet, 2,000 acres in St.

Manor	To Whom Granted	Acres	Date	In Which Hundred Located
Trinity	Gov. Leonard Calvert	600	1634	St. Michael's
St. Gabriel's	Gov. Leonard Calvert	900	1634	St. Michael's
St. Michael's	Gov. Leonard Calvert	1,500	1634	St. Michael's
St. Elizabeth's	Capt. Thomas Cornwaleys	2,000	1639	St. Inigoes
Manor of Cornwaleys Cross	Capt. Thomas Cornwaleys	2,000	1639	St. Inigoes
St. Clement's	Thomas Gerrard	1,030	1639	St. Clement's
Snow Hill	Abel Snow	1,000	1639/40	St. Mary's
St. Richard's	Richard Gardiner	1,000	1640	Harvey
St. Inigoes	Ferdinando Poulton	3,000	1639	St. Inigoes
St. Joseph's	Nicholas Harvey	1,000	1642	Harvey
Westbury	Thomas Weston	1,250	1642/43	St. George's
De la Brooke	Rev. Robert Brooke	2,000	1650	Resurrection
Resurrection	Capt. Thomas Cornwaleys	4,000	1650/1	Resurrection
Basford	Thomas Gerard	1,500	1650/1	St. Clement's
Fenwick	Cuthbert Fenwick	2,000	1651	Resurrection
Mattapany Sewell	Henry Sewell	1,000	1663	Harvey
Wolseley	Philip Calvert	1,900	1664	St. George's

George's Hundred. The term "hundred" merely designated specific tracts of land from which many subdivisions were made.

When one speaks of Catholic life in Colonial Maryland, the mission of the Jesuits demands the most attention. One may traverse Southern Maryland today and find the sites of so much Catholic history, a significant amount of which has been remarkably preserved. Two of the most significant, both in St. Mary's County, are St. Inigoes and Newtown.

The Jesuit Missions

St. Inigoes has the distinction of being, along with St. Mary's City, the oldest mission founded in British North America. It is the oldest Catholic settlement with permanent residency and activity in the Thirteen Colonies, the oldest Jesuit establishment in the United States—and perhaps the oldest in the world remaining in the continuous possession of the Jesuits.

It was purchased from Thomas Gerrard and named for St. Ignatius Loyola, founder of the Society of Jesus, using, appropriately, the Spanish spelling and pronunciation in honor of his Spanish Basque origins. Father Ferdinand Poulton, after some years in London representing the contingent of Jesuits who had accompanied the first settlers, was named the first Jesuit Superior of the mission by Father Thomas Copley. After Poulton's death, Copley obtained a second warrant for the manor and assigned it to Cuthbert Fenwick on July 27, 1641; Fenwick, in turn, conveyed the property to another Jesuit, Father Henry Warren in 1663. This and other Catholic properties were conveyed through a series of owners until 1792, when the "Corporation of Roman Catholic Clergy of Maryland" was chartered by the Maryland Legislature to hold all the lands belonging to the Society prior to 1775.

The Society built the original St. Inigoes House in 1638, which was described as being

> of English birth, the walls being very thick and massive. The ground floor had five rooms. Entering the south front you came to a hall which led to the pastor's room on the left and to the assistant's room on the right. On crossing it you were in the grand parlor or reception room, and in the front the north entrance door was before you. A door leading from the left of the large room was the Bishop's apartment, and from the right there was another leading into the ordinary dining room. The central or main room was an elegant one and must have been twenty-four feet square with high ceiling. From the north front there was a superb view of the upper St. Mary's, historic Rose Croft, Porto Bello, and old St. Mary's City, where Leonard Calvert made his first settlement, and where the first genuine seed of religious freedom was planted in the New World.[84]

Our chief source of information about the mission is Jesuit Brother Joseph Mobberly. A native of Montgomery County, Maryland, he had studied at Georgetown and later entered St. Mary's Seminary, Baltimore, in order to study for the priesthood. When this did not materialize, he entered the Society of Jesus with the specific intent of being a religious Brother; he took up his duties at St. Inigoes in 1806. By Mobberly's time, the mission was eighty-eight miles from Washington, D.C., by water, and eighty by land. He described the land as having a variety of trees, an abundance of game and various species of birds, and, supplied by surrounding waters, a plentiful supply of fish. Sea breezes swept in from the Chesapeake, keeping the air pure and the inhabitants healthy. In its long history, the manor house was twice attacked by British troops: first during the Revolutionary War and again during the

[84] Edwin Warfield Beitzell, *The Jesuit Missions of St. Mary's County, Maryland* (Abell, MD: E.W. Beitzell, 1960), 55.

War of 1812. Barns, stables, workshops, and storehouses surrounded the imposing edifice; in later years, a windmill, a miller's house, a weaving house, a smith's shop, and buildings housing cows and hens were added. The church, also dedicated to St. Ignatius Loyola, was located at the eastern end of the manor, and saw much activity and change:

> Time and fortunes of war took their toll on the church; consequently in 1816 Father Joseph Carberry, S.J. (who remained pastor of St. Ignatius until 1849) began making extensive repairs. He erected the sacristy, arched the ceiling, added pews, redecorated the interior, and probably installed the beautiful stained glass windows. St. Ignatius continued to serve the Catholics of St. Inigoes well into the twentieth century, but the population shift from river to road caused its decline. After 1946 St. Ignatius was no longer an active parish; fortunately, a dedicated local group saved the church from slow deterioration. They restored St. Ignatius in the early 1950's, and today this beautiful little church stands as a reminder of a rich, historic past. [85]

Nine years after Brother Mobberly's arrival, forty-three slaves lived and worked there; within five years the number had grown to fifty-six. Their quarters were located one-half mile east of the manor house. The overseer, upon orders from the plantation's manager, dispensed food and clothing to the slaves. Since this was a Catholic mission, the overseers strictly enforced the Church's laws of fast and abstinence, and most clothing was produced on the manor.

[85] Joseph Agonito, "St. Inigoes Manor: A Nineteenth Century Jesuit Plantation," *Maryland Historical Magazine* 72, no. 1 (Spring 1977): 89.

> A male slave received in the summer one pair of trousers and two shirts. For the winter he obtained, in addition, one pair of double soled shoes, one pair of stockings, one pair of pantaloons, and one homemade coat. A female slave received one habit and two shifts for summer wear, while in the winter she was allotted one pair of double souled shoes, one pair of stockings, one petticoat, and one short gown. More fanciful apparel—such as hats and Sunday dresses—came out of her own pocket.[86]

Some fourteen slaves worked in the fields; a few others served as craftsman or domestics in the manor house; and the rest were too young or old for serious work. Brother Mobberly took very seriously the instruction of the slaves in the Catholic Faith, and their sacramental life centered on the little church of St. Ignatius. However, one Jesuit visiting the Society's manors in the early years of the nineteenth century recommended that his colleagues "devise more effectual means to promote morality and the frequentation of the sacraments. The crimes that are reported of our slaves and the neglect of duties the most sacred to a Christian are a reproach to [our] society."[87] Disappointingly, this particular Jesuit did not apparently regard slavery itself as a reproach to their society.

Stories are replete at St. Inigoes and the other Jesuit manors throughout Maryland of the Fathers making great efforts to see that their slaves did not marry into bad situations; at the same time, they made every effort to keep slave families from being separated through the slave trade—a commerce that the Society not only did not participate in but also strongly opposed. In all, Mobberly found the ownership of slaves a trying experience; he continually argued against the use of slave labor—interestingly, for economic

[86] Ibid., 91.
[87] Ibid., 95.

reasons. Slavery, he said, forced the Maryland planter to depend on corn and tobacco, both of which proved nonbeneficial: Corn required great labor but fetched little revenue, since it went to feed the slaves and the farm animals; tobacco, on the other hand, exhausted the soil. For their part, several of the manor slaves were not beyond criticizing Mobberly's administration, though it appears that specific complaints were never recorded in the mission's official records.[88]

Newtown, under the patronage of St. Francis Xavier, one of the original "Company" Ignatius gathered around him to form the Society of Jesus, came after St. Inigoes between 1638 and 1640. The manor house, church, cemetery, and so on were built on land granted to William Bretton, a "gentleman" who arrived in the Maryland colony in January 1637, accompanied by his wife, Mary, in-laws, and son, William, who was four years of age. Bretton immediately occupied a position of prominence in the colony; he became the first clerk of the lower house of the assembly, and later clerk of the council and of the provincial court. He was a lawyer, a judge, and a devout Catholic layman. His title indicates a fair degree of education in England, and he obviously was a man of means, since he transported his entire family with him. The Brettons had a daughter after their arrival in Maryland, and then, sometime before 1650, Mary Bretton died; she is believed to have been buried in Newtown. About one year later Bretton married Mrs. Temperance Jay; the two were known to be very active in the practice of their Faith and became close to the Jesuit Fathers. From this friendship grew their decision to give a generous gift of land for the beginning of a Catholic center at Newtown.

It seems that Father Thomas Copley, S.J., was the first missionary to serve the people of Newtown. Records indicate that he

[88] Ibid., 97–98.

gathered a flock of people at the home of Luke Gardiner, a prominent Catholic living near St. Clement's Bay. Others who would join the party were John Pile, Robert Tuttey, John Medley, William Thompson, Walter Peake, Edward Cotton, Robert Cole, John Greenwell, George Reynolds, Robert Clarke, Thomas Matthews, Francis Van Enden, and John Jarboe.[89] The manor comprised 850 acres and was described as a "beautiful and rich neck of farm land reaching out into the Potomac River between Bretton Bay and St. Clement's Bay in St. Mary's County."[90]

Father Copley continued to serve Catholics at Newtown, as well as the congregation at St. Mary's City, until 1644. The church, however, was not built until 1662; prior to that, Father Copley offered Mass in homes, most often those of Luke Gardiner and William Bretton. Around 1653 Ralph Crouch, a layman who would eventually become a Jesuit Brother, opened a school at Newtown in which Catholics and Protestants could both be educated. This was made possible by an allocation of funds in the will of Edward Cotton; the school was the first attempt at Catholic education in the British Colonies.

Once established, the "Hundred," as the settlement at Newtown was called, was distinctive.

[89] Beitzell, *The Jesuit Missions of St. Mary's County*, 25. Beitzell also lists the following original settlers: William Assiter, Richard Banks, Dr. Luke Barber, Thomas Bassett, Ralph Beane, Walter Beane, Joseph Cadle, Thomas Carpenter, William Cole, Thomas Conant, John Dandy, Thomas Diniard, William Evans, Henry Fox, Walter Guest, John Greenway, Walter Hall, John Hammond, Barnaby Jackson, Thomas Jackson, Robert Joyner, Thomas Langworth, Philip Land, Richard Lloyd, Charles Maynard, Robert Newchant, John Nunn, Christopher Oldfield, James Pettison, Bartholomew Phillips, Thomas Phillips, John Price, Paul Sympson, Zachary Wade, William Whittle.

[90] Ibid.

> The scene in Newtown Hundred must have been picturesque during this period. Along the shores could be seen the cabins and huts of the freemen, while in scattered clearings stood the more pretentious brick homes of the planters. Both St. Clement's Bay and Bretton Bay were dotted with the sails of small boats plying up and down the Potomac River and across the river to Virginia, for water, at this time, was still the chief means of transportation. At the port anchorage the great square–rigged ships of England loaded hogsheads of tobacco, corn, and furs to be exchanged for products needed by the Colonists. After loading, they sailed down the river to the Chesapeake Bay for a rendezvous with their sister ships to form a flotilla for protection against pirates or enemy fleets lurking about the capes.
>
> A narrow road, overshadowed by a forest of virgin pine, oak, gum and chestnut, branched at the head of Newtown neck to lead the travelers to St. Mary's City or the Patuxent River. Bands of wild horses roamed about preying upon the planter's crops, while wolves and other wild animals played havoc with his stock. At the "Quarter" could be seen the bark wigwams of the Indians who dwelt in peace with the settlers, except that on occasion some luckless pig found his way into the communal pot of the Redman instead of the smokehouse of the Colonist. The provincial youngsters skylarked across open field and through shadowy woods to the school at Little Bretton, no doubt envying the freedom of the little redskins who were not bothered by such tiresome doings.[91]

Not every memory of Newtown was happy, however. A colonist named Charles Peake ran a plantation on Bretton Bay; he was one

[91] Ibid., 27.

of the earliest settlers and was a successful planter. Unfortunately, he was also given to excessive drink, and on one occasion he was indicted by a Grand Jury for causing the death of a fellow settler of Newtown following a quarrel during which Peake was under the influence of liquor. He was sentenced to death by hanging; the facts that he was drunk and that the person killed had an unsavory reputation made little difference. He was hanged expeditiously, and life went on.

On a more positive note, the Jesuits went on to open a school for the humanities at Newtown in 1677. It would quickly grow in numbers, and two of its students went on to the College of St. Omer's in French Flanders: Robert Brooke, the first native Marylander to enter the Society of Jesus, and Thomas Gardiner, son of Luke Gardiner, one of the earliest settlers in the colony. Newtown was ideally located for such a school, midway between St. Inigoes and St. Thomas Manor at Chapel Point.[92] The two Jesuits who

[92] St. Thomas Manor, adjacent to St. Ignatius Church at Chapel Point, overlooking the Port Tobacco River in Charles County, followed Newtown in foundation by just one year (1641). It was established by Father Andrew White, and eight years later, Jesuit Father Thomas Copley deeded it to Thomas Matthews, Esq., who, in 1662, handed all rights over to Father Henry Warren, S.J., then pastor. During the suppression of the Society of Jesus (1773–1805), the Fathers continued to operate it as secular priests. After the restoration of the Society, Fathers Robert Molyneux, Charles Sewall, and Charles Neale renewed their vows, becoming the first Jesuits of the new United States. Among the many priests to have served at Chapel Point were: George Hunter, Ignatius Matthews, Francis Neale, Aloysius Mudd and James Brent Matthews. All of these men were from Charles County except Hunter, who came from England. At this foundation the superiors of the Jesuits lived for several years, acting as vicars for the vicar apostolic of the London District, the bishop under whose jurisdiction the colonies fell. Many of the earliest missionaries of the

opened the school were Fathers Michael Foster and Francis Pennington; later they were joined by Brothers Gregory Turberville and John Berboel. Mr. Thomas Hothersall, a Jesuit Scholastic, taught humanities and grammar at the school from 1683 until his death in 1698.[93]

While places such as St. Inigoes, Newtown Manor, Chapel Point, and so many others that joined them in subsequent years[94] served as places for worship and for the ministration of the sacramental life of the Church, a closer look at the makeup of both Catholic devotional life and the structure of Catholic living tells even more about the contribution of the Jesuits—as well as the fiber of the early generations of English colonial Catholics.

American Colonies, including John Carroll, who was to become the first bishop in the United States, met here, and it was here also in 1833 that the Maryland Province of the Society of Jesus was first established. Archbishop Carroll's successor, Archbishop Leonard Neale, brother of Father Francis Neale, lived nearby; another brother, Father Charles Neale, was instrumental in settling the first convent of Carmelite Nuns within the parish boundaries. In later years, slave quarters and a Catholic cemetery were located near the Manor House; most of the cemetery's tombstones were destroyed when Union Soldiers camped there during the Civil War and used them for target practice. The Jesuit Cemetery, located by the side of the present church, dates from 1794.

93 Beitzell, *The Jesuit Missions of St. Mary's County*, 39. Beitzell gives a rather detailed account of the school's faculty for several decades of its existence.

94 Examples in St. Mary's County: Our Lady's, Medley's Creek, 1776; St. Joseph's, Morganza, 1700; Sacred Heart, Bushwood, 1755; St. Francis de Sales, 1785; from Charles County: St. Peter's, Waldorf, 1700; St. Joseph's, Pomfret, 1763; St. Ignatius, Bel Alton, 1641; the Carmelite Monastery, La Plata, 1790; St. Mary's, Newport, 1695; St. Mary's, Bryantown, 1795; from Calvert County: St. John's, Hollywood, 1690; St. Aloysius, Leonardtown, 1710.

Distinctively Catholic Settlements

The chapels on the estates of gentry Catholics grew more numerous as the seventeenth century gave way to the eighteenth. Soon parishes sprung up, which the Jesuits served as itinerant missionaries. One such member of the Society who had grown up near one of the "stations" served by the Jesuits of Newtown was John Mattingly. His memory of the activities of the clergy describes a scene enacted many times in many locales:

> On Sundays and feast days they go to minister at various stations, called "congregations," at a distance of 10, 15, or even more than twenty miles, all widely scattered. In this manner in each station at least once a month they celebrate Mass, administer the sacraments, and preach the word of God; in the main stations they do this two or more times a month, depending on the numbers and … the needs of the faithful.… From very early in the morning until 11 o'clock, they hear confession. Then they celebrate Mass, and distribute Holy Communion. At the end of Mass there is a sermon, in which the priest explains Christian doctrine.

Jesuit Father Joseph Mosley explained to his sister:

> I allow our fatigues are very great, our journeys very long, our rides constant and extensive. We have many to attend, and few to attend them. I often ride about 300 miles a week, and never a week but I ride 150 or 200: and in our way of living, we ride almost as much by night as by day, in all weathers, in heat, cold, rain, frost or snow. Several may think the colds, rains, &c, to be the worst to ride in; but, I think to ride in the heats far surpasses all, both for man and horse.[95]

[95] Both references cited in Curran, *Papist Devils*, 178–179.

Mass would be offered, of course, entirely in Latin, with the priest facing *ad orientem*, with his back to the people. He would offer the Mass silently while his congregation would assist by reciting the Rosary privately or by the pious recitation of prayers from one of the many Catholic devotional manuals prominent at the time. Sermons would be catechetical lessons focusing on the doctrines of the Faith explained in simple fashion. In a sense they were meant to be apologetical tools for the hostile environment Catholics found around them. Following Mass, the people would recite novena prayers of one sort or another or possibly the prayers of Vespers, and all would conclude with Benediction of the Blessed Sacrament. Following this, catechetical instructions would be given to the children and instructions on marriage would be given to young couples. Often, in certain mission stations, adoration of the Blessed Sacrament was also encouraged. At Chapel Point, the Society for Perpetual Adoration of the Blessed Sacrament was established in 1768, with members pledging to spend a certain amount of time in adoration of Our Lord's Real Presence in the Eucharist.

A unique aspect of Jesuit spirituality was the idea of the sodality, or gathering of faithful men or women, for a common purpose. One such sodality in honor of the Sacred Heart was especially popular in Southern Maryland, as was one dedicated to adoration of the Blessed Sacrament. In the former, one could see the "private nature of Maryland Catholicism," with individual love of the Heart of Christ being stressed; in the latter, one could see "a communal form of devotion taking place in the domestic or public chapel."[96]

In addition, Jesuit lending libraries, usually found in manor houses run by the Society, were very popular. Catholic colonists

[96] Ibid., 183.

could take books for a time and then return them, just as we do today. The books were often apologetic texts or lives of the saints.

If there were not sufficient missionaries to go around—some areas waited several weeks for a priest—Catholic families were expected to gather together for prayers, for the mutual discussion of an agreed-upon book, or for other devotions. Following the English liturgical calendar, they were expected to keep a large number of Holy Days of obligation throughout the year: This meant they were obliged to follow the contemporary strict laws of fast and abstinence. Mitigating factors, such as the obligatory work of tobacco farmers, allowed for some leeway in fasting and the obligation to rest on Sundays, but modern Catholics would find the seventeenth-century regulations much more demanding than today's. Church authorities in England were aware of the hardships of the colonists in this regard, and so obligations were, in time, moderated.

This was the sort of Catholic life colonists experienced almost from the beginning; it was to be a life that both grew with and was challenged by political and cultural events of the late-seventeenth and early-eighteenth centuries. Colonial life would often test the fiber of these souls. In some cases, trials strengthened an already firm faith; in others, there was a falling away that took its toll on succeeding generations.

Chapter 6

Political and Religious Life in Maryland from the Restoration to the Glorious Revolution

Conditions improved for Catholics in Maryland following the collapse of the Cromwellian regime and the restoration of the Stuart monarchy. Charles II, whose father had been executed not too many years earlier, arrived in London to assume the English throne in May 1660. The newly elected Parliament, intensely royalist in its sentiments, declared that the new government should be headed by a king, and both houses soundly approved the new monarch. The crowning in Westminster Abbey was so crowded, according to diarist Samuel Pepys, that he had to assume his seat seven hours before the beginning of the ceremony. This is an indication of the true nature of British sentiment—that the restoration was a return to normalcy that many were convinced would occur.

Changing Circumstances in England and America

Charles was almost immediately confronted with the Great Fire of London, which destroyed thirteen thousand homes and businesses within the city and left one hundred thousand homeless. It would take much effort not just to rebuild London but to restart everyday life, but the king faithfully promised the citizenry that he would construct a new, magnificent city on the ashes. Within two years of his accession, he married the devoutly Catholic princess Catherine of Braganza, daughter of the king of Portugal; the Catholic ceremony was conducted privately and followed by the public Church of England pageantry. Charles did not lead a particularly moral life, however, fathering a number of illegitimate children—but his queen remained loyal to her husband throughout their marriage.

Besides matters at home, Charles II was faced with a new set of circumstances in America: His reign saw the beginnings of the colonies in New York, New Jersey, and the Carolinas—as well as William Penn's Holy Experiment in religious toleration in the colony of Pennsylvania. Over a quarter century, Charles would witness the unforeseen political and economic maturation of his transatlantic subjects:

> From one colony in 1607 [the number of British colonies] rose to twenty-five after 1713, and thirty-three after 1763; and as these colonies advanced rapidly in wealth and prosperity, they formed habits of self reliance and developed methods of government that were in many ways more free, more individual, and less stereotyped than were those prevailing in the mother country at the same time. Secondly, in her foreign relations, Great Britain was confronted with a constantly shifting international situation that presented new obligations and new perplexities, and demanded frequent enlargements and alterations of policy to enable her to meet, with efficiency and dispatch, the various emergencies that arose. And, thirdly, the British Constitution itself was undergoing far reaching changes in form and spirit: much that was old was giving way to much that was new, old powers became vested in new hands, and authority in

matters that concerned administration and control was often transient and uncertain.[97]

What is clearly traceable from the beginning of the Restoration, and that would continue to the American Revolution, is England's transformation from a commercial to a political empire—a mercantile to an imperial nation. Her relations with her colonies—and theirs with her—would, for the next century, reflect this change. In 1660, the passing of the Navigation Acts signaled this shift. The object of the law was to protect British shipping against competition from Holland and other competitors. No goods could be brought into or taken out of any British colony in Asia, Africa, or America except in British vessels—that is, vessels that were English owned and whose crews were at least three-quarter British natives. Further, Asian, African, or American products coming into England could be brought only in English ships. The result was to give Englishmen and their ships a legal monopoly of all trade between colonial ports and home country.

Also, certain colonial products—such as tobacco, sugar, indigo, cotton, wool, ginger, and various dyewoods—could be exported from their place of production only to England or one of her other colonies. This list was extended to naval stores, hemp, rice, molasses, beaver skins, furs, copper ore, iron, and lumber. These "enumerated clauses" of the Navigation Acts were enforced by a system of bonds that required each ship's master to comply with the particulars of the system.

The Trade Acts, passed a few decades later, were another component of this system. Parliament envisioned that the comprehensive

[97] Charles M. Andrews, *The Colonial Background of the American Revolution* (New Haven, CT: Yale University Press, 1924), 69. In citing these facts, Andrews is including far more than the British Colonies along the Atlantic Seaboard.

mercantilist system would ensure the prosperity of the whole British Empire, with each section complementing the other. So long as these pieces of legislation were limited to the regulation of trade and commerce, they were generally popular in America; the attempt to use them as taxation measures, however, was strongly resisted.[98]

Against this background, Charles II restored proprietary rights in Maryland to Cecil Calvert, who appointed his son Charles as governor and instructed him to reinstate religious toleration. While all seemed well on the surface, the Calvert form of governing had begun to be seen as autocratic, and many were not as pleased as they might have been if earlier members of the family had proceeded more tactfully. Charles would govern until his father's death in 1675; during this time, Catholicism expanded in the Maryland Colony and extended beyond its borders to the neighboring colony of Virginia.

Catholicism Crosses the Border

The Brent family made the journey from England to Maryland, and then to the Old Dominion. The family's origins at Lark Stoke in Gloucestershire begin, for our purposes with the life and career of Richard Brent and his daughter Catherine, who was the first in the family to embrace the Catholic Faith. She, in turn, convinced her parents and her siblings to follow her example. Catherine then informed her father of her desire to enter religious life. He consented, not only to her entrance, but that of her sister Elizabeth as well, and the two entered the Benedictine Community of Our Lady of Consolation, an English Abbey at Cambrai in the Low

[98] Wayne Andrews, ed., *Concise Dictionary of American History* (New York: Charles Scribner's Sons, 1962), 645–646.

Countries. Some five years later, they were joined there by a third sister, Eleanor.[99]

Shortly before the outbreak of the English Civil War, four of Richard Brent's children had emigrated to Colonial Maryland. Of these, Giles would become particularly significant; he was appointed a member of the governor's council almost immediately and, sometime after, treasurer of the colony. His two sisters, Margaret and Mary, rather conspicuously for those times, assumed active roles in colonial life.

> For ten turbulent years Giles Brent remained in Maryland. Exhibiting a fondness for litigation and a determination to maintain his property rights, which proved characteristic of the family both in England and in Virginia, he acquired a manor on Kent Island in Chesapeake Bay and sought to enlarge his acres by a marriage, probably in 1644, with the elder daughter of the Tayac, or Emperor, of the Piscataway tribe. Brent argued that she was her father's heiress, but Indian laws of descent, proving different from those of England, [made it possible for] a distant male relation [to succeed] on the Tayac's death. Not only was Brent's estate not improved, it was soon diminished in the rising which began

[99] Little is recorded of these three Brent sisters. The first two, Catherine and Elizabeth, made their religious profession on August 15, 1629. Catherine took the religious name of Christina, and was twice abbess of the community. Eleanor would take the religious name Helen. A Benedictine monk from Yorkshire, Laurence Lodowik, died at Lark Stoke in 1633 and very likely had served as chaplain in Richard Brent's household. If so, he would have been the influence leading the young women not only into religious life, but also into his specific community. In 1652 Elizabeth Brent, with several other nuns, left Cambrai for Paris, where they founded the English convent of Our Lady of Hope.

in Maryland in 1645. Captured by the insurgents and carried as a prisoner to England, he secured his release and made his way back to Maryland. About 1650, however, after a bitter quarrel with the Calverts, which climaxed several years of disputes, he removed to Virginia and established himself on a wilderness plantation near the mouth of Aquia Creek.[100]

A curious aspect of this story is a piece of legislation passed in Virginia in 1642 that directly penalized Catholics in a number of areas. Any Catholic who failed to attend services in the established Anglican church was fined twenty pounds monthly once the court determined them to be guilty of recusancy.[101] The same court might insist on a Catholic's taking the Oath of Allegiance, and, on his refusal, imprison him for life and confiscate his goods and property. Religious acts were also prohibited: No Catholic could assist at Mass or receive the sacraments without incurring substantial fines. Fines were also given to those who hired a tutor to instruct their children in the rudiments of the Catholic Faith; if parents sought to get around this restriction by sending their children to Catholic schools on the Continent, they were to be deprived of their property and imprisoned for life.[102] So, why were the Catholic Brents left alone? Why did the bill's particulars seem not to affect them?

[100] Bruce E. Steiner "The Catholic Brents of Colonial Virginia: An Instance of Practical Toleration," *Virginia Magazine of History and Biography* 70, no. 4 (October 1962): 393–394.

[101] The term, carried over from England, simply meant a refusal to attend or pay tithes to the established church. Such English Catholic families, usually of great means, were usually left alone in these matters, particularly those who lived on manors and estates at considerable distance from London.

[102] The act can be read in full in Ellis, *Documents*, 113–114.

> At first glance the freedom enjoyed by the Brent family might, indeed, appear inexplicable. But practical considerations had modified the harsh penal statutes in their operation even in those infrequent times when they were carefully enforced in England, and practical considerations likewise determined that anti-Catholic laws should not be enforced against the first Virginia Brents. As in England so in Virginia: the letter of the law was not an accurate measure of Catholic restriction. Public service as guardians of the frontier, relative isolation on the fringes of settlement, important ties with fellow gentry, and an unobtrusive practice of their religion all operated together to secure for the Brents a practical, limited, but very real toleration. [103]

The Brents became the most northern settlers in the colony. Giles Brent had a knowledge of military organization from his young days in England, and a deeply anti-Calvert bias. As such, he could prove useful to Virginia authorities in the event of an invasion from Maryland forces. Further, the Brents brought many new settlers into Virginia and provided needed supplies to many others who were settling on the Virginia frontier . Not given to any missionary spirit, Giles did not force his religious views on his fellow settlers. These factors accounted for their peace, and, in time, prosperity.

The Northern Neck of the Old Dominion—the peninsula bounded on the north by the Potomac River and on the south by the Rappahannock—soon became peopled with arrivals from other colonies and from Europe. As the population grew, certain individuals became more concerned with who was or, more pertinently, *was not* attending Anglican services. Fortunately, this did

[103] Steiner, "The Catholic Brents," 396.

not have to concern Giles, whose death in the winter of 1671–1672 brought the first generation of Virginia Brent settlers to a close. Prudent as he had learned to become, his will was worded in such a way that it requested that "three thousand pounds of good tobacco with cask are to be given ... to my executors unto pious uses where and unto whom they shall see fit for which doing and how and for whom I Will that to none else but God they shall be accountable.[104] He was also willing that Masses be offered for the repose of his soul.

Headship of the family passed to his son, Giles Brent II. He was part English gentleman, part Piscataway Indian. Raised on the Virginia frontier since childhood, he could speak the Indian language with fluency. He succeeded his father as a captain of the colonial militia; at the time of his death, he had reached the rank of colonel. He moved freely in Virginia society, did not hide his Catholicism, and married his cousin Mary Brent—but, at her request, the two were judicially separated because of his cruelty. His death at age twenty-seven left his widow and several children.

Leadership of the Brents of Stafford County now passed once again to a branch of the family at Woodstock, Virginia, headed by George Brent, nephew of Giles, Margaret, and Mary. George had come to Virginia in 1673 from Worcestershire, England and developed his Woodstock Plantation near his Stafford relatives. He took up the practice of law with one William Fitzhugh, a devout Anglican, who appears not to have minded having a Catholic partner. George's brother Robert Brent joined him in 1686, and the two, in time, enjoyed a lucrative law practice in several Virginia counties.

In England, the Catholic James II had succeeded to the throne in 1685, and colonial penal laws were suspended, making the various troubling oaths unnecessary. In such a climate, the governor of

[104] Ibid., 398.

Virginia, Lord Howard of Effingham, was able to appoint George Brent his receiver general for colonial taxation in the area north of the Rappahannock River. Following this, his fellow landowners chose him to become one of the county's representatives in the Virginia Assembly.

In a spirit of religious toleration, which so often characterized Catholicism in the colonial period, Brent and others were open to a plan to settle a group of French Huguenots—the Reformed Protestants who had attracted the ire of the Catholic monarchy—on a large tract of Virginia land. Little came of the plan, however, since, in the end, the Huguenots themselves seemed minimally inclined to migrate; in England the toppling of the Stuarts and the permanent ensconcing of Protestantism made the European climate less hostile. These events brought, at the same time, a certain foreboding to Catholics in Virginia, the Brents in particular:

> Since 1682 the politics of Stafford County had been marked by a bitter feud between Tories led by William Fitzhugh and Whigs commanded by George Mason II and the Reverend John Waugh. George Brent as a Tory, business partner and close friend of William Fitzhugh had naturally taken part in the quarrel: he sat in the 1688 Assembly as the elected candidate of the Stafford Tory faction. In the early months of 1689, when reports of the happenings in England gave rise to rumors of a Papist invasion from Maryland, Waugh and his lieutenants (whose following seems to have come from the idle and ignorant elements in Stafford) saw a chance to strike down their political enemies.... [A] story was concocted that the Catholics of Maryland, supported by the Seneca Indians and captained by George Brent, were plotting to take over Stafford. Fearing for their lives, the Protestant farmers of Stafford sprang to arms and made for

> Woodstock, Parson Waugh leading the way. Members of the Council, sensing the political motivation behind the agitation, now intervened to avert serious trouble. Brent was ordered to Fitzhugh's house for safety.... For some months Stafford was a scene of disorder, but quiet was eventually restored.[105]

George Brent survived this scare and went on to live until 1699. Strangely enough, some years later, his brother Robert served as lawyer for Reverend John Waugh in a legal dispute. The Brents remained a socially prestigious family, largely not interfered with in religious matters. Through the years, Mass was offered at Woodstock at least occasionally. At the time of the Glorious Revolution in England, when things again became difficult for colonial Catholics, a complaint was made by a Protestant insurgent in Maryland to the Virginia Council requesting the apprehension of enemies of William and Mary, the newly enthroned Protestant monarchs. Among those cited was a Franciscan priest, Richard Hobart, who, it was claimed could be found "at his Popish patrons, Mr. Brent's in Stafford County."[106]

George Brent's death marked the close of the family's public activity in Virginian affairs. William Brent of Richland, grandson of Giles Brent II had been raised an Anglican and filled several offices in the eighteenth century. His Woodstock cousins, however, remained true to the Faith and lived quietly, if not elegantly.

Across the Chesapeake

In addition to Virginia, the mid- and late-seventeenth century also witnessed Catholic expansion on Maryland's Eastern Shore.

[105] Ibid., 404.
[106] Ibid., 407.

The times were ripe for such expansion: By 1669, King Charles II had confided to his wife his wish to be reconciled to the Catholic Church. Though it would be some time in coming, he did make certain concessions, including a "Declaration of Indulgence for Tender Consciences," suspending all laws against those who refused to take the Oath of Supremacy. English Catholics at this time accounted for only one-fifth of the population, yet the more than 250 Jesuit priests working in England were able to move about freely, in spite of the very stringent laws remaining on the books. In 1671, Charles's brother, James, Duke of York, openly proclaimed himself a Catholic, and in a very public Catholic ceremony two years later married Mary of Modena, a devout Catholic woman.

If Catholics in England were only one-fifth of the population, those in Colonial Maryland numbered no more than one-twelfth. Of these, a great many lived around the Wye, Miles, and Choptank Rivers east and south of Kent Island—so many, in fact, that the population warranted the founding of a new county, Talbot, named in honor of Cecil Calvert's sister, Grace, wife of Robert Talbot of County Kildare, Ireland. The Wye River basin became an enclave for numerous Catholic families.

> Henrietta Maria Neale was the eldest child of Captain James Neale, one of Lord Baltimore's chief lieutenants. Her father and mother were personal friends of King Charles II and his brother, the future King James II. The Neales made their principal home at Wallston Manor in Charles County. A number of families of high rank also settled around Neale Sound and, as gentry of the colony, lived rich and gracious lives on their vast estates. The Neale children were all born and baptized in Spain and were naturalized as citizens of Maryland in 1666.... Richard Bennett, a Puritan like his father, and Henrietta Maria Neale were married in 1665.

> They made their home at Pitney Point on the back Wye River, near the home of Major Peter and Frances Sayer, another prominent Catholic family.[107]

Bennett died at an early age, and Henrietta Maria married Philemon Lloyd, a Protestant, who, while tolerant of his wife's staunch Catholicism, insisted their children be raised Protestant. She agreed to his request, though their sons subsequently, through marriage, continued the Catholic connection for later generations. Following Lloyd's death,

> Madame Lloyd lived for a dozen years, managing the estate at Wye House and supervising the education of her children. Her background, wealth and beauty dazzled those who might otherwise have snubbed her for her open espousal of Catholicism. Until her death she continued to support the priests' activities with gifts of cash and land. Her nephew, the son of Anthony Neale and Elizabeth Digges, became the Reverend Bennett Neale, who lived through the American Revolution. The Neale family gave several other sons and daughters to careers in the church, notably Leonard Neale, the second Archbishop of Baltimore. Around 1675 the first Catholic Church on the peninsula was built on Morgan-Sayer property adjoining "Wye Town" at Peter Sayer's Morgan's—St. Michael's, with Father Nicholas Gulick, S.J. as the first resident pastor. Madame Lloyd attended and supported the church, and in her will left three hundred acres near the chapel "for the use and benefit of the Chapel at Wye." Her resolute faith was praised by [one] historian who said of her "She threw over the Roman Catholic priests

[107] Thomas J. Peterman, *Catholics in Colonial Delmarva* (Devon, PA: Cooke Publishing, 1996), 92.

> the protection of her long social standing in Maryland on both shores and no Archbishop could have been more of a stay and prop to American Catholicism than this estimable woman."[108]

Finally, the legacy of the Sewall family on the Eastern Shore is notable. After the restoration of the Calvert family's proprietary rights in 1660, Charles Calvert, who had married Mary Darnall of Herefordshire, England, migrated with his wife to Maryland. Henry Sewall of London accompanied them as Calvert's secretary. The Sewalls were themselves of a distinguished Catholic family in Coventry, in the county of Warwick. When the new governor arrived at St. Mary's City in 1663, he was feted with a grand reception given by his uncle, Philip Calvert, and shortly thereafter made an extensive tour of the Eastern Shore. Henry Sewall, along with his wife—the former Jane Lowe—and their three children accompanied Charles Calvert and, prior to their departure, were given an estate on the Patuxent River. The Sewalls soon became part of Maryland's upper class; next to Philip and Charles Calvert, Henry was the most influential man in colonial affairs. Calvert made grants of land on the Eastern Shore to "my secretary" in 1664 in what is now Dorchester County.

> Near the head of Secretary Creek (now called Warwick River), which is a tributary of the Great Choptank, Henry Sewall is said to have built a one-and-a-half story brick, gable-roofed manor house, which was known until the last third of this century as "My Lady Sewall's Manor House." Though their permanent residence was in St. Mary's County at Mattapony, the Sewalls are thought to have used this as an alternative home, and Nicholas Sewall, the son, may

[108] Ibid., 94–95.

> have made his chief residence there after his exile as a Catholic in 1689. . . . The house was purchased by the Diocese of Wilmington in 1927 and survives today, with an historical marker, as the rectory for Our Lady of Good Counsel Parish, Secretary, Maryland.[109]

The Glorious Revolution in England and Maryland

After a reign of a quarter century, Charles II's life ended in 1685. Though he had procrastinated for years, he died a Catholic, apparently finding peace by listening to his conscience:

> King Charles II died on 6 February, 1685. On his deathbed he secretly converted to the Catholicism espoused by his wife and feared by his subjects. He was severely unwell for four days after suffering a stroke, but maintained his good humor and before he died made his peace with his queen and many illegitimate offspring. Queen Catherine, who had loved him powerfully throughout his years of philandering, sat patiently with him during the illness, but was absent at the end because she grieved so fiercely. When she sent an apology for not being present, the King exclaimed, "Alas, poor woman. She begs my pardon? I beg hers with all my heart!"[110]

The Whig Party had long been fearful of the ascendancy of Charles's brother James II because of his unabashed Catholicism. Various plots to prevent this outcome had been hatched, all of which were unsuccessful. James was crowned in Westminster Abbey in April 1685, and immediately had to deal with Protestant

[109] Ibid., 104–105.

[110] Charles Phillips, *The Illustrated Encyclopedia of Royal Britain*, 165.

challenges to his authority. Charles's illegitimate son, the Duke of Monmouth, and later the staunchly Protestant Earl of Argyll both launched campaigns of significance, only to be thwarted. In the brief years of his reign, James II instituted religious toleration, began promoting Catholics to positions of authority in the privy council, and made public statements that seemed to indicate, at least in the minds of some of his enemies, his desire to restore Catholicism as the official religion of the state. After his wife, Queen Mary, gave birth to a son in 1688, these fears became even more pronounced. The king reissued the "Declaration of Indulgence," and when the archbishop of Canterbury and six Anglican bishops asked him to withdraw the order, he had them put in the Tower of London and tried for seditious libel.

Although the churchmen were acquitted of the charge, the event marked a shift in public opinion against the monarch. Crowds cheered in London streets when they were released, and on the same day, seven leading Protestant noblemen wrote to Prince William of Orange—husband of Mary, the king's eldest daughter by his first marriage, to Anne Hyde—and asked him to lead an invasion from the Netherlands to secure Protestantism as the religion of the realm. The result of that request has been known ever since as the Glorious Revolution. Leading a sizeable army, James had to retreat on two occasions and ultimately fled to France, where he was apprehended and returned to London. He escaped once again to France at the close of 1688.

William and Mary jointly succeeded to the throne in February 1689, not by royal succession, but by the decision of both houses of Parliament—the first time such had occurred in British history. They ruled as constitutional monarchs—over the objections of some in the House of Lords who favored the concept of absolute monarchy and felt that Mary, as James II's daughter, should rule alone. In any event, after a mere five years, Mary died an untimely death, and William, so overcome with grief, could not issue a reply to Parliament when offered condolences by the members. William truly felt that God was punishing him for an extramarital affair he had carried on for years. He would rule alone for six more years, when the death of the young Prince William of Gloucester, son of Princess Anne and grandson of James II, put the Protestant succession in some question once again. Though Anne did become queen upon the death of William, setting the stage for a contested succession the next time around, Parliament stepped in and passed the Act of Settlement, which stated that the next heir was to be Sophia, Electress of Hanover and the daughter of Charles I's sister Elizabeth and her husband Fredrick V, the Elector Palatinate. All those relationships might be confusing, but the upshot is this: Such legislation made it very clear that ultimate power was now in Parliament, including the choosing of the monarch. Anne would reign over what most historians view as very successful years for the burgeoning British Empire.

In Maryland the Glorious Revolution left Catholics with a feeling of foreboding that proved to be warranted. The anti-Catholic backlash took the form of Coode's Rebellion, named for its leader John Coode, a former Anglican Minister who had migrated to the colony in 1672. He has been described as "clubfooted, with a face that a sheriff's warrant once described as 'resembling that of a baboon or monkey', he was quick tempered, boastful, and resentful of all authority."[111] Despite his intense anti-Catholicism, he married the daughter of a leading Catholic, Thomas Gerrard, whose landholdings quickly made him a major figure in the colony. When news of the Glorious Revolution reached Maryland, Coode gathered around him a group calling themselves the

[111] Brugger, *Maryland*, 36.

Associators.[112] They purported to rule the colony in the name of King William, forcing the members of the council to take refuge in one of the large plantations and to promise, for their future safety, that no Catholics would henceforth hold political office in the province.

> The Associators, after establishing themselves in power, proceeded to threaten, plunder and imprison all citizens who attempted in any way to oppose them—Protestant and Catholic alike. They petitioned the Protestant King William to take the government of the Province into his own hands, a proposition most pleasing to the King, who approved the revolutionary action of the Associators, but ordered them to await his further commands.... The Charter was vacated on the ground of "political necessity," and on June 27, 1691, a commission was issued to Sir Lionel Copley to be the first Royal Governor of Maryland. Thus Coode and Cheseldyne, who had gone to England to plead the case of the "Associators", were entirely successful despite the petitions of many of the leading Protestants of the Province.[113]

Another scene captures poignantly events in the mother country:

> Coode styled himself commander and chief of the Protestant Associators, whose spokesman issued a high-sounding "Declaration of the reasons and motive for the present appearing in arms of His Majesties Protestant Subjects in the

[112] All non-Catholics, they included Kenylm Cheseldyne and Nehemiah Blakiston of St. Mary's, Henry Jowles and Ninian Beale of Calvert, and John Addison and John Courts of Charles County.

[113] Beitzell, *The Jesuit Missions of St. Mary's County*, 43.

> Province of Maryland." The manifesto listed the grievances that long had divided the proprietor and so many of his people, declared allegiance to the new monarchs, William and Mary, and prayed them to take Maryland under their protection. Armed and resolute, members of the Association marched toward St. Mary's City, gathering strength all the way.... Proprietary government fell virtually without a shot.[114]

The loss of the colonial charter and of the Calverts' proprietary rights in Maryland marked the end of any official religious toleration. Shortly after Lionel Copley assumed power, the first act of the assembly was an official recognition of William and Mary as monarchs, which included thanking them for "redeeming us from the arbitrary will and pleasure of a tyrannical popish government under which we have so long groaned."[115] The Anglican church became the established church of Maryland; every county was divided into parishes; and annual taxes were imposed on all citizens for the support and upkeep of the established church. The first colonial legislation in 1692 attempting to establish Anglicanism did not actually receive royal approval, and the following year, the king ruled that liberty of conscience should be extended to all. One year later, however, the colonial government submitted another bill that did receive royal sanction, and Anglicanism did become the official religion in the colony until the American Revolution.

Under the new regime, Catholic attorneys were disbarred and all Catholics were prohibited from holding any official position in the province. Most stringent of all was the 1704 *Act to Prevent the Growth of Popery*, which made it a penal offense for Catholics to practice their religion, for priests to offer Mass publicly, and for

114 Brugger, *Maryland*, 39.

115 Beitzell, *The Jesuit Missions of St. Mary's County*, 43.

Catholics to maintain schools or teach children. In later years, Queen Anne, seeing the unjust nature of this act, permitted priests to say Mass in private chapels. Under these conditions once again the custom developed of erecting chapels in manor houses or adjacent to the homes of wealthier Catholics; these chapels, called Mass houses, continued to function until the revolutionary era. Even the Jesuits operated under a great deal of pressure, writing in their annual letter to the provincial in England that "great difficulties are suffered. Our Fathers yet remain to render what consolation they can to the distressed Catholics."[116]

As the eighteenth century began, the lot of Catholics seemed rather dim—but still no one creed had emerged decisively victorious:

> Although the Revolution in Maryland had been a distinct triumph for Protestants, the Protestant majority was far from united, even in its attitude toward the revolution that had occurred. It is impossible to speak in any but the most general terms regarding the religious affiliations of the people. Many doubtless were nominal Anglicans in the sense that they had no fixed allegiance to one of the dissenting sects or to the Roman Catholic Church, but an Anglican minister had reported to Canterbury in 1676 that there were only three Anglican priests in the entire province. Baltimore himself had replied for a subsequent request for information by declaring that three-fourths of his people were Presbyterian, Independents, Anabaptists and Quakers, which at this time in English history was to say little more than that they were a varied assortment of dissenters.[117]

[116] Cited in ibid., 44.

[117] Wesley Frank Craven, *The Colonies in Transition* (New York: Harper and Row, 1968), 274.

Chapter 7

Eighteenth-Century Religious and Political Life in Maryland

Somber as things were for Catholics at the beginning of the eighteenth century, particularly with the passage of the 1704 anti-Catholic laws, there were some bright spots, especially on Maryland's Eastern Shore. Until now the only educational endeavor of the Jesuits had been at St. Francis Xavier at Newtown in St. Mary's County. But in 1704, they took steps toward expanding their educational mission by establishing St. Xaverius Mission in Cecil County, located a significant distance northeast of Annapolis, now the colonial capital. The school, however, would have to wait some four decades for the initial planning to become a reality.

The Expansion of Jesuit Education

Father Thomas Poulton has traditionally been credited with starting Old Bohemia Academy in the 1740s. At least one reason for the increased enthusiasm to open such a school was a significant event in Scotland. In 1745, Charles Edward Stuart—known to many as Bonnie Prince Charlie, the grandson of James II and the last Catholic King of England—made an abortive attempt to regain the British Crown at the Battle of Culloden, with an army of about two thousand. Easily thwarted, all Stuart hopes of recapturing power died that day.[118] A shipload of largely Catholic political prisoners who had survived the battle made the voyage to Oxford on Maryland's Eastern Shore in 1747. Many were enrolled in the Jesuits' new enterprise, and as the school's numbers increased, the student body included several from the more prominent Catholic families in the colony:

> The earliest students were Daniel Carroll II and James Reynolds.... Daniel Carroll II was a member of the Maryland Catholic gentry. His father had married Eleanor Darnall, daughter of Henry Darnall II. Daniel Carroll II prepared at Bohemia for an education abroad and left there in 1742 for six years of study on the Continent.... He became prominent in the political life of the new nation after the Revolution, was a framer of the American Constitution, and served as a Commissioner for the new District of Columbia before his death in 1796. James Reynolds was the son of a farmer in New Castle County, Delaware.... [He] took only the basic course at Bohemia and returned to the farm, where, during and after his schooling he helped his father. He inherited Eleanor's Delight from his father, and continued to farm it until his death in 1787.... Two cousins of the Reynolds ... enrolled as students were Matthew and Peter Lowber, both from farms in Kent County, Delaware. Their grandfather, Peter Lowber, a Catholic from Amsterdam, Holland, had purchased land near Dover in 1684.... Two students were from

[118] Charles Edward escaped to France, the nation that had always supported his family and their claims. In this instance, King Louis XV denied him any aid, clearly seeing that the family's political power had long since ended. Charles Edward died in 1788, leaving no offspring. Priest brother Henry was made a cardinal and lived for many years in Rome. The two brothers, along with their father, James, lie in a tomb in St. Peter's at the Vatican.

> nearby Worsell Manor, James and Daniel Charles Heath. The Heath brothers were aristocrats, destined to study in Europe. James Heath became a Jesuit in Europe before his father's death, and remained there the remainder of his life; Daniel Charles Heath inherited Worsell Manor.... From Queen Anne's County in Maryland came two other aristocratic students, Bennett and Edward Neale.... Two Neale cousins, Leonard and Charles, are alleged to have received early educations at Bohemia Academy, but are not mentioned in the Account Book.... Rev. Leonard Neale became President of Georgetown University, is credited with the establishment of the Georgetown Visitation Monastery in Georgetown, was consecrated coadjutor-Bishop of Baltimore in 1800, and succeeded to the Archbishopric in 1815.... His brother Charles also studied in Europe, joined the Jesuits, and returned to America with a group of Carmelite nuns to found the first Carmelite Monastery in the United States in Port Tobacco, on the Western Shore of Maryland.[119]

Among this excellent company, by far the most notable student enrolled at Bohemia was John Carroll of Upper Marlborough, Maryland, destined to become the nation's first Catholic bishop.[120]

[119] Rev. Thomas J. Peterman, *Bohemia: A History of St. Francis Xavier Catholic Shrine in Cecil County, Maryland* (Devon, PA: William T. Cooke, 2004), 32–34. During the years Daniel Charles Heath owned Worsell Manor, he once hosted George Washington, who dined and lodged there on May 14, 1773. In his party were Governor Robert Eden of Maryland, and John Parke Custis, Washington's stepson. Governor Eden was en route to Philadelphia, while Washington was taking his stepson to New York to enroll him in King's College, now Columbia University.

[120] Peterman states that there is a tradition, though no documentary evidence, that Archbishop Carroll's cousin, Charles Carroll of Carrollton, the only Catholic signer of the Declaration of

Bohemia was not only an academy but a Jesuit residence and plantation at the same time.[121] As such, Bohemia had many slaves through the years. The Jesuits depended on them both here and at other plantations to man the farms, which provided the income to cover the household, missionary activities of the Fathers, and, in the case of Bohemia, educational expenses. Much Jesuit literature of the time expressed the strong belief that families should not be separated through the slave trade and that all attempts be made for the education of their slaves in the Catholic faith.

> The Jesuit owned estates were managed by priests and the old Jesuit records indicate the considerable manner in which they avoided the terms "slaves" and referred to them usually as "servant men, servant women, negroes and members of the family." Such consideration is an indication of the position these domestics held under the Jesuit management and the moral care taken by them.[122]

The Penal Period and French Newcomers

This is not to say life was without conflict on the Eastern Shore. As the number of Catholics increased, at least one Anglican divine complained of the number of "papists" living within his church boundary, and various newspapers, the *Maryland Gazette* among them, were only too quick to print anti-Catholic editorials aimed at stemming the tide of Catholic immigration into the various counties

---

Independence, also attended Bohemia Academy before going to Europe to study. Ibid., 34.

[121] Jesuits who were at Bohemia in the years following its establishment were Fathers John Digges, James Farrar, Richard Molyneux, and Henry Neale.

[122] Ibid., 36.

of the Eastern Shore and Southern Maryland. Nevertheless, it is apparent that Catholics stood steadfast in the Faith, even if their performance, for whatever reason, seemed less than it should be:

> In spite of the antagonistic legislative environment, Catholicism survived in Maryland—and the Catholic population itself grew more than fivefold throughout the Penal Period—because the people who made up the Catholic community refused not to be Catholic. They did not always attend Mass as frequently as they or their priests would have liked, and they did not always approach their fasting obligations with the reverence and consistency that were required of them by their Church. Very few of Maryland's Catholics ever took the step of renouncing their Catholic Baptism and joining a Protestant denomination, however—even though the gains to be gotten from such a move were substantial—and the fact that many Catholics requested dispensations from their priests before failing to observe a religious obligation testifies to the respect that they still had for the idea of religious obligations, and to the depth to which they identified themselves as Catholics.[123]

After the Act of 1704, one of the severest against Catholics in Maryland's history, chapels in manor houses took on the importance they had in generations past, often with resident priests serving as chaplains for the many who frequented Mass and the sacraments. In the earlier part of the century, Bishop Richard Challoner, vicar apostolic of the Midland District in London, under

[123] Maura Jane Farrelly, *Papist Patriots: The Making of an American Catholic Identity* (New York: Oxford University Press, 2012), 136–137. Farrelly does note five cases of prominent Catholics who apostatized for political gain or social prestige in Maryland. Ibid., 145–148.

whose ecclesiastical jurisdiction the colonies fell, had a census taken that reported that approximately 8,500 of Maryland's 16,000 Catholics received Holy Communion frequently—a goodly number when one considers there were only 18 priests working in Maryland at the time with an average age of more than fifty years, old indeed for the eighteenth century. The bulk of these priests were still to be found in St. Mary's and Charles Counties, as well as on the Eastern Shore.[124] As in years gone by, sodalities and confraternities were active in Jesuit foundations, and the Jesuit lending libraries, begun years earlier, took on a new significance as colonists became more educated and more numerous.[125]

The final and very conspicuous addition to Catholicism in Maryland in this century was the arrival of the French Acadians. A great many of Maryland's Catholics were quite wealthy, so it was relatively easy for them to settle these Catholic refugees in a certain degree of comfort. The Acadians were the victims of the Seven Years' War, known in the United States as the French and Indian War, between France and England. By the terms of the Treaty of Utrecht, ending the hostilities, France ceded Acadia (present-day Nova Scotia, New Brunswick, and Maine) to England. The British

[124] In Southern Maryland such names as " Boarman, Carroll, Darnall, Digges, Greene, Neale, Rozer, Sewall, Slye, and Van Sweringen were most conspicuous.

[125] The works most often read by eighteenth century Catholics were: *The Three Conversions of England* by the English Jesuit Robert Parsons; *The Touchstone of the Reformed Gospel* by Matthew Kellison, in which major tenets of Protestantism are refuted; Joseph Mumford's *The Plea of the Roman Catholics*; Robert Manning's *The Shortest Way to End Disputes about Religion*; and Richard Challoner's *The Catholic Christian Instructed*. Finally, Challoner's *The Garden of the Soul*, a book of devotions which opened with a summary of Catholic doctrine and continued with numerous devotional and prescribed prayers. See ibid., 159–160.

formally removed more than fourteen thousand French-speaking Catholics from their homes, supposedly because of the fear of favoritism for France, but surely due to religious motives as well. Many historians have described this as one of the most inhumane actions taken by the British government of that time. Approximately one-third of the removed Acadians died while aboard prison ships taking them to various destinations. Of the entire number of refugees, nine hundred arrived in Maryland in 1756. Due to their upheaval and their French language, these newcomers were clannish; it took many years for them to become accustomed and integrated into their new environment.

Rumblings of Revolution

The eighteenth century also saw much change in the British monarchy. The Act of Settlement passed in 1701 was quite clear that on the death of Queen Anne, the crown would pass to the Protestant Sophia, Electress of Hanover. As the Queen was nearing death in 1714, many supported the succession of Anne's Stuart half brother James Francis Edward. He was the Catholic son of James II, and on the very day of Anne's death, some were ready to proclaim him king—but, in the end, his partisans acquiesced to their Whig opponents in Parliament in the selection of a Protestant. Sophia had died two months before Anne, and so succession passed to her son, Prince George Louis of Brunswick-Luneburg, who became George I, reigning until 1727. The House of Stuart was finished, and a German line had begun. George was succeeded by his son George II, who reigned until 1760, and then, with the accession of George III, grandson of George II, the country had its first member of the Hanoverian line who was born in England and spoke English without a distinct German accent. With a name change to Windsor, this royal family continues to reign into the twenty-first century.

George III is particularly remembered for ruling during the American Revolution:

> King George III saw it as his duty to maintain the authority and power of the British monarchy, but failed in his struggle to do so. The king, remembered as the ruler who lost Britain's North American colonies, who saw the rise to independence of the United States of America, was increasingly sidelined at home, as powers of government passed to ministers in Parliament. The monarch became a figurehead, who reigned more than he ruled. In his final years, Parliament appointed the Prince of Wales to serve as Regent during his father's mental illness.[126]

The year 1763 has always been considered the beginning of the era of the American Revolution. Maryland and all the other colonies were caught up in political events that would profoundly affect their future and in political sentiments that quickly snowballed to a point of no return.

By 1763, England was the most powerful nation in the world. In order to hold this power together, they had to begin tightening the reins. The national debt had increased to 130 million pounds and the general expenses of running the government multiplied threefold. Land taxes were raised throughout the empire, and a decision was made to station an army in America to safeguard their territory from Indian attacks and invasions from French Canada. All these factors combined to force English officials to wonder: If costs are so high, why should not the colonies pay their fair share? Americans, on the other hand, were already paying church taxes, colonial taxes, and certain imperial taxes; they could not understand why these revenues were not sufficient.

[126] Phillips, *The Illustrated Encyclopedia of Royal Britain*, 195.

By the spring of 1763 the government in London was seriously studying the question of further taxing the colonists. The Treasury board set up commissioners to regulate the customs service in America. These people, known as the British Board of Customs Commissioners (BBC), were not cabinet rank; rather, policy was set by the Treasury board and carried out by the commissioners. The BBC related to Treasury that existing laws were being flagrantly violated and recommended that the custom service should be reorganized for more efficiency and effectiveness. All customs officers were ordered to their posts throughout the empire, and many additional officials such as collectors, controllers, surveyors, tide waiters, land waiters, and so on were appointed. The BBC sent a letter to all colonial governors telling them to enforce the laws or there would be serious consequences.

In the spring of 1764, Prime Minister George Grenville's government introduced the Sugar Act, a very high tax on rum and molasses, and a complete reversal of previous British economic thinking. The act cut in half the import duty on foreign molasses, but provided for strict enforcement; the government wanted to increase revenues and strengthen the already existing Navigation Acts. The old tax was designed to stamp out foreign trade entirely; this one, however, was the first purely revenue-raising tax in the history of the mother country's relationship with her colonies. It was also the first piece of legislation shifting Britain from a mercantile to an imperial system. The mercantile system had been designed to protect merchants, farmers, and manufacturers and was based on the idea that government control would help these stakeholders. Under the imperial system, the government was simply trying to maximize revenue. No clearance could be given to ships going to England unless the entire cargo was headed there; every accusation against a vessel was to be tried in admiralty courts, and the burden of proof was on the owner.

The Sugar Act, as might well be imagined, generated objections, protests, and petitions, especially from New England and New York, whose markets were hardest hit. Opposition was still only local and sporadic, but opponents of the London regime began working on constitutional themes that in a few years would be fully developed arguments. The same year, the Currency Act forbade bills of credit as legal tender. Any governor approving such bills would be fined one thousand pounds and forced to leave office. This act was very unpopular since it forbade any substitution for hard money.

In 1765, the Stamp Act was the first attempt to solve the problem of liberty and order in the relationship between colonists and their home country. It also, of course, emerged because Britain had accumulated an enormous debt and a vast empire. Stamp taxes, which required certain paper products to be produced on special stamped paper, were very much in vogue in England, and some of the colonies themselves had moderate stamp taxes. By May 1764, Grenville was already signaling that he had no intention of allowing the colonies to tax themselves, as some felt he should; he insisted on a tax levied by Parliament and sent a letter to all colonial governors asking for a list of what could legitimately be taxed. The legal controversy was whether Parliament had the right to levy a tax on internal commerce among the colonies, since, in 1765, all the colonies were not royal ones. Meanwhile, colonials living in England immediately began applying for positions as stamp collectors at home—not even beginning to realize how much opposition the act would engender.

The stamp tax would take effect on November 1, 1765, and was imposed on legal and commercial documents, wills, deeds, licenses, leases, mortgages, bonds, insurance policies, playing cards, advertisements, newspapers, magazines, and the like. The tax was to be collected in specie—that is, gold or silver—not local currency.

All offenders were to be tried in the admiralty courts, since these had no juries. Money from the tax was to be spent in the colonies, and all stamps were provided by England. The government hoped to raise sixty thousand pounds, but before any money was collected, an organized opposition developed: The more literate upper class seethed, and colonial newspapers were full of condemnatory editorials.

The most significant protest was the Stamp Act Congress, which met in New York City in October 1765. Three petitions were drawn up: to the King, to the House of Lords, and to the House of Commons. It was too late to set up an effective boycott, so the emphasis was on opposition to the stamp collectors. Some were hanged in effigy while others suffered significant damage to their properties. Non-importation associations sprang up throughout the colonies, declaring that there would be no importation of colonial goods until the Stamp Act was repealed—and the Sugar Act modified, for good measure. This developed into a unified, well-enforced boycott that was felt in England. While the militant Sons of Liberty played an important role in the agitation and protest in each colony, at this point not even the most radical protestors spoke of independence.

After Grenville's deteriorating political situation compelled him to resign, Lord Rockingham formed his new government. By March 1766, London had repealed the Stamp Act and modified the Sugar Act—but, at the same time, passed the Declaratory Act, which stated that Parliament had the right to regulate for the colonies in all cases whatsoever. Some have seen this as a statement of strength developed to save face after acceding to the colonists' demands, but, in fact, for years there had been pressure within the British government to make such a declaration to put the colonists on notice.

The events surrounding the Stamp Act proved to be a unifying force in the colonies, leading to the development of a more sophisticated form of constitutional argumentation. The Congress in New York has been described as a monument to colonial initiative and a moment of unique colonial unity. The atmosphere was made more tense by the passage of the Quartering Act, affecting New York and Halifax, which strongly asserted what colonists had to supply to troops living in their colonies.

The Rockingham ministry fell in the summer of 1766 and was replaced by that of William Pitt, Earl of Chatham, and Augustus FitzRoy, Duke of Grafton. During this time, Charles Townsend became chancellor of the exchequer and proceeded to institute his now-famous duties. Upon Pitt's retirement, Grafton was not up to the task of governing, and so Townsend assumed leadership by default. Townsend had always been an ally of former Prime Minister Grenville, agreeing with him that the American colonies must pay their way. Hence, there would be new custom duties designed to pay for the existence of all colonial officials and America was to receive its own Board of Customs Commissioners who would be present and very active in the colonies. This American Board of Customs Commissioners (ABC) represented, in the minds of many historians, the point of no return for the American colonies.

The ABC was independent of all colonial governors—and let them know it.[127] The commissioners controlled all thirty-two ports, including Bermuda and the Bahamas, and their headquarters were in Boston. They reorganized the customs service, increased the number of lesser offices, and, at one point, wanted to build a coast guard. Had their headquarters been elsewhere than Boston, already a center of opposition to parliamentary authority, there might not have been a revolution.

The commissioners set up a system of "General Letters," sent to each of the individual ports, along with a detailed questionnaire

[127] Its members were Robinson, Hulton, Burch, Paxton, and Temple.

asking for very specific details about their operations. They had inspectors general and an enormous bureaucracy, establishing an elaborate system of books, reports, and so on. Every port was given a copy of everyone else's seal to test for authenticity, and officials in England who discovered smuggling were instructed to write ahead to warn officials in America. The ABC sent details to the home government, especially noting Boston as a hotbed of rebellion; as a result, troops were sent to Boston for the express purpose of putting down any possible revolt.

The ABC tried often to secure writs of assistance, allowing customs officials to search premises for illicit goods, but American courts would not comply; England told them these orders were legal, but, for the most part, courts continued to refuse. The new dispensation increased revenue, taking in thirty thousand pounds annually against thirteen thousand in costs—but at the cost of losing the colonies themselves.

Accelerating Toward Conflict

The Townsend Acts became law in 1767. They were enacted on the colonies solely to raise revenue: taxes were levied on paper, glass, painter's colors, and tea. This was seen as an attempt to undermine the authority of the colonial assemblies; it was a complete abandonment of the mother country's previous mercantile policy. There was not the unified opposition there had been to the Stamp Act, but criticisms were raised in the publication of John Dickenson's *Letters from a Farmer in Pennsylvania to the Inhabitants of the British Colonies*, as well as the *Massachusetts Circular Letter*. Dickenson admitted Parliament's right to regulate trade but denied its right to tax to raise revenue in America; Sam Adams, author of the second document, denounced the duties as violating the principle of no taxation without representation. These two strong statements, along with a program for austerity, all contributed to a powerful uniting of the colonies.

Clashes between citizens and soldiers were not uncommon, especially in Boston, where so much resistance was to be found. An event in March 1770, however, was to have lasting repercussions. Called the Boston Massacre, it began quite simply:

> A fist fight between a worker and soldier at Grey's ropewalk on the afternoon of 5 March quickly became a small riot. That evening belligerent bands of both civilians and soldiers roamed the streets of Boston. The pent up tension exploded about 9 P.M. when a beleaguered sentry in King St. near the State House called the main guard ... to his aid. When the swelling crowd pressed upon this detachment, the soldiers, upon the command of a person never identified, fired into the mob, killing 3 outright and wounding 2 mortally. A general uprising was averted only when Lt. Governor Hutchinson bowed to a demand by Sam Adams and withdrew the troops from the town to islands in the harbor.[128]

There is some evidence that the patriots had organized this confrontation, but the truth remains unknown. The soldiers were all acquitted, except two privates, and even they received "benefit of clergy"—that is, an exemption from the jurisdiction of the American court—and went free.

The non-importation boycott was quite successful; imports dropped one million pounds in one year. Further, revenue from the Townsend Acts did not measure up to the expected forty thousand pounds, producing only slightly more than half of that figure. Townsend himself had died in September 1767 and was succeeded

[128] Richard B. Morris, ed., *Encyclopedia of American History* (New York: Harper and Row, 1965), 79.

by Lord North as chancellor of the exchequer. George III now established personal rule, in which he took on expanded authority and responsibility in the parliamentary structure, and he set up a ministry that was to be led by North. In the spring of 1770, all the Townsend duties were repealed—except that on tea, which was kept purely to maintain the principle that Parliament had the right to legislate in the colonies.

The period from 1771 to 1773 was one of peace and prosperity—the lull before the storm. Colonial merchants seemed quite happy. Meanwhile, though, the always-plotting Sam Adams was setting up committees of correspondence to organize further opposition to London, though it is not certain if even he was thinking in terms of independence at this point. The purpose of the committees was simply to provide information and to ensure cooperation among the colonies.

In May 1773, Parliament passed the Tea Act, not so much to generate revenue as to save the British East India Company—specifically to enable tea dealers to undersell smugglers. The company had to be rescued because of its corrupt and inefficient management; they paid high dividends but at the same time owed great debts to the British government. Many members of Parliament were shareholders, and a general panic was feared if the company went under. The British continued, of course, to export their tea to colonial ports, but the act imposed barriers to non–East India Company importation. When one East India Company ship, eventually joined by two others, came into the port of Boston and refused to turn back, the Sons of Liberty organized the famed Boston Tea Party, dumping some ninety thousand pounds of tea into the Charles River on the night of December 16, 1773. When the news reached England, the Boston Port Bill immediately became law, closing the city's port until the tea was paid for. In addition, a further bill was passed changing the colonial charter: The governor was to appoint and remove all judges; jurors were to be picked by sheriffs; and there were to be no town meetings. A third act passed dealing with unfair trials, and a new quartering act brought additional troops to the city. Once again, this legislation served as a tremendous unifier of the colonists.

There seemed to occur at this point a total transformation of American society:

> Among those who were opposed to extreme measures were the conservatives, British or colonial born, men who were actuated by sentiment rather than principle, were loyal to their oath of allegiance to the King and sincerely believed in the existing constitutional order. They represented all grades of society, rich and poor alike; some held office under the crown and some contented themselves with private life. Secondly, there were the merchants and other members of the propertied class ... whose instincts were conservative, and whose preferences, little influenced by questions of political and constitutional theory, were for friendly co-operation with their fellow merchants of Great Britain in order to preserve a business connection that was profitable to all. Thirdly, there were those, neither bold enough nor reckless enough to court disaster, who opposed a declaration of independence, because they believed that an armed contest with Great Britain would end in defeat and the consequent ruin of the colonies. Among members of all these groups were thousands who were patriotic at heart and devoted to America, whose moderate views were due not to moral cowardice or self-interest only, but to honest convictions and a natural instinct of self-preservation. At the other extreme were the radicals, many of whom ... had banded together as Sons of Liberty. At first these groups

> were composed of moderates and radicals alike, but later, as the movement advanced, only radicals remained, young and fiery souls with none too much respect for constituted authority and intensely antagonistic to all phases of British policy.... Many of the more temperate among them were high-minded, well-educated thoughtful men who ... raised the issue from a mere dispute about money to the dignity of a cosmic event. Others ... were radical by nature, and willing to sacrifice even their property interests for a cause in which they profoundly believed and which they upheld with a vociferousness that often bordered on hysteria.... Still others were born political agitators, gifted with a genius for persuasion, propaganda and organization.... Last of all were those whom the conservatives called the inferior sort, the populace, or the mob, to many of whom the colonies had never granted the right to vote, who bore few of the responsibilities of citizenship, paid a minimum of taxes and were without property or civic obligations.... They were the terrorists of the period, many of whom did their thinking with their muscles.... Their influence lay in their physical ability to override law and order, destroy property and intimidate their enemies.[129]

Much of this description of American society changed drastically in light of the events just described. The First Continental Congress, held in Philadelphia, was the first in a series of steps in the colonial attempt to bring about liberty and order. Catholics, no more than their fellow colonists, were acutely aware of political developments in the decades preceding the revolution, and

[129] Andrews, *The Colonial Background of the American Revolution*, 146–148. Some have seen in Andrews's last description an anti-Catholic reference.

their subsequent response can be understood only in light of this background.

Catholicism in the Revolutionary Consciousness

The delegates who convened in Philadelphia from early September until late October 1774[130] tended to several items of business, including considering a proposal by Pennsylvania's Joseph Galloway for a new political union with the mother country; passing a resolution of "sympathy and approbation" to the Suffolk Resolves of Massachusetts,[131] adopting a *Declaration of Rights*, and forming an association for the implementation of non-importation, non-exportation, and non-consumption regarding trade and commerce with England. Prior to the convention, the Boston Port Bill had been followed by the Administration of Justice Act, protecting crown officials in Massachusetts from major suits before hostile provincial courts, and the Massachusetts Government Act, virtually annulling the Massachusetts Charter. These three pieces of legislation constituted the Coercive Acts, which, when combined with the Quebec Act, became known as the Intolerable Acts.

Parliament passed the Quebec Act, which had particular significance for Catholics, on May 20, 1774. The act provided a permanent civil government for Canada; in keeping with the French tradition of the inhabitants, the administrative power was placed

[130] Twelve of the thirteen colonies sent delegates, but as late as 1774 they were not talking independence.

[131] The Suffolk Resolves adopted by a local convention in Suffolk County, Massachusetts, declared the Coercive Acts unconstitutional, and therefore not to be obeyed, urged the people of Massachusetts to form a government to collect taxes and withhold them from the royal government until the repeal of the Coercive Acts, advised the people to arm and form their own militia, and recommended stringent economic sanctions against Britain.

in a council appointed by the crown. The acts of this council were subject to the royal veto; only in matters of local taxation were they free to act on their own. Perhaps the most significant—and to American Protestant colonists, outrageous—portion of the bill stated that "Catholics were granted religious toleration and civil rights; their Church's privileges confirmed."[132] The Continental Congress reacted swiftly to this, stating to the government and people of Great Britain:

> As men and Protestant Christians, we are indispensably obliged to take all proper measures for our security ... nor can we suppress our astonishment, that a British Parliament should ever consent to establish in that country a religion that has deluged your island in blood, and dispersed impiety, bigotry, persecution, murder and rebellion throughout every part of the world.[133]

Even more to the point was the reaction from prominent Americans of the day:

> "They have made a law to establish the religion of the Pope in Canada," Sam Adams announced. Americans up and down the eastern seaboard would soon be forced to "submit to Popery and Slavery." John Adams worried that "the barriers against popery, erected by our ancestors" would be "suffered and destroyed" by the Act, "to the hazard even of the Protestant religion." In Connecticut, Ezra Stiles, the future president of Yale College, was astonished that "the king and Lords and Commons, a whole Protestant Parliament" had "establish[ed] the Romish religion and IDOLOTRY" over "Two Thirds of the Territory of English America." ... "Does

[132] Morris, *Encyclopedia of American History*, 83.

[133] Ellis, *Documents*, 138.

> not your blood run cold, to think an English Parliament could pass an act for the establishment of Popery and arbitrary power?", Alexander Hamilton asked his colleagues in New York. In South Carolina, Judge William Henry Drayton predicted that a "tyranny under which all Europe groaned for many ages" would sweep the colonies, now that the King had approved the Quebec Act, and a "most cruel tyranny in Church and State" would be "fed with blood by the Roman Catholic doctrines."[134]

It was not long until the convoking of the Second Continental Congress, in May 1775. From 1774 to 1776, the colonies were governed by provincial assemblies, not terribly dissimilar from the colonial assemblies, and it was, for the most part, these provincial assemblies who sent delegates to the Second Continental Congress. John Dickenson's *Olive Branch Petition* professed the attachment of the American people to George III, expressed hope for a restoration of harmony, and begged the monarch to resist any further hostile acts until reconciliation, of whatever sort, could be carried out. George III rejected the *Olive Branch Petition* since it was produced by what he considered to be an illegal body and responded with a *Proclamation Against Rebellion and Sedition*; in October 1775, he declared the colonies to be in a state of open rebellion. Two months later, the Prohibitory Act was passed; it established "a complete naval blockade of America, authorized the seizure of American goods whenever found upon salt water, and called for the forcible enlistment in the royal navy of merchant sailors captured in American vessels."[135] To this, the colonists responded by opening all their ports to foreign vessels.

[134] Farrelly, *Papist Patriots*, 238–239.

[135] John Richard Allen, *The American Revolution: 1775–1783*. (New York: Harper and Row, 1962), 65.

One of the more powerful pieces of American literature turning many people's minds to the cause of independence was Thomas Paine's *Common Sense*. Paine convincingly argued that independence would prevent American involvement in European wars, expand American access to international trade, and give the young country access to the kind of foreign aid that would allow her to achieve her aims. In June 1776, Richard Henry Lee of Virginia submitted a resolution, which was passed on July 1, calling for just such a statement officially severing the colonies from England. The congress convened a committee to draw up the Declaration of Independence, and formal hostilities with the mother country commenced.

Maryland in Revolutionary America

Throughout these years, Maryland had been a reluctant observer of and then a reluctant participant in colonial tensions. One observer notes that in the year leading up to the Second Continental Congress, "resistance to the revolution, both internal and external, had continued to mount in forms ranging from slave and militia insurrections, particularly on the Eastern Shore, to the taunting threat from British warships commanding the Chesapeake and its tributaries."[136] The advocates for colonial self-determination decided, in this environment, to pursue a policy of "institutional conservatism and economic radicalism,"[137] undermining British economic interests without directly challenging the mother country's right to rule. Catholics did serve on the Maryland Committee

[136] Curran, *Papist Devils*, 257–258.

[137] Ronald Hoffman, *A Spirit of Dissension: Economics, Politics, and the Revolution in Maryland* (Baltimore: Johns Hopkins University Press, 1973), 2.

of Correspondence,[138] but the question continually surfaces: Why, in the face of several generations of colonial bigotry, would Catholics have favored the patriot cause?

> The Catholic community in Maryland endorsed, contributed to, fought for, and died for an ideology that rested upon republican principles and came wrapped in the rhetoric of anti-Catholicism. On the surface, it was an almost absurd incongruence—one that the British essayist Samuel Johnson seized upon in 1776, when he noted with great sarcasm that all of Maryland's residents "are now become such excellent Protestants," that they "totally forget that their own existence as a Colony is owing to this very religion which [the Sons of Liberty] abhor.[139]

One of the reasons, but by no means the only one, was the presence in Maryland of the Declaration of Independence's only Catholic signer, Charles Carroll of Carrollton. Born in Annapolis in 1737, he represented the third generation of his family in the Maryland Colony and would die in Baltimore, in his ninety-sixth year, in 1832. His grandfather had arrived in the colony in 1688 from England, and because of a longtime friendship with Lord Baltimore, he enjoyed a certain prestige and, after the Calverts regained their proprietary rights, a degree of political power. Charles Carroll the settler began a Catholic family that left a great legacy to the Church and to the state.

The Carrolls' fondness for the name Charles can lead to some confusion. The first Charles in America had a son Charles who

[138] Charles Carroll, Benjamin Hall, Ignatius Fenwick, and Jeremiah Jordan were the four Catholics elected out of seventy-six as delegates to the Maryland Provincial Convention held at Annapolis in the summer of 1776.

[139] Farrelly, *Papist Patriots*, 222.

settled in Annapolis; his son Charles, who signed the Declaration, was given land at Carrollton. The middle Charles Carroll's education gave him great appreciation for Jesuit qualities: steadfastness, discipline, austerity, and a reasoned use of the mind.

> Charles Carroll of Annapolis' Catholicism reflected the influence of the Jesuits who had shaped him. He did not question the teachings of the Church; he was (as his son would become) a devout Roman Catholic, who believed that strict doctrinal adherence was essential for salvation.... When his father died, he engaged priests to say Mass for him. He married Elizabeth Brooke in a ceremony that complied precisely with the format prescribed by the Council of Trent, and upon her death he had Masses offered for her in Maryland, and forwarded (his son) money for similar services in England. He prayed regularly, and maintained a "Priest's Room" at Doughregan. He wanted a priest nearby to say Mass, to help him make his Easter duty, which included Confession, to give him the Last Rights, to absolve him from sin.[140]

This legacy he passed on to his son, whom he first sent, it is believed, to the Jesuits at Bohemia Manor on the Eastern Shore, where his cousin John Carroll was also a student. In 1748 he enrolled in the Jesuit College of St. Omer in French Flanders, where

[140] Ronald Hoffman, *Princes of Ireland, Planters of Maryland: A Carroll Saga, 1500–1782* (Chapel Hill, NC: University of North Carolina Press, 2000), 280. Carrollton was a tract of land given to Charles Carroll the Signer by his father. It contained a manor house and was located near present-day Buckeystown, Maryland. Carroll himself never lived there but resided at the ancestral manor house, Doughregan Manor, near Ellicott City, Maryland. It is here, in the house chapel, that he lies buried in the sanctuary.

he remained for six years. After a year at the college of the Jesuits at Rheims, he went to the college Louis le Grand at Paris, then to Bruges, Belgium, to study civil law, then back to Paris, and finally to the Inner Temple in London to complete his legal studies.

Upon his return to America in 1765, Charles quickly became embroiled in the patriot cause, to which he gave his all. In 1770, the governor of Maryland, by proclamation, imposed certain fees on the colonists. "Fees," however, seemed to be just another word for "taxes," and so the bold executive move was seen as a violation of the people's right to tax themselves. As a result, Carroll found himself drawn into a debate with a leading Maryland political figure, Daniel Dulany, a member of a highly placed Protestant (though formerly Catholic) family. Both Carroll and Dulany contributed four articles in the *Maryland Gazette*, Dulany taking the pen name "Antillon," and Carroll using "First Citizen." The Dulanys were close friends of the proprietary interests; Daniel accused his newspaper opponent of being a less-than-patriotic Marylander, while he claimed to present a rational and conservative argument.

> Importantly, these debates went well beyond mere politics, power, and interest and stood at the very heart of Maryland's identity. Dulany desired an English Protestant community, rooted in the court tradition of proprietary government. His anti-Catholicism was not just a rhetorical strategy against Charles to gain the support of anti-Catholic voters.... While such intent must have existed on Dulany's part, his anti-Catholicism was too deep-seated to be merely Machiavellian rhetoric.... Anti-Catholicism stood at the very center of Maryland's legal, religious, and political cultures.... Charles Carroll, as an open, educated, and extremely wealthy member of the Roman Catholic Church, and of a family despised by the Dulanys, represented all that Dulany feared. The

> tensions between Catholicism and anti-Catholicism had defined the essential characteristics of Maryland up to this point, with Catholicism being the clear loser.... Likewise, by entering the debates and using his considerable intellectual prowess, Charles was protecting his family and hoping to reshape the politics and culture of the community to allow the common law—and ultimately natural rights—to offer a serious protection of his family. To protect these things, he hoped to apply the lessons of the English constitution to all Marylanders.[141]

These debates with Dulany established Charles Carroll's reputation as a scholar and apologist for the patriot cause. In 1774, he was elected delegate to the Maryland Provincial Convention; he became a member of the Provincial Committee of Correspondence; and he participated in the Maryland Convention of 1775 that adopted the "Association of the Freemen of Maryland," which became the governing charter of the colony until the Maryland Constitution was adopted in 1776. The association pledged itself to an armed resistance to Great Britain.

As a member of the Second Continental Congress, he formally affixed his signature to the Declaration of Independence on August 2, 1776. Earlier, he, along with Samuel Chase of Maryland and Benjamin Franklin, undertook a journey to Canada, which even more firmly established his patriotic convictions. The purpose of their journey was to secure an alliance with the Canadians in the War of Independence. This was not achieved, though it was not for lack of zeal or ability. Carroll's cousin, Father John Carroll, also accompanied the group and became fast friends with the deist Benjamin Franklin. It was a friendship that would later prompt

[141] Bradley J. Birzer, *American Cicero: The Life of Charles Carroll* (Wilmington, DE: Intercollegiate Studies Institute, 2010), 42.

Franklin to recommend to Rome the selection of "Mr. John Carroll" as America's first Catholic bishop.

The mission ended in early June 1776:

> The Journal of Congress records that on June 11th Mr. Chase and Mr. Carroll of Carrollton, two of the Commissioners being arrived from Canada, attended and gave an account of their proceedings and the state of the army in that country, and on the same day Dr. Franklin laid before Congress an account of his expedition to Canada. The next day the Commissioners sent in their formal report in writing, but this document, unfortunately, has been lost.[142]

Charles Carroll later helped to draw up the Maryland State Constitution and served as a member of the board of war, as a United States senator, and as a leading member of the Federalist Party in the new nation. Years later, reflecting back, he noted:

> To obtain religious as well as civil liberty, I entered zealously into the Revolution, and observing the Christian religion divided into many sects, I founded the hope that no one would be so predominant as to become the religion of the State. That hope was thus early entertained, because all of them joined in the same cause, with few exceptions of individuals. God grant that this religious liberty may be preserved in these States, to the end of time, and that all believing in the religion of Christ may practice the leading principle of charity, the basis of every virtue.[143]

[142] Kate Mason Rowland, *The Life of Charles Carroll of Carrollton, 1737–1832: With His Correspondence and Public Papers*, vol. 1 (New York: G. P. Putnam's Sons, 1898), 173.

[143] Charles Carroll to the Reverend John Stanford, October 9, 1827, cited in ibid., vol. 2, 357–358.

Such a life and presence surely played a part in Maryland's Catholics joining the patriot cause. But there were other reasons given, all of which carry merit:

> The implications of the severance of time-honored ties, the repudiation of hallowed loyalties, and vivid memory of opposition and open hostility extending through generations served as deterrents to their ranging themselves on the side of the new leaders who proclaimed a new liberty. If the past had been hard, what might the future bring under a regime in which individuals conspicuous for anti-Catholic sentiments were vested with authority?... Even if they were not especially indebted to the government of George III, the past seemed to preclude wholehearted cooperation with the new leaders in America.... Should they repudiate a government whose legitimacy they had never questioned hitherto, sever hallowed ties, and renounce British authority? If they could not blink the fact that England's enemies were in many cases notoriously hostile to Catholics, *it was soon apparent that neutrality was not possible and that loyalism would engender persecution without a guarantee of effective protection by England.*[144]

And so, no fewer than thirteen Catholics were members of the General Committee for St. Mary's County, and the Committee of Correspondence had among its members Catholics Athanasius Ford and Jeremiah Jordan. Ignatius Fenwick and George Plater were both elected to the convention of delegates from the

[144] Charles H. Metzger, S.J., *Catholics and the American Revolution: A Study in Religious Climate* (Chicago: Loyola University Press, 1962), 178–181, emphasis added.

counties of Maryland.[145] St. Mary's and Charles Counties in Southern Maryland provided the greatest amount of Catholic manpower in the revolutionary army; these areas also produced grain, tobacco, meats, and general provisions on which Washington's army relied. For this reason, British forces paid particular attention to them, occasionally carried out raids, and confiscated many of the needed goods themselves.

Colonel William Smallwood is well remembered for the regiment he organized prior to the signing of the Declaration of Independence; it contained many Catholics from the Southern counties and along the Eastern Shore.[146] Raids continued throughout the war along the Southern Maryland coast, prompting Catholics John Drury, John Drury, Jr., Francis Drury, Ignatius Moore, and Nicholas Moore to petition "for compensation for ejection from their homes and possessions on St. George's Island by a British Squadron under Lord Dunmore."[147] Such invaders met their match, however, and were often turned back.[148]

[145] Catholic members of the Maryland General Committee were William Neale, Athanasius Ford, Maffey Leigh, Edward Fenwick, Henry Carroll, Nicholas Sewell, John Fenwick, John Greenwell of Ignatius, Ignatius Combs, William Jenkins Jr., Enoch Fenwick, Nicholas L. Sewell, and Ignatius Taylor.

[146] Among the better remembered were Ignatius Douglas, Clement, Edward and John Edelen, Ignatius Boon, John Neale, Joseph Mattingly, and Francis and William Baggott. A branch of the militia, the Maryland "Flying Camp" included Catholics Edward Mattingly, Ignatius Sims, Edward Spalding, Ignatius Knott, Ignatius Watkin, Luke Cusick, and others whose names were not recorded.

[147] Ibid., 192.

[148] In Captain Alex McPherson's company, for example, Henry Boarman was lieutenant; Edward Boarman Jr., sergeant; Raphael Boarman, corporal; Ignatius Francis Garner, ensign; Joseph and William Boarman and Henry, Thomas, and Ignatius Mudd, and Richard Spalding, privates. Similarly, under Captain Yates, John

In Charles County to the north of St. Mary's, census figures listed eighteen hundred young men at least eighteen years of age. Not all would have served, of course, but to an even higher degree than St. Mary's County, certain Charles County family names, many notably Catholic, appear over and over.[149]

Priests serving in Maryland were, like everyone else, given to political opinion. Since the Society of Jesus had been suppressed in 1773, letters to the Jesuit General had ceased. Political topics would never have been introduced in the pulpit, and men busy with pastoral concerns would have had much less time than others to sit around engaging in opinion, much less military strategy.

Neale served as second lieutenant, Raphael Boarman as ensign, and William Neale, Joseph Neale, and Richard B. Ignatius, and William Boarman as privates; and serving under Captain Burnham were Raphael Boarman Jr., John Boarman, and Zachariah Mattingly, all Catholics. Ibid., 192–193. In the lower battalion the number of Catholics was also significant: Ignatius Fenwick, colonel; Ignatius Taylor, major; Ignatius Abell, captain; Philip Fenwick, first lieutenant; and Ignatius Combs and Bennett Combs, second lieutenants. Still other Catholics in the militia of St. Mary's County were: Athanasius Thompson, Athanasius Joy, two by the name of Cuthbert Abell, Cuthbert Clarke, Cuthbert Fenwick, Cuthbert Smoot, Basil Howard, Basil Bright, Basil Hall, and Basil Brooke. With the 1778 call for increased militiamen, hundreds more enlisted, and one would be hard-pressed to list the number of Catholics who, in the end, served the revolution. Ibid., 194–195.

[149] Twenty-one of the name Boarman, fourteen named Mudd, thirteen named Spalding. The county also had its Neale and Purcell families, and Ignatius Adams. Sergeant Bennett Mudd and Sergeant Jeremiah Mudd were regulars wounded in action, and Privates Richard Mudd, Richard Fenwick, George Spalding, Henry Spalding, and Aaron Spalding served in the Maryland line. A Daniel Spalding saw Marine service, and William Fenwick is classified as captain of militia and privateer.

While Catholic presence in loyalism was quite noticeable in Pennsylvania, this does not seem to have been the case in Maryland, especially in the Southern Counties. The Eastern Shore was, however, a hotbed of Toryism, but it seems unlikely the Catholics were members in any measure. Father Joseph Mosley, who labored there, on hearing the arguments for both sides, soon gave his complete personal assent to the cause of the revolution:

> The very silence of Tories and of those unfriendly to Jesuits or to Catholicism is tacit admission of Mosley's contention. Mosley, however, did more than pledge personal loyalty, for, assuming the new role of political advisor to his people, he urged them to do as he had done, and "every Catholic ... not one excepted" followed his example. Such a generalization by Father Mosley would have been impossible unless it corresponded with fact. Otherwise it would have evoked instant challenge and denial.[150]

Charles Carroll rendered any number of significant contributions during the war years. One letter to George Washington argues for what ultimately became the Treaty of Amity and Commerce, signed with the French government in 1778, by which each country received most-favored-nation status with the other. This was followed by the Treaty of Alliance, which brought about the military aid of vessels and manpower needed to help continental troops in the battle with Great Britain. Carroll had confided to Washington:

> I flatter myself our struggles for Independence will, in the end, be crowned with success, but we must suffer much in the meantime, and unless we continue to receive powerful

[150] Ibid., 205.

> assistance in arms, ammunition, and clothing, and other warlike stores, and supplies of cash or a credit in Europe, equivalent thereto, we must sink under the efforts of a rich and inveterate enemy, mistress of the ocean, and determined, it seems, to run every hazard in subduing these States to unconditional submission.[151]

Not only did this become a reality, but Washington himself, on receiving a letter of congratulations from a group of Catholic laymen upon assuming the presidency, responded with his thanks and his hope that they would not soon forget the aid given the revolutionary cause by a "nation in which the Roman Catholic faith is professed." Such sentiments were also expressed during the war years (1776 to 1781) when Washington, in his role as military commander, publicly banned the celebration of Guy Fawkes Day among American soldiers:

> As the Commander in Chief has been apprized of a design form'd for the observance of that ridiculous and childish custom of burning the effigy of the pope—He cannot help expressing his surprise that there should be Officers and Soldiers in this army so void of common sense, as not to see the impropriety of such a step at this Juncture; at a Time when we are soliciting, and have really obtain'd, the friendship and alliance of the people of Canada, whom we ought to consider as Brethern embarked in the same Cause. The defence of the general Liberty of America: At such a juncture, and in such Circumstances, to be insulting their Religion, is so monstrous as not to be suffered or excused; indeed instead of offering the most remote insult. It is our duty to express public thanks to these our Brethren, as to them we are so

[151] Rowland, *The Life of Charles Carroll of Carrollton*, vol. 1, 207.

> much indebted for every late happy Success over the common Enemy in Canada.[152]

Carroll also played a decisive role in putting down a plan referred to as Conway's Cabal—an attempt on the part of New England in general, and Massachusetts in particular, to regain control of the Continental Army. Named for Major General Thomas Conway, it centered on an indiscreet letter he had written to General Horatio Gates, urging the removal of Washington and the restoration of Massachusetts' control of the army. Conway's letter and subsequent revelations "rallied to Washington a support that overwhelmed the conspirators both in Congress and in the army," and it was Carroll's quick, decisive action that both exposed and terminated the plan.[153]

The Other Carroll

Catholic Maryland was also strongly affected during the war years by ecclesiastical events in Europe, particularly the suppression of the Society of Jesus in 1773. The reasons for this move by the Church were primarily political, especially the perception that Jesuits were gaining political power among the European royal courts. The Society would cease to exist in the Church for a quarter century, and Jesuits throughout the world found themselves, literally overnight, secular priests. This affected Maryland, where they had labored as missionaries since 1634; Charles Carroll, writing to a friend, left no doubt about his sentiments:

> General accusations against a body of men, of great crimes and misdemeanors, without particular proof, are to me strong

[152] Ellis, *Documents*, 140–141.
[153] Andrews, *Concise Dictionary of American History*, 250–251.

> confirmation of the falsity of those accusations. It is my private opinion that the Roman Catholic princes are desirous of rooting out the regular clergy in their dominions, not only with a view of seizing their estates and enriching with their plunder a few court favorites, but to ease their people of a dead weight and themselves of a political encumbrance.[154]

One of those deeply affected was former Jesuit Father John Carroll, cousin of Charles, and destined to be the first Catholic bishop (later archbishop) in the United States. Son of Daniel and Eleanor Darnall Carroll, he was born in Upper Marlboro in 1735, and probably baptized at Boone's Chapel, near Rosaryville, Maryland. At the age of twelve he was sent to Bohemia Manor in Cecil County, and from there, like his cousin, to St. Omer's, where he studied for six years. His father died in 1750, and three years later John entered the Society of Jesus, began his studies in philosophy and theology at Liege, Belgium, and was ordained to the priesthood in 1769. The next four years were spent both in Liege and at St. Omer's, teaching the same disciplines he had studied, and, for a short time before returning home, he served as chaplain for Lord Arundel and his family at Wardour Castle, not far from London. He received word of the suppression of the Society in 1773:

> [He was] utterly distraught.... He became a recluse in his family's home in Rock Creek and brooded there for months. "I am not, and perhaps never shall be, fully recovered from

[154] Charles Carroll to William Gates, November 7, 1767, cited in Annabelle M. Melville, *John Carroll of Baltimore: Founder of the American Catholic Hierarchy* (New York: Charles Scribner's Sons, 1955), 23. See also Rowland, *The Life of Charles Carroll of Carrollton*, vol. 1, 86. In this letter, Carroll is reacting to the suppression of the Society in Spain, which preceded by six years the general suppression of the Society.

> the shock of this dreadful intelligence," he wrote in September 1773. "The greatest blessing which in my estimation I could receive from God would be immediate death."[155]

God was not to grant such a wish, however; Carroll still had much to accomplish. His life on his mother's Rock Creek farm afforded him lodging while he lived the life of a missionary in Maryland and Virginia. He built a small frame chapel on his mother's estate and on Sundays offered Mass there for a congregation; on weekdays, he said Mass in her home when he was present. The first indication of his value to the emerging government came when he accompanied his cousin Charles, Samuel Chase, and Benjamin Franklin on the ill-fated mission to Canada. When the thirteen new states adopted constitutions after winning independence, only four drew up documents that removed the old penal legislation against Catholics; it is curious, though, that those four were Maryland, Virginia, Delaware, and Pennsylvania—those in closest proximity to Father Carroll's missionary endeavors.

Beginning in June 1783, Carroll and several priests working in the Maryland mission met at Whitemarsh Plantation, the previous home of the Jesuits.[156] They discussed ways to keep their missionary work intact and their property holdings safe. A few months later they sent a letter to Rome asking for permission to nominate a superior who would have some of the powers of a Bishop. Cardinal Lorenzo Antonelli, Prefect of the Congregation Propaganda Fidei, made inquiries to the nuncio in Paris—the seat of government of the nation friendliest with the new United States—and the following year, Father Carroll received official notification of his appointment:

[155] John Carroll to Daniel Carroll, September 11, 1773, cited in Farrelly, *Papist Patriots*, 248.

[156] The site is today Sacred Heart Parish in Bowie, Maryland, in the archdiocese of Washington, D.C.

> Rev. Sir, you have given conspicuous proofs of piety and zeal, and it is known that your appointment will please and gratify many members of that republic, and especially Mr. Franklin, the eminent individual who represents the same republic at the court of the Most Christian King, the Sacred Congregation, with the approbation of his Holiness, has appointed you superior of the mission in the thirteen United States of North America, and has communicated to you the faculties which are necessary to discharge of that office; faculties which are also communicated to the other priests of the same States, except the administration of confirmation, which is reserved for you alone, as the enclosed documents will show.[157]

One of the earliest difficulties the new superior had to contend with, which persisted for several years, was the shortage of clergy; this was particularly true in the counties of Southern Maryland. At the time of the suppression of the Jesuits nine years earlier, there were twenty-one priests laboring in both Maryland and Pennsylvania.[158] This, among other factors made up the content of an

[157] Ellis, *Documents*, 147–148.

[158] They were Fathers John Ashton, John Bolton, Thomas Digges, James Framback, Ferdinand Farmer, Luke Beisler, Robert Harding, George Hunter, John Lewis, John Lucas, Mathias Manners, Ignatius Matthews, Robert Molyneux, Peter Morris, Joseph Mosley, Bennet Neale, James Pellentz, Louis Roels, Bernard Rich (Diderick), John Baptist de Ritter, and James Walton. These were joined during the next few years by John and Sylvester Boarman, John Boone, Ignatius Baker Brooke, Anthony and John Carroll, Joseph Doyne, Augustine Jenkins, Charles, Francis, and Leonard Neale, Henry Pile, and Charles Sewall, all native Marylanders, who, having completed their studies abroad, returned to serve in their native land. At the time of the restoration of the Society in Maryland in 1805, of the original group of twenty-one Jesuits stationed in Maryland

official report Carroll sent to Propaganda in 1785, one that has traditionally given the historian one of the earliest glimpses into Catholic statistics in the new republic.

In his report, Carroll estimated the number of Catholics in Maryland to be about 15,800; in Pennsylvania, 7,000; and in Virginia, no more than 200. There were many Catholics in other states, but he did not know how many; he did know they were without the ministrations of priests. He understood there were 1,500 Catholics in New York served by only one Franciscan, to whom he could not extend faculties because of the limits of his Letter of Appointment. There were many Catholics in western areas near the Mississippi, though again, he had no idea how many. In Maryland, he spoke of the affluent families present since the seventeenth century who were still devout in practicing and passing on the Faith, and in Philadelphia, much the same was true among the planters, merchants, and mechanics. He noted, among other evils, the "unavoidable intercourse with non-Catholics, a free intercourse between the sexes, a fondness for dances and amusements, and the reading of love stories brought over from Europe." Also of concern was a certain neglect in the instruction of some children and of slaves in the rudiments of the Faith. Of all the priests serving in the new nation, nineteen were in Maryland and five in Pennsylvania. Two were over seventy years old, and two others very near that age. Some were in bad health, while those who were robust worked hard and were zealous in carrying out their priestly duties. They were maintained chiefly from the estates of the clergy and the charity

---

only Fathers Ashton, Bolton, and Molyneux remained alive. Of the second group, Fathers John Boarman, Boone, Doyne and Jenkins had passed to their eternal reward, so that only twelve of the Fathers remained alive to carry on. Beitzell, *The Jesuit Missions of St. Mary's County*, 156.

of many Catholic laity. There was one college in Philadelphia and two in Maryland to which Catholics might be admitted.[159]

The anti-Catholicism that had been so ubiquitous in Fr. Carroll's formative years would come again to the forefront when an attack on the Faith was made by one Charles Wharton—an ex-Jesuit who had apostatized and became a popular writer and lecturer on the anti-Catholic circuit, much as the Nativists and Know-Nothings would become in the mid-nineteenth century. Wharton's *Letter to the Roman Catholics of the City of Worcester* rehashed all the traditional prejudices built against the Church over the decades, and Carroll knew he needed to respond. He was acutely aware of the climate of American public opinion but also of the strides Catholics had made, especially during the Revolutionary War, to overcome their countrymen's hostility. Any response on his part had to be a model of diplomacy, filled with charity, that clearly explained the Catholic position on all disputed points. The fact that Carroll was able to accomplish this in his *Address to the Roman Catholics of the United States of America* was a tribute to his ability and a sign he was destined for even greater things.[160]

That would happen soon with his appointment as Baltimore's first bishop in 1789, the same year George Washington was inaugurated first president of the new nation. When the premier see was erected, it included all territory between Canada and Florida, and from the eastern seaboard to the Mississippi River. This vast expanse would be under Carroll's jurisdiction until 1808, when Baltimore was raised to an archbishopric and the suffragan sees of

[159] Thomas T. McAvoy, C.S.C., *A History of the Catholic Church in the United States* (Notre Dame, IN: University of Notre Dame Press, 1969), 50–51. The term "college" did not carry a present-day understanding. Rather, it more closely resembled a prep school.

[160] Ellis, *Documents*, 149–151.

New York, Philadelphia, Boston, and Bardstown, Kentucky, were created.

Carroll traveled to England in 1790 to be consecrated in the chapel of Lulworth Castle in Dorsetshire, the ancestral home of the Weld family, friends of the Maryland Carrolls for many years. He had long since moved from his mother's estate in Rock Creek to St. Peter's Church in downtown Baltimore, the diocese's first cathedral prior to the building of the Basilica of the Assumption a few years later. He took an active part in municipal affairs; became president of the Female Humane Charity School of the City of Baltimore; was one of three trustees of St. John's College, Annapolis; began Georgetown Academy; and brought the Sulpicians from France to engage in seminary work. He was also head of the library company, a founding member of the Maryland Historical Society, and president of the trustees of Baltimore College.

He was a particular friend of George Washington, and wrote to the Archbishop of Dublin that it was impossible "for a person not thoroughly acquainted with our situation to know how much depends at this time on one man for the happiness of the nation."[161] He was none too happy at the thought of the great patriot leaving the presidential office:

> You will see in the public papers an admirable address of our excellent president Washington to the people of this state on retiring from public life. He has far other principles of the necessity of Religion than the superficial French theorists on government. Tho I cannot help rejoicing at the prospect before him of enjoying some repose at the expiration of his quadriennium of service ... yet I am fearful for this country

[161] Carroll to Archbishop John Thomas Troy, O.P., July 19, 1794, cited in Melville, *John Carroll of Baltimore*, 168.

> when he is no longer the head of it to overawe the sowers of sedition and wild democracy.[162]

Bishop Carroll's eulogy on the death of Washington in 1799 was a masterpiece of patriotic rhetoric and was published as a book. Well circulated in its time among Catholics and non-Catholics alike, it was another rite of passage for Catholics in America, and gave proof of their sincere attachment to the new republic.

The Bluegrass Connection

Yet another significant story in eighteenth-century Catholic life in Maryland was the migration of substantial numbers of Southern Maryland Catholics to Kentucky—a replanting of the English Catholic Faith, as it were. There were several reasons for this exodus, which amounted to a loss of nearly three thousand people from St. Mary's County over two decades.

The availability of western land played a large part. Citizens read with great interest in the *Maryland Gazette* and the *Maryland Journal and Baltimore Advertiser* about the vast western territory available due to England's victory in the French and Indian War. Land grants were being offered to those who had served in the Continental Army, which was a powerful incentive. There were also religious factors: Since the late seventeenth century, Catholics in Maryland had been denied the right to hold political office; they were far more familiar with that legacy than anything the new government promised in the Constitution or the Bill of Rights. Such platitudes sounded fine on paper, but there was little trust in their implementation. In 1785 a group of Southern Maryland

[162] Carroll to Rev. Charles Plowden, S.J., September 24, 1796, cited in Melville, *John Carroll of Baltimore*, 168.

families formed a Catholic League, deciding to move to Kentucky as soon as it was feasible. John Carroll, by then bishop of Baltimore, promised to send a priest who would serve as founding pastor of a parish, if the migrants promised to settle together in a way that would make a parish geographically possible.

Another reason for migrating was British plundering along the Maryland coast during the war. British fleets, constantly present in coastal waters, confiscated slaves and stock and plundered homes, taking whatever pleased them and living off stolen supplies. This practice did not cease at war's end and was one of the factors leading to a second round of hostilities with England, the so-called second war of independence, in 1812.

Economic reasons were also present. Many residents of St. Mary's County who had worked on the many proprietary manors lost their jobs when these large properties were confiscated by the British. These manors had previously been leased by residents of the county, who paid the proprietor a rather small annual fee. They were given preference in purchasing the farms they desired on the lands they had worked, but purchase prices were often high, and subsequent taxes could become burdensome. All these factors led many Catholics to desire a new life in which they could prosper economically and practice their faith in such a way that it was not an encumbrance on any other area of their lives.

The geographic pattern of migration over the next two decades changed little:

> The usual route from St. Mary's County was overland to Pittsburgh. At that point the families boarded flatboats and traveled down the Ohio River to Maysville, Kentucky. They disembarked at Maysville to avoid the area above the falls of the Ohio which was known to be infested with Indians. From Maysville they travelled overland to one of the

half-dozen "stations" located near their area of settlement. These stations played a vital role in the settlement of the Kentucky frontier. The danger of Indian attack made isolated homesteads impractical. Between 1774 and 1790 every neighborhood boasted a blockhouse station which provided a degree of safety until homesteads could be established. It is likely that many countians who emigrated prior to 1790 left their wives and children at one of the stations temporarily and traveled the additional twelve to fifteen miles to establish their homesteads.[163]

No complete list of those who left St. Mary's County over the decades has ever been compiled, though many partial statistics give valuable information. Many family names were recorded during the first decade of the migration, and the occupations of the travelers showed a cross-section of American labor and business: farmer, physician, merchant, mill owner, pilot, elite, mariner, clergy, tavern keeper, attorney, ship owner, carpenter, blacksmith, schoolmaster, bricklayer, ship carpenter, and so on.

Migration from Maryland led to north-central Kentucky, where the newcomers established communities such as Pottinger Creek, Hardin Creek, Bardstown, Cartwright's Creek, Scott County, Woodford, Rolling Fork, Cox Creek, and Breckenridge. The League of Catholic Families began the Pottinger Creek community in 1785 near the present town of Boston in Nelson County. Basil Hayden—whose name has been adopted by a popular bourbon brand—was the group's leader, and traveling with him was a settler named Philip Lee, who was known for meticulous notetaking.[164]

[163] Hammett, *History of St. Mary's County*, 93.

[164] Lee lists the original, and earliest, Catholic Settlers as Basil Hayden, Philip Lee, Leonard Johnson, Stephen Elliot, Ignatius Cissell, Ignatius Hagan, Ignatius Bowles, Thomas Bowlin, Harry

While the Pottinger Creek Settlement was the earliest, it was surely not easiest. The practical hardships of the newest arrivals on the Kentucky frontier were well summarized in this anecdote:

> When I was a boy, there was a tradition rife here to the effect that when the old pioneers from this section used to meet Saturday evenings in Bardstown as soon as they had shaken hands, one would turn his back to the other and beg him for a half-dozen kicks under his coat tail and when they were duly administered, the other would turn around and ask his friend for his kicking.... Not infrequently, half a dozen pairs have been noticed exchanging civilities of this nature, in the course of an afternoon. Why was this done, you ask? Why, in order to get temporal punishment inflicted, to expiate the grievous sin they had committed in abandoning the peaceful shores of Maryland for the wild forests and savage Indians of Kentucky. But the plunge had been made, the labor and exposure of

---

Hill, John Spalding, William Bowles, Bernard Nally, Washington Boone, Thomas Mudd, Philip Mattingly, Joseph Dent, Joseph Howe, Monica Hagan, William Bold, Charles Payne, Henry McAtee, James Mollihorne, Ignatius Byrne, Jeremiah Brown, Hezekiah Luckett, John Baptist Dent, John Hutchins, William Mahony, James Queen, James Stevens, Francis Bryan, Raphael R. Mudd, Joseph Spalding, Urban Speaks, Joseph Mills, Rhodolphus Norris, Bernard Cissell, William Brewer, Joseph Clark, Henry Norris, Randall Hagan, Robert Cissell, Stanislaus Melton, Philip Miles, Isaac Thawles, Henry Lucas, Ignatius French, Jeremiah Wathen, Walter Burch, James Dent, Joseph Edelin, Harry Mills, and Francis Peake. Ibid., 98. In these, as in all lists of Catholics from this time, it is interesting to see the influence of the Maryland Jesuits in the men's first names, Ignatius and Francis (Xavier) in particular.

going forbade the idea of return, and it was a clear case of "root hog or die."[165]

The Hardin Creek settlement followed some ten miles east of Pottinger Creek, founded in 1786 by Catholic settlers Edward Beaven and his brother Colonel Charles Beaven. Four of the Cissell brothers—Zachariah, Sylvester, Matthew, and Jeremiah—were also early leaders. They all lived to an old age and were admired for their "exemplary character, intelligence, and wise leadership."[166]

The next area of settlement, which would play a prominent role in the development of Catholicism in the late eighteenth and early nineteenth century, was Bardstown, incorporated as a town by the Virginia legislature in 1788 and county seat of Nelson County. It had become a prosperous community by the time Kentucky was admitted to the Union in 1792; among its early settlers were found men named Anthony Sanders, Captain James Rapier, Edward Howard and his son Thomas, Basil, Robert and Alexius Hagan, William Coomes, Thomas Gwynn, Dr. George Hart, Raphael Lancaster, and Edward Hayden.[167]

Bardstown was to see the great missionary work of Bishop Benedict Joseph Flaget, one of a number of Sulpicians John Carroll was instrumental in bringing from France. Kentucky would also be the scene of the missionary efforts of Father Stephen Theodore Badin, the first priest to receive all minor orders and be ordained in the United States. He is often called the "apostle of Kentucky," and his work has become legendary in Kentucky Catholic history.

[165] This was described by Mr. J. Edwin Coad in an article reprinted in an 1897 issue of the *St. Mary's Beacon*, cited in ibid., 98.

[166] Ibid., 99. As with many of these settlements, Regina Combs Hammett lists at least sixty of the founding families of Hardin Creek. Among them are found such familiar Maryland names as Lancaster, Mudd, Miles, Fenwick, Jarboe, Hagan, Medley, and Sims.

[167] Ibid., 99.

Bardstown was created a diocese in 1808 and was absorbed into the diocese of Louisville in 1841. St. Joseph's Cathedral in downtown Bardstown has traditionally marked the seat of the transplanted Catholicism brought by Marylanders.[168]

Cartwright's Creek was next, in 1787. It was located about twenty miles from Bardstown and eventually became part of Washington County. Thomas Hill and his brother-in-law Philip Miles led the expedition, and they and their families were soon joined by many from Leonardtown, in St. Mary's County. Their original intent was to settle closer to their fellow Marylanders, but, being the victims of a particularly bad Indian raid, they escaped, went to Bardstown, and eventually chose the area around Cartwright's Creek.[169]

Scott County was settled the same year as Cartwright's Creek, and Rolling Fork the following year. Clement and Ignatius Buckman and James Raley were among its earliest settlers. Robert Abell, son of St. Mary's County sheriff Samuel Abell, migrated to the area shortly after its foundation, and two years later, Benedict Spalding led another group of settlers. By 1791, still more had arrived, making Rolling Fork very substantially populated.

Cox's Creek, later called Fairfield, began in 1795, starting with only a dozen families led by Clement Gardiner and Nicholas Miles. The settlement soon grew, containing at least fifty families within

[168] The first "elders" of the Bardstown cathedral were nearly all born in Maryland: Henry Wathen, Charles Drury, Elish Gates, James Warren, John Merriman, John McArdle, James McArdle, Thomas Aud, George Ross, Thomas Beaven, Ambrose Aud, Mr. Cooper, Mr. Deavers, Alexius Adams, Daniel Harkins, Patrick Blocklock, Robert Livers, Mr. Blandford, Roger Smith, Lewis Hayden, Charles Jarboe, Bennett Smith, Walter Osborne, John Stuart, John Stevens, Henry Livers, and William Osborne. Ibid., 99.

[169] Well over seventy-five family names of the Leonardstown settlers are included by Ms. Hammett. Ibid., 100–101.

the first year of its establishment.[170] Breckenridge County was later renamed Hardin County (the county of Abraham Lincoln's birth). Richard Mattingly and Vietchel Hinton led the original settlers there, and were joined sometime later by a group led by Elias Rhodes and Barton Mattingly.

The names of settlers are numerous, but their names are not nearly as significant as their faith. This was truly a Catholic migration, and, as such, a significant saga in the annals of Maryland Catholic history. Since these Marylanders came from a culture of tobacco, this crop became an important staple in the economy of Kentucky, from which it spread to Ohio, Tennessee, and Missouri.

> Former Southern Marylanders and their Kentucky descendants earned distinction in many fields. They were especially prominent figures in the field of religion. Mother Catherine Spalding became the first superioress of the Sisters of Charity. Rev. Edward Fenwick became the first Bishop of Cincinnati, and Rev. R.P. Miles was the first Bishop of Nashville. Rev. Martin John Spalding became the first Bishop of Louisville and served as Archbishop of Baltimore from 1864 through 1872. Archbishop Spalding was the son of Richard Spalding who emigrated in 1790, and he is only one example of the many Kentucky cousins to whom St. Mary's Countians point with pride.[171]

[170] All names provided in ibid., 103, as well as those lesser numbers who first settled Breckenridge County in 1799.

[171] Ibid., 103. Also to be included is Rev. John Lancaster Spalding, nephew of Archbishop Spalding, one of the intellectual lights among the American hierarchy in the nineteenth century and a scholarly writer of huge proportion; he became one of the founders of the Catholic University of America in Washington, D.C., and the first bishop of the Diocese of Peoria, Illinois.

Opening a Monastery to Close a Century

The story of eighteenth-century Maryland Catholicism concludes happily, with the establishment of the first monastery of religious women in the thirteen colonies: the Discalced Carmelites in Port Tobacco, Charles County.

Just as it was impossible to secure a Catholic higher education in colonial Maryland, so was it impossible for women to enter a religious order. In addition, the expectations for dowries were high and not always affordable for families. These difficulties notwithstanding, there were those in the colony who were able to answer the Lord's call.

As early as 1753, Ann Matthews, a native of Southern Maryland and sister of Father Ignatius Matthews, was accepted at the Carmel of Hoogstraeten, near Antwerp. In religious life, she became known as Sister Bernardina Teresa Xavier of St. Joseph. In the 1770s she received two of her nieces, sisters of Father William Matthews, into the same Carmel: Ann Teresa became Sister Mary Aloysia of the Blessed Trinity, and Susanna became Sister Mary Eleanora of St. Francis Xavier. Both uncle and nephew were active priests in Southern Maryland: Father William had been the first colonial native ordained to the priesthood.

One of the most influential persons in making the Maryland Carmel a reality was Father Charles Neale, S.J., a native Southern Marylander who had gone to Europe at the age of ten to study. His second cousin, Mother Margaret Mary Brent (a sister of the Giles Brent who had come to Maryland from England and subsequently settled in Virginia), was superior of the English Carmelite Monastery in Antwerp. Stationed with her in this monastery was London-born Mother Clare Joseph, formerly Frances Dickenson. In 1783, a group of Catholic Southern Marylanders petitioned the bishop of Antwerp for the establishment of a monastery to be located at Port Tobacco. The sudden death of Mother Margaret Mary Brent in 1784 brought discussion to a close for a time; she would have been the Maryland monastery's first superior. Six years later, the time was right, and Mother Bernardina was named superior; she, her two nieces, and Sister Clare Joseph set sail from Texel, a small island off the coast of Holland, on May 1, 1790. It was to be a difficult journey.

> Our passage was very disagreeable on account of the passengers—a man and his wife and three little children who were crying almost morning to night, and the man and his wife were very disagreeable people who were often quarreling and wrangling.... The captain was a poor little mean-spirited, stingy sort of man who had provided very slender provisions or necessaries for the passengers. The bread from the first was mouldy and not fit to eat.... The water was so bad it was not fit to drink. We were forced to strain it through a cloth for a day to sweeten before we could drink it.[172]

The Sisters were, of course, dressed in lay clothes, since no religious garb would have been allowed. They were, one would guess, overjoyed to see the Port of New York in July 1790. They proceeded to Norfolk, then through the Chesapeake Bay and up the Potomac River to Brentfield, home of Robert Brent, Mother Margaret Mary's brother. During their tumultuous voyage, Mother Bernardina's brother, Father Ignatius Matthews had died, something she had a strange premonition would happen.

The Sisters lived briefly in a mansion—Chandler's Hope—above the town of Port Tobacco. It had been the boyhood home of Father Neale and was unoccupied at the time of their arrival.

[172] *Who Remember Long: A History of Port Tobacco Carmel* (Port Tobacco, MD: Carmel of Port Tobacco, 1984), 19–20.

It was, however, not especially suited to being a monastery, and they eventually secured the property of Mr. Baker Brooke, about four miles from the town of Port Tobacco. It was a large farm that produced wheat, corn, and tobacco and was manned by slaves. Besides the normal work associated with monastic life, the Sisters also did spinning, copied and bound prayer books, and did their own watercolors. Sister Clare Joseph Dickenson, who was to succeed Mother Bernardina following her death, compiled one of the first prayer books printed by Catholics in the United States.

The first woman admitted to the Carmel was Elizabeth Carberry, a native of Southern Maryland who would become Sister Teresa of the Heart of Mary. She was the first woman to pronounce religious vows in the United States, and was, at age forty-seven, an older vocation, especially for the time. Her grandfather John Baptist Carberry came from Dublin and settled in the Maryland Colony in 1690. By 1712, his son, also John Baptist, owned twenty-one acres of land near Newtown in St. Mary's County. His estate was Hopton Park, and much of the land was sold or rented through the years. Elizabeth's mother, Mary Thompson Carberry, was a great-granddaughter of the gentleman William Bretton, who had first established the Newtown settlement. It was at Hopton Park that Elizabeth was secretly baptized by one of the Jesuits from Newtown, since all such sacramental life was at the time forbidden.[173]

Sister Teresa was to spend twenty-two tranquil years at the monastery, which quickly became known as Mount Carmel. She left a telling bit of information about life in the early years of the Maryland monastery in a letter written to fellow Carmelites at the

[173] Much of the recorded information on Teresa Carberry was compiled by her nephew, Thomas Carberry II, who became the third mayor of Washington, D.C.

monastery at Lanherne, England, where the Antwerp community fled after the armies of Napoleon had invaded Belgium.

> Without rent or revenue we depend on Providence and the works of our hands, productive of plentiful crops of wheat, corn, tobacco, a good will supplying our large and healthy community with every necessary of life. We raise a large stock of sheep, yielding a considerable quantity of wool, black and white, which we spin and weave to clothe ourselves and negroes. The situation of our monastery is pleasant, rural and healthy, being on top of a large hill. We have excellent water and extensive enclosure containing nearly three acres of land. The place is solitary, suitable to our eremitical order.[174]

Some years later, Sister Teresa Coudray, writing from England to Sister Teresa Carberry added this sparkling compliment: "... and yourself ... .who having the honor to stand first in the profession book are a kind of model for all the rest to look at."[175] Sister Carberry died in the seventieth year of her life, 1814, and Mount Carmel's record noted that "she was our first religious in this country and was remarkable for her gratitude to God and to us for entering religion."[176]

[174] Cited in Rose Martin, *The Story of Elizabeth: Our Country's First Nun* (Los Angeles: Twin Circle Publishing, 1968), 26.
[175] Ibid., 27.
[176] Ibid.

Chapter 8

Catholic Colonial Pennsylvania

The story of Catholic Colonial Pennsylvania takes on a very different cast than that of Maryland. Maryland had been an almost completely English colony in origin, tradition, and outlook. Pennsylvania, on the other hand, took on a cosmopolitan look with the early rise of cities and the diversity, manufacturing, and commerce that went with them. In Pennsylvania one found not only Englishmen but Germans, Swedes, Scots, and Irish; while the Anglican church eventually became the established one in Maryland, a wide variety of denominations were present from Pennsylvania's outset. William Penn, the founding proprietor of the colony, which bore his name, did significant promotional work in Germany to attract new settlers. Penn, a Quaker, boasted of the religious freedom that would be enjoyed by new settlers, not to mention the location of the colony with its easy access by water and land to both the interior and the eastern seaboard of what would become the United States.

These German settlers, Catholic and non-Catholic alike, were not inheritors of the British political system, nor would they have felt reason to be aggrieved at the apparent deprivation of the political privileges enjoyed by Englishmen that British colonials so often decried. The banks of the Delaware River, by the time of the American Revolution, would not be nearly as accessible to raids by British forces as was the coast of Maryland; hence, the need to develop a militia was never as acute in Pennsylvania. Because of the lateness of its development—nearly fifty years after Maryland—there would never be distinctly Catholic areas of Pennsylvania like St. Mary's and Charles Counties in Maryland. Nor, for that matter, would records be as meticulous as in Calvert's colony. The best one could often hope for in a city such as Philadelphia in order to determine religious affiliation would be the names of pew holders in the earliest churches.[177] These differences aside, it would be Pennsylvania where religious liberty was most robustly practiced and deeply felt for many years, due to both the mind of the Quaker proprietor William Penn and the religious dispositions of the sect to which he belonged.

Quaker Roots

The Society of Friends, the formal name for the Quakers, had their origins in England in the person of George Fox, who desired yet a further break from Puritanism. As much as Puritans wanted to get away from the hierarchical, sacramental form of Christianity of the Middle Ages, Fox, his followers, and their movement became "the most important and enduring manifestation of Puritan radicalism in either England or America."[178]

Fox was a weaver's son, born in Leicestershire in 1624. He had manifested a serious religious conviction since childhood, and when he was in his twenties he began to give witness to a deeply spiritual faith; after the minister had completed his discourse, Fox often rose to give public expression to what the Holy Spirit had

[177] Metzger, *Catholics and the American Revolution*, 208–210. Father Metzger develops these colonial differences in some detail.

[178] Sydney E. Ahlstrom, *A Religious History of the American People* (Garden City, NY: Image Books, 1975), vol. I, 229.

said to him in the course of listening. For such outbursts, he was frequently ridiculed by mobs and sometimes even imprisoned for disorderly conduct. He persevered, however, and gradually won people over by his "powerful witness, homely eloquence and wonderful tenderness."[179] The date traditionally given for the foundation of the Quakers is 1652, when Fox brought "convincement" to a group who ardently sought the same kind of spirituality in, of all places, old Catholic Lancashire.

Quaker belief is the direct revelation of Christ to the soul, though this in no way is considered separate from or contradictory to revelation in Scripture. Their faith falls within the broadly defined Christian tradition, and specifically within the Puritan theological dissent from the Church of England. With such a background, Quakers were initially looked at suspiciously by the English government and were feared by many as disturbers of an established order.

> [The Quaker's] belief that the "Inner Light" might guide mankind to salvation seemed to strike many Christians as a repudiation of scriptural revelation, and so to strike at the very foundation of a well ordered Christian society. Perhaps the most maddening thing about the Quaker was his insistence upon carrying the logic of the Protestant position to an uncompromising extreme. For him, "the priesthood of all believers" was no mere phrase; it was a principle to be literally followed. To men who had agreed to abandon most of the traditional sacraments of the Christian Church, the Quaker proposed that they all be abandoned. When Protestants were still debating the place of ritual in their worship, [the Quaker] insisted upon no ritual at all. Moreover, he was a pacifist; he refused to take an oath; and he rejected the conventional forms of deference for both office and social position. The "leveling" implications in [Quaker] teachings became the more disturbing because of the role women were allowed to

[179] Ibid.

play in the movement, not to mention the readiness of the Quaker to preach his radical doctrines to servants.[180]

William Penn both epitomized and transcended this description. Born in 1644 as the son of the British Admiral who had conquered the Island of Jamaica for Oliver Cromwell, he would become a friend of Charles II (who died a Catholic) and his brother James, Duke of York, the last Catholic monarch of England. The diversity of his life and talents have been well captured by many, but, succinctly put:

> He was almost "all things": the pacifist son of a naval hero; the favorite of kings (Charles II and James II) who was also the friend of the philosophers John Locke and Algernon Sidney; the sometime student of Christ Church (Oxford), Saumur, and Lincoln's Inn who was also a Quaker convert, friend of George Fox, and author of a minor devotional classic, *No Cross, No Crown;* the devout adherent of a radical Protestant sect, democratic theorist, and champion of religious freedom who was yet an aristocrat, accused of Jesuitry and suspected of Jacobitism; the visionary idealist who was also the founder and longtime proprietor of the most successful colony in the British Empire. A practical man of affairs, yet truly a man of the spirit. His long life charts an important path across the terrain between the age of Puritanism and the dawning Age of Reason.[181]

Finally, it seemed almost incongruous that a man of penetrating intellect could be converted to a sect known for its strong antidoctrinal and anti-intellectual convictions. He was described as a writer with "a passion for elegance which flashes through the

[180] Craven, *The Colonies in Transition*, 185.
[181] Ahlstrom, *A Religious History*, vol, I, 265–266.

general dullness of his style in a number of apt and polished maxims," one who pursued profits from his Holy Experiment "almost as ardently as he pursued the Quaker interest and the principle of toleration":

> Converted to the Quaker faith at twenty-three, Penn found himself at twenty-four a prisoner in the Tower of London ... for having preached illegally to a Quaker assemblage. During his subsequent imprisonment in Newgate he wrote the first of several appeals for liberty of conscience that he published in the 1670's and 1680's. His tract, *The Great Case of Liberty of Conscience* (1671), which was the most complete statement of the theory of toleration to be written under the later Stuarts, anticipated by more than fifteen years a substantial part of the case argued by Locke in his famous *Letter on Toleration.* At first Penn wrote simply as a Quaker, crying out with the familiar urgency of left wing Protestants for liberty of conscience. Later he supplemented this appeal to human rights with a shrewd statement directed to practical considerations of state and to the desire for prosperity—a change reflected in the title of his essay of 1675, *England's Present Interest Discovered.*[182]

Penn's Woods

In 1681, Penn received from King Charles II a charter giving him and his heirs the area lying between Maryland and New York and extending westward through five degrees of longitude. On the south, the boundary was fixed at the 40th parallel, which was the upper limit of Lord Baltimore's grant under the Maryland charter

[182] Richard Hofstadter, *America at 1750: A Social Portrait* (New York: Alfred A. Knopf, 1971), 194–195.

and a line close to the later site of the city of Philadelphia. The charter also gave Penn rights along the Delaware River to a point twelve miles above the present-day city of New Castle, Delaware. This was actually well below the 40th parallel, and the issue was further confused by a statement that "the boundary should follow a circular line bending southward at twelve miles distance from New Castle until it intersected the 40th parallel."[183] Such stipulations inevitably caused confusion and would lead to one of the best-remembered boundary disputes in colonial history, between Maryland and Pennsylvania.

In 1682, while still in England, Penn drew up his long-remembered *Frame of Government*, the thirty-fifth clause of which laid to rest any fear a newcomer to his colony might have regarding the freedom to exercise his religious creed in freedom:

> That all persons living in this province, who confess the Almighty and eternal God, to be the Creator, Upholder and Ruler of the world; and that hold themselves obliged in conscience to live peaceably and justly in civil society, shall, in no ways be molested or prejudiced for their religious persuasion or practice, in matters of faith and worship, nor shall they be compelled at any time, to frequent or maintain any religious worship, place or ministry whatever.[184]

Catholics and Quakers had a bit in common: They were both persecuted minorities in England, and had many enemies. Lest he incur the wrath of the Puritans or the Church of England, or, for that matter, any other religious denomination interested in

[183] Craven, *The Colonies in Transition*, 190.

[184] Francis Newton Thorpe, ed., *The Federal and State Constitutions, Colonial Charters, and Other Organic Laws* (Washington, D.C., 1909), V, 3063, cited in Ellis, *Catholics in Colonial America*, 371.

colonizing Pennsylvania, Penn realized he had to walk a fine line. At the end of 1682, he made a bold statement for that time when, at the first session of Pennsylvania's assembly, he declared that office holding would be open to all who professed a belief in Jesus Christ as Savior of the world. Jews, Unitarians, and those professing no religious creed would be excluded, but, from a Catholic perspective, this seemed almost unbelievable. Penn's idea of religious toleration came under immediate fire, however, and differences within Pennsylvania and between Philadelphia and London were pronounced.

Penn's broad-mindedness was not going to go unchallenged: In 1693 the British government insisted that all colonial officeholders take the specific oath demanded of all British officeholders. The colony delayed a response as long as possible, but the demand was repeated in 1701, and, two years later, Queen Anne's government became insistent. The Quakers had not established sufficient strength to defy Britain, and the colonial legislature, much to Penn's displeasure, went along:

> This oath not only continued the exclusion of Jews, Unitarians, and unbelievers, but it expressly demanded an abjuration of the Catholic doctrines of transubstantiation, veneration of the Mother of God and the saints, and the sacrifice of the Mass, and it was not until 1776 that this requirement was eliminated in the broad liberties embodied in Pennsylvania's declaration of rights of September of the year.[185]

Despite this, Catholic colonists apparently had few misgivings about what life in Pennsylvania offered them. Religious freedom was still robust, so many were determined to seek a better life for the practice of their Faith—and for their economic betterment.

[185] Ibid., 372.

Pioneer Priests and Makeshift Altars

Catholic life didn't take long to get started. Reverend John Talbot, an Anglican divine in New Jersey, wrote a curious letter to the Society for the Promotion of the Gospel in England in 1707 or 1708, telling his confreres of the worst of rumors—that a "popish Mass" had been conducted in Philadelphia:

> I saw Mr. Bradford at New-York, he tells me mass is set up and read publicly at Philadelphia, and several people are turned to it amongst which Lionel Brittain the Church-warden is one and his son another. I thought that Popery woul'd come in among Friends the Quakers, as soon as any way.[186]

The Conewago Chapel

Between 1680 and 1720, traces of a Catholic presence in Pennsylvania could often be detected among itinerant missionaries and small congregations gathering for the celebration of Holy Mass. These priests were almost exclusively Jesuits and traveled through southeastern Pennsylvania to and from New York. Central to this operation was Bohemia Manor on Maryland's Eastern Shore; the work of the missionaries was incessant. As so many Maryland Catholics would later settle Kentucky, so, it appears, did they settle Pennsylvania:

> Land-hungry citizens of Maryland, including Catholics seeking relief from religious intolerance, began to move northward along the Susquehanna River and its tributaries in the early years of the eighteenth century. A group proceeded up the upper reaches of Conewago Creek and settled with

[186] Talbot to George Keith, Westchester [New York], February 14, 1707–1708, *American Catholic Historical Researches* XXII (April, 1905): 122, cited in Ellis, *Catholics in Colonial America*, 373.

the hope of attaining quick and easy title to the land. It was then Indian territory but never a battleground between the various tribes. Therefore, the non-violent reputation of the area as well as its close proximity to the intersection of Indian trails leading northward from Baltimore to Carlisle and the east-west axis from Lancaster and Philadelphia proved a strong attraction.[187]

The area today that is made up of Lancaster, Philadelphia, Chester, and Bucks Counties hosted a combination of German and Celtic-Irish peoples professing the Catholic Faith who, by 1785, numbered approximately seven thousand. The network of roads, trails, and waterways that sprang up in these areas provided easy access to the port cities of Baltimore and Philadelphia and from there to European markets. German Catholics had been as attracted to Pennsylvania as their Protestant counterparts by the promotional work of the agents of William Penn, while English and Irish Catholics, feeling the effects of religious intolerance in Maryland, were eager to move northward in search of peace.

Titles to land around the Conewago settlement were first given by Lord Baltimore in 1730, though Maryland settlers were present long before. The largest grant was over ten thousand acres to John Digges and came to be known as Digges Choice. The English Jesuit Joseph Greaton had arrived in Maryland in 1719 and is the first known priest to have ministered in the Conewago area; it would be some years before a church could be erected, so Mass houses were used with frequency, with the Catholic faithful coming for miles to assist at the Holy Sacrifice, to go to Confession, to have

[187] Robert Edward Quigley, *Catholic Beginnings in the Delaware Valley*, in James F. Connelly, S.T.L., Hist. E.D., ed., *The History of the Archdiocese of Philadelphia* (Philadelphia: Archdiocese of Philadelphia, 1976), 13.

their children baptized, and to receive ongoing instruction in the truths of faith. The first such Mass house was reportedly that of Robert Owings, near the present-day Conewago Road near McSherrystown. A German Jesuit named William Wapplier, who had been sent to look after German Catholics in particular, built the first church, dedicating it to St. Mary of the Assumption. Almost immediately it took on the name "Conewago Chapel" and became the headquarters of the St. Francis Regis Mission Band of the Jesuits, covering the territory west of the Susquehanna River, Western Maryland, and the Shenandoah Valley of Virginia.

Yet another German Jesuit, James Pellentz, arrived in 1758 and became pastor of Conewago a decade later, remaining there until 1800. With a congregation now comprising over one thousand souls, he was compelled to erect a new edifice, built of stone, and dedicated to the Sacred Heart of Jesus.[188] By the early nineteenth century, with five thousand Catholics, it was thought to be the largest parish in the United States.[189]

[188] Conewago was the first church in the United States dedicated to the Sacred Heart, thought to be perhaps the first in the western hemisphere, and is currently the oldest Catholic church building in the United States built of stone. Prince Demetrius Gallitzin spent the earliest years of his priesthood at Conewago. The son of Prince Dimitri Gallitzin, envoy of Catherine the Great of Russia at the Hague, and his German wife, Amelia, the daughter of Field Marshal von Schmettau, who served under Fredrick the Great of Russia, the young prince was ordained by Bishop John Carroll in Baltimore in 1795 and spent four years at Conewago. He founded the Catholic parish at Loretto, Pennsylvania, and in the forty-one years he spent there, he grew in religious stature. He has been known since as the "Apostle of the Alleghenies."

[189] The parish cemetery was opened in 1752 to receive the body of Dudley Digges; the oldest existing gravestone is that of Samuel Lilly, who died in 1758. He came from Bristol, England, to Philadelphia in 1729, and, hearing of a Catholic settlement at

The Church in Philadelphia

Father Joseph Greaton was the first regularly appointed pastor in Pennsylvania and the first priest resident in the city of Philadelphia prior to 1741. He had been born in London, and a personal notation made in a family Bible stated that he had converted to Catholicism at fifteen. This was a conversion he took very seriously; years later, he begged forgiveness for what he thought might be an impediment to Holy Orders, namely, that he had once professed heresy. After his profession as a Jesuit and his ordination to the priesthood in Flanders, he spent a decade working in the Low Countries, where he learned German, Flemish, and Spanish. His fluency in German would greatly enhance his pastoral capabilities in southeastern Pennsylvania. Greaton came first to the Jesuit mission in Southern Maryland, and only in later years to Pennsylvania. For several years, he served as an itinerant missionary and a circuit rider:

> Across the Chesapeake Bay, through Kent and Cecil Counties to Bohemia and thence to Philadelphia, coming into the city by way of Concord, Chester County, where the Wilcox family was settled from 1727; or, at times through Cecil, Hartford, Baltimore Counties to Conewago, thence to Lancaster, to Concord, and so to Philadelphia.[190]

Conewago, moved there in 1730. His home, "Eden," was along the Conewago Creek. A school under the direction of the Jesuits was begun as early as 1800. One century later, the Society of Jesus formally transferred the parish to the Diocese of Harrisburg, Pennsylvania. Pope St. John XXIII bestowed the title of Minor Basilica on the Conewago Chapel on June 30, 1962.

[190] Joseph L. J. Kirlin, *Catholicity in Philadelphia* (Philadelphia: John McVey, 1909), 27, cited in Quigley, *Catholic Beginnings*, 16.

About 1729, Father Greaton took up residence in Philadelphia, saying Mass in private homes. The possibility for doing this was far better at this time than it would have been in Maryland, though even here there were strong Protestant forces, largely in opposition to William Penn, who were only too happy to report Catholic liturgies to the British government, hoping, at least, to cause some embarrassment to the proprietor.

Once the English Jesuit knew that Philadelphia was to be his principal residence, he began plans for constructing a church and was able to buy land through friendly offices in the city. He named the church in honor of St. Joseph, and constructed it in 1733 and 1734. Located in Willings Alley near Fourth and Walnut Streets, it was described as being tucked away in "a place of quiet seclusion." It caused consternation to a certain set in the city, but there was no Pennsylvania statute prohibiting its presence. As such, Catholic life in the city began to take permanent hold. Early estimates counted twenty-two Irish, the rest German, for a total of merely thirty-seven parishioners. A later inquiry increased these figures somewhat, but it is certain that Catholics were a distinct minority in 1730s Philadelphia.

Father Greaton labored without help for several years, not only pastoring St. Joseph's but riding the circuit as well. In 1741, a young Jesuit of Maryland English heritage, Henry Neale, arrived to assist the pastor. Later that year, the two German Jesuits, William Wapplier and Theodore Schneider, arrived to augment the mission band. Neale stopped first in the present-day city of Lancaster, where he found a population of some twelve to fifteen hundred, mostly German, but some English and Irish as well. His letters to his Jesuit superior in London describe the harshness of life on the circuit, which may well have accounted for his death at the early age of forty-six. Father Greaton, for his part, died in his early seventies at Bohemia, where he spent a few brief retirement years after his profound apostolic work.

Father Wapplier was a native of Westphalia who had entered the Lower Rhine Province of the Society of Jesus in 1728. He literally exhausted himself in missionary effort for seven years in America and returned home, where he died at age seventy in 1781. Father Schneider had had a brilliant academic career before coming to America. He hailed from the Palatinate in southwest Germany and entered the Upper Rhine Province in 1721, studying medicine in addition to philosophy and theology. He taught for several years in Liege and at the University of Heidelberg, where he was elected Rector Magnificus. The two men traveled together often, but it appears Wapplier kept up a more frequent correspondence with Jesuit superiors. He writes of their first visit to Lancaster:

> The English people call it Nemororon or Lancastertown. The Germans call it Neustatt. There we lodged with a certain Catholic Hibernian Thomas Doyle, to whom we gave favorable introductory letters about ourselves from our English missionaries in Philadelphia. Our appearance among the German Catholic inhabitants of the city was as pleasant as it was unexpected. They had always been under the false impression that the entry of German Catholic priests in the land of Pennsylvania was strictly forbidden. They likewise thought that even if it were permitted, no one would decide to minister to such a small group of German settlers amid such danger and inconvenience.[191]

Lancaster was to become the second city in importance in Pennsylvania after Philadelphia, though Father Wapplier noted that the small band of Catholics was so scattered it was difficult to gather them for "Divine Service." He decided to tend to the needs

[191] Sister Janet McCauley, master's thesis, Seton Hall University, 1960, cited in Quigley, *Catholic Beginnings*, 20.

of those residing in the western portion of Lancaster County, while Father Schneider would work in the counties of Philadelphia and Bucks. There were, at that time, no Catholics residing in Chester County. Wapplier's procedure varied little at each mission outpost:

> As soon as I arrive at my mission place I enclose myself in my little wooden church where my lambs are either awaiting my arrival or gradually gathering. Usually I preface all activities with the Holy Sacrifice of the Mass. After that I read the gospel from an English book, until I know the language more thoroughly, for the English members, who often mingle with the German. Then I address an allocution to my compatriots in their mother tongue. Lastly I take a Catechism question and discuss it fully for the necessary instruction of both old and young. [192]

These counties would grow and develop; German Catholicism would become more and more significant; and the German Jesuits and their successors in these mission outposts would truly become heroes in the spread of the Faith.

Father Greaton's congregation at St. Joseph's, Willings Alley, small as it was, had grown by the mid-1750s to nearly four hundred. While not a spectacular number, it did necessitate the building of a larger edifice on the same property and allowed the Jesuits to consider beginning another church to accommodate both permanent and transient parishioners. They purchased a lot on Fourth Street, south of Spruce, in 1760 and began construction on St. Mary's, one day to be the first cathedral of the diocese. Important also in this planning was the inclusion of a sufficiently large graveyard—one in which, in later years, numerous Catholic patriots would be interred. This work was directed by another English Jesuit, Father Robert

[192] Ibid., 21.

Harding, a native of Nottingham, who had previously served the Maryland mission. Harding would distinguish himself in the city of Philadelphia, in both civic and ecclesial matters, and in his own career would foreshadow a pattern of Catholic assimilation that would continue for generations.

On two occasions the Continental Congress would gather at St. Mary's, once for an official requiem for a Spanish Diplomat, the other for a Te Deum on achieving independence. It was to St. Mary's as well that John Adams strolled on a warm fall afternoon when Congress had recessed. Mass was going on, and he sat and observed. His recollections, written to his wife, Abigail, have become standard lore in United States Catholic history:

> This afternoon, led by curiosity and good company, I strolled away to mother church, or rather grandmother church. I mean the Romish chapel. I heard a good, short moral essay upon the duty of parents to raise their children, founded in justice and charity, to take care of their interests, temporal and spiritual. This afternoon's entertainment was to me most awful and affecting; the poor wretches fingering their beads, chanting Latin, not a word of which they understood; their pater nosters and ave Marias; their holy water; their crossing themselves perpetually; their bowing to the name of Jesus, whenever they hear it; their bowings, kneelings and genuflections before the altar. The dress of the priest was rich white lace. His pulpit was velvet and gold. The altarpiece was very rich, little images and crucifixes about; wax candles lighted up. But how shall I describe the picture of our Savior in a frame of marble over the altar, at full length, upon the cross in the agonies, and the blood dropping and streaming from His wounds! The music, consisting of an organ and a choir of singers, went on all afternoon except

sermon time, and the assembly chanted most sweetly and exquisitely. Here is everything which can lay hold of the eye, ear, and imagination—everything which can charm and bewitch the simple and ignorant. I wonder how Luther ever broke the spell. Adieu.[193]

Philadelphia Catholics had begun to achieve a certain amount of business success, and with it social prestige. At the same time, the spiritual democracy that is Christianity knows no boundaries. Ethnic groups were fairly intermixed in the areas around St. Joseph's and St. Mary's, and division by income and occupation does not seem to have been in the norm in central Philadelphia.

Jesuit Outposts in Eastern Pennsylvania

A census taken by Father Harding in 1757 indicates only four Jesuits throughout Pennsylvania. But Catholicism had taken root all around Penn's Colony and would continue to radiate from Philadelphia for years to come.

Jesuit missionaries moved to Pennsylvania from several directions; one of the best remembered routes is the path from Bohemia Manor in Cecil County, Maryland, through Coffee Run, Delaware, and finally to Ivy Mills, Pennsylvania. As early as 1720 Mass was offered there in the Thomas Willcox home. The settlement took its name from the ivy-covered mills, owned by Willcox, in which paper was manufactured. It was a very high grade of paper, exported internationally, and used by several of the colonial governments to print their currency. The Willcox firm for many years had the patronage of Benjamin Franklin, who used their product to supply his printing press. From the notebooks kept by the nineteenth-century

[193] Ellis, *Documents*, 136–137.

saint John Neumann of Philadelphia, it is possible to deduce that Mass was said at Ivy Mills for well over a century in the Willcox Manor and that official permission to have a house chapel was ultimately granted by Bishop Francis Patrick Kenrick.

Thomas Willcox was a convert to Catholicism after his marriage to Irish-born Elizabeth Cole; Mary Brackett Willcox, the wife of Thomas's grandson James M. Willcox, became a Catholic after "protesting for twenty years under a Catholic roof and beside a Catholic altar in her own home."[194] These two converts stood out in the family annals, and the zeal with which the entire family approached the Faith was noticed and commented on by Catholics and non-Catholics alike. The large home was a stopover for numerous individuals prominent in both journalism and business, but "no matter how many strangers were on hand, Mass was said in the family oratory."[195] The family also had slaves, and were conspicuous for their efforts to instruct them in Catholicism, as well as doing everything possible to have them marry within the Faith. While the Jesuits were the first to minister to the Catholics of Ivy Mills, Augustinians, Vincentians, and diocesan clergy were all prominent for their apostolic activity.[196]

The first Jesuit missionaries to arrive in the area now called Bally, Pennsylvania, in between Reading and Allentown, discovered friendly Indians and German pioneers, mostly Mennonites.

194 Leo Gregory Fink, *Old Jesuit Trails in Penn's Forest* (New York: Paulist Press, 1936), 27. In later years, the Willcox Mansion gave way to the parish church of St. Thomas the Apostle, Chester Heights, Delaware County, in the Archdiocese of Philadelphia.

195 Ibid., 25.

196 In the mid-nineteenth century, the Willcox family opened their home to seminarians from St. Charles Borromeo Seminary in Philadelphia for a summer respite. The seminary was in Ivy Mills for a time but later was sold and became the Mother House of the Sisters of St. Francis. See ibid., 27.

Father Greaton began to acquire land in 1742, and within five years the Jesuits had nearly five hundred acres of rich farmland and forest. The area was first called Goshenhoppen, and Father Schneider was the first active missionary to minister among his fellow Germans. The early Masses were offered in the homes of Catholic farmers, and when Father Schneider took up permanent residence, he quickly opened a school to which Catholic and Protestant children were equally welcome. By 1743 he was ready to build a church, which he dedicated to St. Paul. Local Protestants, grateful for the rudimentary education he provided to their children, even helped to build the structure. But Father Schneider did not remain stationary in Goshenhoppen:

> From Goshenhoppen a missionary trail was opened to Reading, Douglasville, Mount Pleasant, Obolds, Moselem Springs, Hamburg, Port Clinton, Schulykill Haven, Pottsville, Ashland and as far as Sunbury; they also branched off at Pottsville and passing through the Schulykill Valley, visited all the little towns such as Port Carbon and Middleport where the old Catawissa trail was used to pass over the mountains towards Hazleton on the east and on the west toward Williamsport. From Middleport ofttimes the Fathers traveled on a straight line through Brockton (then called Patterson), Tuscarora and Tamaqua towards Buck Mountain and Mauch Chunk, with northeastern Pennsylvania as their objective. From Bally they also went to Reading, Kutztown, Tulpehocken, Moselem Springs, Mount Pleasant, through Wernersville to Lebanon and the western sections. Another favorite trail was Bally, Macungi, Vera Cruz, Emaus, Maxetani, Cedar Creek, Allentown, from which one trail led to Bethlehem, Easton, and down along the Delaware to Haycock, while the other trail branched off

> at Allentown to Catasauqua, Hokendauqua, Slatington, Berlinsville, Weissport, Walnutport, Parryville, Lehighton, to Mauch Chunk.[197]

One of the larger towns for which Goshenhoppen served as a base for other missionary activities was Reading:

> Sight must not be lost of the work done by the selfsame missionaries in Reading and its immediate environment. The old Church of St. Peter which was mentioned by a certain writer in 1753 as a "Roman Catholic Meeting-house" was a block house on the east side of old Duke Street.... Alongside the church was a graveyard.... The Jesuits consistently cared for the Catholics of Reading, and the probable date of St. Peter's Church and its founding was in 1751.[198]

An incident of particular note occurred at Goshenhoppen during Father Schneider's pastorate, in 1755. It involved the annual Corpus Christi procession, which occurred both inside and outside the church, and then through the cemetery, the churchyard, and the adjoining fields. Familiar and beloved to Catholics for centuries, it looked strange indeed to others. It was thought that Catholics were participating in a military drill so that they might be better prepared to massacre Protestants. Conrad Weiser, a local justice of the peace, wrote to Pennsylvania's governor, informing him that 117 adult Catholics lived in Berks County, and of those, about fifty worshipped in the small church in Goshenhoppen:

> As all our Protestant inhabitants are very uneasy at the behavior of some of the Roman Catholics, who are very numerous in this country, some of whom show great joy at the bad

[197] Ibid., 67–68. The name Goshenhoppen was later changed to Bally.
[198] Ibid., 82.

> news lately come from the army, we have thought it our duty to inform Your Honor to enable us, by some legal authority, to disarm, or otherwise disable the Papists from doing injury to other people who are not of their vile principles. We know that the people of the Roman Catholic Church are bound by their principles to be the worst subjects, and worst of neighbors; and we have reason to fear just now that the Roman Catholics at Cussahoppen, where they have a magnificent chapel, and lately had large processions, have bad designs.[199]

Apparently, the report was not taken seriously, but it reveals the deep-seated suspicion always present in the American Protestant mind.

Goshenhoppen was served by a series of priests, largely but not exclusively Jesuits, the best remembered being Father Augustine Bally, for whom the town was later renamed. Though he served the town in the nineteenth century, beyond the scope of this study, his service was of an extraordinary nature and is worthy of note. Born in Belgium and arriving in America as a young man full of spiritual energy and vigor, he quickly won the respect of all residents. He served in the same capacity as his eighteenth-century counterparts in missionary travels and won numerous converts to the Faith. It was said that in him, "the happy combination of St. Vincent de Paul's spirit of self-denial and practical helpfulness was always found." He began a parish school described as "praiseworthy," took keen interest in his young men fighting in the Union Army in the Civil War, and for forty-five years was Christ's presence in countless ways.[200]

[199] Ibid., 70.

[200] Ibid., 75–81. Fink develops the career and spirituality of Father Bally at length.

Finally, when the Jesuits came from Maryland into Pennsylvania, they numbered Haycock among their earliest missions. In 1737 the Penn family sold some five hundred acres of land to Thomas and Edward McCarty, who, with fellow Irishmen, came to America to flee religious persecution. It was a very fertile agricultural area at the base of the Haycock Mountain and extended to the Delaware River, midway between the present-day cities of Trenton, New Jersey, and Easton, Pennsylvania. Not only Irish, but many Germans from the Palatinate and especially from Alsace-Lorraine arrived as well.[201]

> The first Catholic settlers around the base of Haycock Mountain were Nicholas, Thomas and Edward McCarty, who with such men as Thomas Garden, John Durham, Patrick McCarty, Charles Poulton, John Fricker, Anthony Greaser, . . . the Lanzinger, Hookey and Bucks families, the Heaneys, Melchiors, McIntyres and Lambings, all combined and contributed toward the organization and development of Catholicism along the Delaware River The very first page of the oldest Catholic Church Register of the Thirteen English Colonies contains a record by the Jesuit missionary, Rev. Theodore Schneider, S.J., and that record pertains to his first Baptism of Albertina, the daughter of George and Barbara Kohl of Haycock. While the Baptism took place in the house of John Utzman in Faulkner's Swamp, nevertheless the importance of the record consists in this, that the first Baptism contained in his oldest Catholic Church Register, was of a child born of parents who were pioneers in Haycock.

[201] Some of the better-known Catholics of the early period were: John George Kohl, who arrived in 1732; John Jacob Eck in 1742; Michael Hartman in 1748; and the conspicuously Catholic Bucks Family in 1752.

> Haycock, therefore, has the honor of presenting to the Jesuit missionaries the first baptism for their valuable register. This selfsame person, Albertina Kohl, whose baptismal record is dated August 23, 1741, was buried in Haycock Cemetery on July 3, 1779.[202]

The first Mass houses in Haycock were those of Edward McCarty and Thomas Garden. As the years passed, both these domiciles became too small to accommodate the increasing Catholic population, and so, not long after the signing of the Declaration of Independence, Nicholas McCarty, Edward's son, decided to construct a much larger home nearby. On the first floor was a room of substantial size where Catholics would gather for Mass, while the second floor had space enough to accommodate any itinerant missionary passing through, as well as a room to store all the sacred vessels used for Holy Mass. The house hosted Baptisms and Marriages. A parish church arose here at the end of the eighteenth century, and yet a larger one in the mid-nineteenth century.

In the Lehigh Valley, Catholic growth may also be traced to Father Theodore Schneider's early visits. There were about 159 Catholics, according to the Jesuit priest's count, in Berks and Northhampton Counties. As early as 1767 a group of Catholics asked permission of the governor of Pennsylvania to collect money for a Catholic Church to be built in Northamptontown, present-day Allentown.

Those plans were postponed due to the Revolutionary War. But the region did have an expanded Catholic presence in a different

[202] Ibid., 91-92. As with generalized statements, Fink's reference to the "oldest Catholic Church Register of the Thirteen English Colonies," given Jesuit activity in Southern Maryland, could be open to serious dispute. This aside, Fink's study is filled with stories of early Catholic Pennsylvania; we have attempted to include only the more significant.

way: The French Engineer Corps under Baron de Kalb, and with orders from George Washington, came from Philadelphia to Bethlehem and Allentown. The unit had a French Catholic army chaplain, who offered Mass for both the French and American soldiers, and many wounded soldiers were brought to a general hospital in Allentown, where they were spiritually tended to by Catholic missionaries. In Bethlehem proper, Father Schneider recorded the baptism of Mary Appolonia Franz on March 4, 1742. In 1768, a Father de Ritter baptized Anna Mary Rose on October 17, in Nicholas Hucki's house near Easton.[203]

Across the Mountains

The story of Catholicism in Western Pennsylvania has a history of its own, and is more related to French colonization in the new world. In the sixteenth and early-seventeenth centuries, French monarchs had tried to stake an active claim in North America, specifically in Quebec, and succeeded in 1608 under the leadership of Samuel de Champlain. The colony of New France, by the latter part of the seventeenth century, had grown to include Montreal and Trois Rivières. Later still, in the 1670s, the French began to settle the Mississippi River valley. In the area west of the Allegheny Mountains they found Shawnee and Seneca Indians, who came under the care of French Catholics, who made a number of converts in each tribe.

It was not until the mid-eighteenth century that France attempted to strengthen its grip on the interior of North America. To protect its lines of communication, extending along an arc from

[203] Ibid., 117–126. Fink gives many particulars of these apostolic visitations, as well as descriptions of the various Catholic families who provided hospitality to the many visiting priests.

New Orleans to Quebec, France sought to control areas where it was vulnerable by expanding into the "buffer area" of the Upper Ohio River valley. By 1753 they had constructed a series of forts from Lake Erie toward the Ohio River. By all accounts, many of the local Indians abandoned their allegiance with England, seeing in the French efforts a surer security.

During the period of French domination, Catholic missionaries often accompanied explorers and military expeditions. The first recorded Mass offered in present-day Pittsburgh was at the site of Fort Duquesne, later rebuilt and expanded as Fort Pitt, in 1754. The French did not remain there any length of time, however, and Pittsburgh became largely a transfer point for westward expansion.

The major settlement in southwestern Pennsylvania occurred between 1769 and 1774, on the eve of the American Revolution, and included the counties of Allegheny, Washington, Fayette, Westmorland, and Bedford. Among the settlers were British, Welsh, Scots, Germans, and a mere 4.5 percent Southern Irish Catholic. Even so, the route of Catholic pioneers was well marked out and came from two directions

> One group of Catholic pioneers went from Goshenhoppen through Huntingdon County ... to Hollidaysburg; it then traversed the Allegheny Mountains to a spot now occupied by St. Vincent's Abbey, at Latrobe. There in the Fall of 1787 "was laid the foundation of the first permanent Catholic settlement in Western Pennsylvania. It became in time the parent of numerous other congregations; and was long a resting place for colonists going farther west." By November, 1799, when Father Peter Heilbron ... took charge of the mission, it numbered about seventy-five communicants.... A second route led westward from Conewago, entering Huntingdon County at Shade Gap in the southeast,

and uniting with the first mentioned route at some point east of Hollidaysburg. A number of families, some German and some Irish, proceeded via this route to Westmoreland County ... and to Loreto, in Cambria County.... It was from this area of western Pennsylvania that in July, 1785, a document containing seventy-three signatures was carried eastward to Father Farmer in Philadelphia petitioning for a priest to be assigned to the west.[204]

Down the River to Delaware

Much as early Catholic Virginia was largely an outgrowth of Maryland Catholicism, so the story of Catholic colonial Delaware is intimately bound up with that of Pennsylvania. Though the early history of the Faith in Delaware remains unclear, settlements along the southwestern portion of the Delaware River did exist, though they were overshadowed by Pennsylvania and, for that matter, by Maryland.

Delaware was first settled by the Dutch in 1631, then seven years later by the Swedes, and finally by the British in 1644. Some eighteen years later, William Penn, fearing that his own colony might be cut off from the sea, secured title to this land from his friend James, Duke of York—later James II. The "lower counties" of New Castle, Kent, and Sussex remained loosely appended to Pennsylvania and shared the same governor with the "upper counties" of Philadelphia, Chester, and Bucks. It was only in the fall of 1776, with the adoption of its own constitution, that the

[204] Quigley, *Catholic Beginnings*, 33. German Jesuit Ferdinand Steinmeyer (later becoming Farmer) was one of the prominent early Jesuits working in Philadelphia. The priest ultimately assigned to the west was Prince Gallitzin.

independent state of Delaware was created. The English, Scots-Irish, and remaining Swedes dominated the colony, thus maintaining the Protestant status quo. It was not until after the American Revolution that the Delaware State Constitution did away with religious qualifications for office holding, and Catholicism in a real way was given a chance to flourish.

The exact origin of the first Catholic settlers to inhabit Delaware remains unknown, but one historian has estimated they were likely

> Maryland farmers who moved back from the Chesapeake Bay seeking fresh lands. Possibly they moved into the Delaware counties purposely in order to assure themselves of religious freedom, but more likely their residence in Delaware was determined by economic considerations—that is, by the abandonment of worn-out tobacco lands along the Chesapeake.[205]

The Jesuits from Bohemia Manor visited occasionally, and for nearly three decades Mass was offered on the estate of Cornelius Hallahan, an Irish Catholic who settled in Mill Creek Hundred, New Castle County. By the mid-eighteenth century, Jesuits were also working in the present-day areas of Dover and Odessa; an Anglican minister named Philip Reading reported to the Society for the Propagation of the Gospel that "a Catholic mission was noticeable at Apoquinimick in lower New Castle County prior to 1750."[206]

In 1772, a German Jesuit named Father Matthew Sittensperger purchased a 200-acre farm from Cornelius Hallahan along a stream that gave the mission the name Coffee Run. Even though the Jesuits were suppressed the following year, various priests, religious

[205] John A. Munroe et al., *Coffee Run, 1772–1960: The Beginnings of the Catholic Faith in Delaware* (Hockessin, DE: Church of St. John the Evangelist, 1960), 11, cited in ibid., 29.

[206] Ibid.

and diocesan, continued to work there—though the number of faithful there and throughout Delaware remained low.[207]

Philadelphia Catholics in the Revolution

As colonial Pennsylvania entered the revolutionary period, Philadelphia became a focal point of political activity. As such, the major Catholic contribution to that activity centered there. Two Jesuits in particular, Ferdinand Farmer and Robert Molyneaux, ministered to the flock at St. Joseph's; the latter is much remembered for his staunch support of the Revolutionary War as well as his later ardent patriotism for the new nation.

It has always been difficult to ascertain the number of Catholics who fought in the Revolutionary Army. The general Catholic population in the war years has been estimated at 25,000, and the greatest number of fighting men must have come from Maryland. In Pennsylvania, numbers were lower, but not insignificant. A 1757 census by Catholic priests of their communicants in the colony, taken at the request of the military, listed 629 as German and 180 as Irish. That number was not greatly altered in the years leading up to 1776, though one calculation put the number of fighting Catholic Irishmen at 300. Yet another tabulator of such statistics noted that the Scots-Irish Presbyterians tended, almost to a man, to favor the patriot cause, while the Celtic Irish were found on both sides of the fight. Statewide, the guess is 1,500 Catholic men

[207] In the early nineteenth century, Father Patrick Kenny, an Irish-born priest took possession of Coffee Run Plantation through arrangements with Bishop John Carroll and the ex-Jesuits who had maintained it. He would remain there for thirty-five years, serving a widely scattered flock of both Irish and French settlers. Also, Father Kenny founded the parishes of St. Peter in New Castle and St. Peter in Wilmington.

would end up fighting in the Revolutionary Army over the course of the war; this figure would include the city of Philadelphia, into which immigrants were pouring in increasing numbers, as well as the rest of the colony. Those attracted to the loyalist cause came almost exclusively from the city.

The names Stephen Moylan, Thomas FitzSimons, George Meade, and John Barry would all be found on gravestones at Old St. Mary's. Each was a revolutionary patriot of the highest distinction, and the career of each bears further scrutiny.

Some hold that what Charles Carroll was to Maryland, Stephen Moylan was to Pennsylvania. Born to a prominent Catholic family in Cork, Ireland, in 1737, his family sent him to be educated in Paris. He then worked in Lisbon for three years for the family's shipping firm. He came to Philadelphia in 1768 with the intention of beginning his own firm, and became one of the organizers and first president of the Friendly Sons of St. Patrick, a nonreligious fraternal organization formed on March 17, 1776. He married Mary Ricketts van Horne in 1778, and they became the parents of two daughters; two sons died in infancy.

A brother of the bishop of Cork, Moylan and several of his brothers were to distinguish themselves on the other side of the Atlantic. Stephen rose rapidly and convincingly in military rank. He came to George Washington's attention, serving first as the general's personal secretary. Washington saw the greater use for his talents, however, and had him named an aide-de-camp in March 1776. Later that summer, John Hancock, president of the Continental Congress, informed Moylan that "from a sense of your merit and attachment to the American cause [Congress] has been pleased to appoint you Quartermaster General in the Army of the Colonies with the rank of Colonel."[208] The office of Quartermaster had not

[208] Metzger, *Catholics and the American Revolution*, 220.

been completely organized at the time of Moylan's appointment, and it is likely he encountered some resistance; it became necessary for Congress to issue a further directive to the colonial army that all orders, directives, and so on coming from Colonel Moylan were to have the same force as those coming from a general.

By early 1777 he was in charge of the Fourth Continental Dragoons, whose activities involved patrol duty, anticipating and thwarting thrusts of the enemy, disrupting their lines of communication, pursuing groups engaged in scouting or raiding, and rounding up and escorting prisoners to their confinement. In late 1783, Moylan was promoted, by act of Congress, to the rank of brigadier general—the highest military rank achieved by a Catholic in the war. He is credited, perhaps apocryphally, with being one of the earliest citizens, if not the first, publicly to use the expression "United States of America." The accomplishments of his family also proved noteworthy:

> In quite various ways three of Stephen Moylan's brothers, James, John, and Jasper, furthered the common cause. About 1778 James became a commercial agent of the United States in France, with headquarters at L'Orient, and when American frigates and privateers preyed successfully on British shipping, even in British home waters, and brought prizes into French ports, he was obliged to undertake the duties of prize agent. In addition, he had a hand in fitting out the *Ranger*, the *Alliance*, and the *Bonhomme Richard*, whose exploits spread dismay in British commercial circles and sent insurance rates soaring. James helped to forge economic ties between our country and France when such bonds were the very lifeline of an almost insolvent United States. Thus, in noncombatant positions James proved himself a worthy emulator of the commander of the Fourth Dragoons. Towards the end of the war John occupied the prosaic post of

clothier general of America's fighting forces, while Jasper, after a tour of duty in Spain, became ensign of the Philadelphia Associators in 1781.[209]

Moylan's contemporary, Thomas FitzSimons, had an equally illustrious career, though more directed to politics. He was born in Ireland, very likely in Ballikilty, County Wexford, in 1741. He arrived in Philadelphia at age nineteen, and his father died shortly afterward. He had enough education, however, to begin work in a mercantile house, and in 1761 he married Catharine Meade and formed a business partnership with her brother George.[210]

Their firm was soon hit by the new revenue measures passed to prop up the finances of the British Empire, including the Stamp Act of 1765. Much concerned with these events, FitzSimons became involved with the merchant community in Philadelphia and, with Moylan and others, became a founding member of the Friendly Sons of St. Patrick. When Pennsylvania began forming a militia to fight the British, FitzSimons soon got involved. He served as captain of a company of home guards, and initially his company served among the soldiers who manned posts along the New Jersey coast for defense. His unit later served as part of the reserve at the Battle of Trenton in 1776. He went on to serve on the Pennsylvania Council of Safety and headed a board to oversee the newly formed Pennsylvania Navy.

Politically, he served as a member of the Committee of Correspondence and participated in a number of revolutionary activities

[209] Ibid., 225. Father Metzger has noted that "circumstances made Stephen Moylan for Pennsylvania what Charles Carroll was to Maryland, but with the difference that, whereas Charles Carroll served his country in civil offices, Moylan served in various military capacities." Ibid., 216.

[210] George Meade was the grandfather of George Gordon Meade, union commander at the Battle of Gettysburg.

prior to the War of Independence. He also became a director of the Bank of North America and later president of the Insurance Company of North America. He was, with George Meade and James White, much involved with the writing of a new state constitution for Pennsylvania, which became a reality in 1790.

FitzSimons was, early on, a Federalist—favoring conservative reform, high protective tariffs, and more power vested in the national government, and pro-British in foreign-policy priorities. As such, he was a staunch supporter of Alexander Hamilton and was closely aligned with the nation's first president, George Washington. Though he was elected to the Confederation Congress,[211] it appeared that Pennsylvania politics were a higher priority for him. As one of only two Roman Catholics to sign the Constitution of the United States,[212] he played a substantial role in the Constitutional Convention:

> He seconded the motion of Governor Morris to restrict the suffrage to freeholders, upheld the submission of treaties to the lower as well as upper house of the national legislature, opposed the full publication of expenditures, and supported the extension of the commerce power of the central government, visualizing even the use of taxes on exports. As with members of the commercial classes generally, the necessity of a stronger government was so apparent to him that it did not need argument.[213]

[211] The Confederation Congress was a loosely knit body that governed while the country operated under the Articles of Confederation.

[212] The other being Daniel Carroll of Rock Creek, Maryland, brother of Archbishop John Carroll, and a cousin of Charles Carroll of Carrollton.

[213] C. J. Nuesse, Ph.D., *The Social Thought of American Catholics: 1634–1829* (Westminster, MD: Newman Book Shop, 1945), 87.

George Meade, FitzSimon's brother-in-law, was an equally prominent Philadelphia Catholic. Before the war, the shipping firm of Garrett and Meade carried on extensive trade with the West Indies. After Garrett's death, FitzSimons became an associate, and the firm was known as George Meade and Company. During the war, the firm engaged in privateering and helped to equip French naval forces in American waters. Also a charter member of the Friendly Sons of St. Patrick, Meade made no attempt to hide his Catholicism. As a patriot, he was active on committees of relief and correspondence.

To his undying fame, when Washington's army at Valley Forge was on the verge of breaking up for lack of food and provisions, it was Meade who contributed very generously to a fund for its relief. "This was commendable generosity," one historian observed, "for as the prospects of repayment were slight, this was tantamount to an outright gift. Thus, in part, the survival of Washington's army was due to Meade's liberality."[214] Along with his brother-in-law, Meade was a member of St. Joseph's Congregation in Willings Alley. When the parish outgrew the limited space in their church, he once again contributed very generously to the building of St. Mary's, a far more commodious structure.

Finally, John Barry was a patriot who vied with John Paul Jones for the title of Father of the American Navy. Barry was born in Tacumshane, County Wexford, in 1745. When his family was evicted by their British landlord, they moved to Rosslare on the coast. A religious man who began each day with a reading from Scripture, he received his first captain's commission in the Continental Navy in March 1776, not many years after his arrival in Philadelphia. He went on to command the USS *Delaware*, the USS *Raleigh*, and the USS *Lexington*. As commander of the USS

[214] Metzger, *Catholics and the American Revolution*, 227.

Alliance, he fought and won the last naval battle of the Revolutionary War. In February 1797, Barry received "Commission Number 1" from George Washington, and this entitled him to use the title Commodore; he is recognized not only as the first American commissioned naval officer, but also as its first flag officer. Barry was twice married: His first wife, Mary Cleary, died only six years after their wedding; he later married Sarah Austin of New Jersey. Though childless, they raised two children of Barry's sister Eleanor, who, along with her husband, died early deaths.

The story of a Philadelphia Catholic physician named Joseph Cauffman was one of tragedy. Living in Vienna, he wrote to Benjamin Franklin at the war's outset, expressing his wish to serve his country and adding his conviction that "his being a Catholic would not prove an obstacle to his doing the duty of an honest and worthy citizen."[215] The government's ready acceptance of Catholics in all capacities ruled out such fears, and Cauffman soon found himself a physician on the frigate *Randolph* under Captain Nicholas Biddle. In March 1778, the *Randolph* engaged the British cruiser *Yarmouth* off Barbados. In the course of the battle, while Dr. Cauffman was attending Biddle, who had been wounded, the *Randolph*, already badly battered, blew up when another American frigate, the *Moultrie*, mistakenly opened fire. The ship sank, and all lives were lost.

Other Philadelphia Catholic patriots, while unnamed, contributed significantly:

> The majority of St. Mary's sons ... engaged in privateering. Common usage sanctioned the issuance, by the federal and state governments, of letters of "marque and reprisal" to privately owned commercial vessels, authorizing them to prey on enemy commerce. Supply ships and transports were

[215] Ibid., 229.

> their special target. No less than fourteen pewholders, or men who were later buried from St. Mary's, . . . challenged British control of the seas.[216]

The Other Side

Of significant mention in the Philadelphia Catholic story is the number of Catholics, St. Mary's parishioners for the most part, who were Loyalists. There were many reasons why certain citizens took this position, all of which are speculative. One line of reasoning is that

> as the war clouds gathered on the horizon the conservative mind reacted in one way, the liberal mind in another. Although the conservative businessman disapproved of certain British commercial regulations, he was inclined to submit to them, or simply to ignore them by nonobservance whenever possible, rather than risk the rupture of established business ties and face the uncertainties incidental to an appeal to arms. Even if America should succeed in her venture, he envisioned a situation so unstable that the status quo was preferable. To the conservative in politics, the overthrow of British rule, which would involve the displacement of an established, experienced official class and the substitution of men who were novices in politics and wholly inexperienced in diplomacy, boded ill for the country. Men of substance, faced with a threat to their possessions, reckoned the old order the lesser of two evils.[217]

In addition, contemporary writers and pamphleteers did much to stir up opposition to the patriot cause. Pennsylvanian Joseph

[216] Ibid., 230.
[217] Ibid., 239.

Galloway is a case in point. The author of a conciliation plan that was almost adopted by the First Continental Congress, he began to see what he perceived as errors in the agitation for independence. Along with other like-minded writers, he tried to convince the colonists that they had no irremediable grievances against Great Britain; that the tyranny of Congress was far worse than that of Parliament; and that nothing could be gained by seeking independence. Many of these writers warned that if independence was unexpectedly won, "we shall inevitably fall under the dominion of some foreign tyrant, or the more intolerable despotism of a few American demagogues." The colonies would become "a theatre of inconceivable misery and horror," filled with "anarchy and confusion."[218]

The flourishing state of the colonial economy was, they argued, "owing almost solely to the protection and patronage of the Parent State": the colonies had been "nourished in their infancy, and supported in their more adult age, with all the attention of a most affectionate parent."[219] Many of the Loyalist writings cited defects in the colonial constitutions, the allowance of constant public complaints against the Mother Country, human neglect, and even a basic stupidity in certain leaders and publicists that caused much confusion for the people. Galloway believed the American governments themselves failed to exhibit "those principles of policy that alone ever have or can bind the members of a free Society together."[220]

[218] Mary Beth Norton, *The British-Americans: The Loyalist Exiles in England 1774–1789* (Boston: Little, Brown and Company, 1972), 20–21.

[219] Jonathan Boucher, *A View of the Causes and Consequences of the American Revolution* (London, 1797), 475, xxxiv; [Joseph Galloway], *Historical and Political Reflections on the Rise and Progress of the American Rebellion* (London, 1780), 4, cited in ibid., 132.

[220] [Joseph Galloway] *Political Reflections on the Late Colonial Governments* (London, 1783), 52, cited in ibid., 136.

The entrance of the Catholic mind into these disputes is even more interesting. Why would "Papists" muster great enthusiasm for the patriot cause? Throughout the colonial period, they had been "victims of discrimination, often of open persecution, at the hands of the authorities of their respective communities. Nowhere had they been accorded the full privileges of citizenship; everywhere they were distrusted and restricted." Added to this, is the very real fact that the leading American Catholic statesmen were, almost to a man, victims of anti-Catholic prejudice. It has been argued that as a result of the Quebec Act and its consequences, the Mother Country might have been in the process of taking a more benign view of Romanists. "At all events," one historian has noted, "it is not surprising that there were Catholic Tories; rather it is amazing that they were not more numerous."[221]

There is little doubt that the majority of Catholics in Pennsylvania and throughout the colonies sided with and fought for the patriot cause. Perhaps it was the forcefulness of the arguments for independence, perhaps the peer pressure of their fellow colonists, perhaps the prevailing view that, in the end, their interests would be better served by the newly envisioned American government. Even so, Catholics were also found among the ranks of Tories, and quite substantially.

When hostilities broke out, British authorities were opposed to the recruitment of Catholics; this was based on their traditional fear of the Church of Rome and distrust of Her members. A certain break with that tradition came with the active recruitment of Irish in the provinces of Connaught and Munster, and the same was proposed for Irish living in America. This was strongly opposed by General Howe out of, one suspects, a personal antipathy. What changed the minds of many in the British government was the

[221] Metzger, *Catholics and the American Revolution*, 240.

purported Treaty of Amity and Commerce that America negotiated with France, in which French military aid and manpower would be forthcoming. If American leaders had no qualms with accepting help from such a Catholic nation, why could Britain not do the same and begin to enlist Roman Catholics wherever they might be?

The first cadre of Catholic officers were submitted to General Howe in November 1777, by Alfred Clifton, "a gentleman of the Catholic faith," and "a prominent member of his religious community," who lived on "Second between Mulberry and Sassafras at the corner of Clifton Alley." His name appeared on the Baptismal and Marriage record of St. Joseph's. The first muster of Catholic men took place in December 1777, with a mere 62; a vigorous recruiting campaign increased the number to 176 within ten days.[222]

The Roman Catholic Volunteers unit was to be relatively short-lived; apparently discipline had always been lax, and several of the enlisted men engaged in conduct forbidden by the rules of war. Still others, mostly with Irish surnames, were court-martialed for a variety of offenses. And finally, their leader, Clifton, died.[223] His final days were troublesome:

[222] Martin I. J. Griffin, *Catholics and the American Revolution*, 3 vols. (Ridley Park and Philadelphia: The Author, 1907–1911), 1, 328, 330. Griffin lists the officers: Lieutenant Colonel Alfred Clifton; Major John Lynch; Captains Kenneth McCulloch, Mathias Hanley, Martin McEvoy, Nicholas Wuregan, John McKinnon; Lieutenants Peter Eck, John Connell, Edward Holland, James Hanrahan, Ebenezer Wilson, John O'Neill; Ensigns John Grashune, Arthur Bailie, Thomas Quinn, Edward Gadwin; Chaplain Fredrick Farmer; Quartermaster John Holland. The reference to Father Farmer, S.J., in this list is incorrect on two counts: First, his given name was Ferdinand, not Fredrick, and second, it is most likely that he never accepted the chaplaincy that was offered to him. Cited in ibid., 245–246.

[223] Ibid., 246–250.

Clifton's Tory activities aroused the wrath of patriot authorities in Pennsylvania, and retribution was prompt. In mid-May, 1778 the Supreme Executive Council of the Commonwealth issued a proclamation that, because he "adhered to and knowingly and willingly aided and assisted the enemies of this State, and of the United States of America," by joining their armies at Philadelphia, Clifton was guilty of high treason. A little more than two years later the Tory *New York Gazette and Weekly Mercury* announced the death in that city of that unhappy man. "Scion of an ancient British family," according to the obituary, he had given years to the service of "his Prussian Majesty, and the Empress of Russia." These antecedents may account for his attachment to England rather than to the state of Pennsylvania, his new home.[224]

Much more durable were the Volunteers of Ireland, to which the remaining men under Clifton's command were assimilated. These Volunteers were the joint effort of British General Henry Clinton and Colonel Lord Rawdon. Clinton argued to the home government that England's chief antagonists in America were the Irish, though they were never fully accepted by their adopted homeland either. To lure them away from the "enemy," Clinton supposed it beneficial to have them fight on the side of the mother country. By the fall of 1779, the Volunteers of Ireland numbered more than five hundred. Since they were a volunteer regiment, the men had been outfitted at the expense of the officers, drawn largely from the regular army, and promoted only one rank.[225]

[224] Ibid.,250.

[225] Clinton supplied a list of these officers: Colonel Lord Rowden; Lt. Colonel Wellborne Ellis Doyle; Major John Despard; Captains John Campbell, John Doyle, James King, William Barry; Capt. Lt.

A thorough study of Loyalists in Pennsylvania concluded that total numbers in the state ranged from 1,700 to 1,800 during the war years.[226] The number of Catholics, finally tabulated, varies from one source to another. The Roman Catholic Volunteers were believed to start out at 82; Clinton then tabulated 331, though this was while they were engaged in fighting in New York. Similarly, the Volunteers of Ireland achieved maturity only after the British gave up the city of Philadelphia and were headquartered in New York; it does not seem likely that more than about 80 who were transferred by Clinton when the Roman Catholic Volunteers were dissolved could have come from Pennsylvania.

Nevertheless, many of the Catholic patriots in Philadelphia were distressed to hear of their coreligionists siding with the British and tried their best to dissuade them. One such case was an open letter to John Dunlap, publisher of the *Pennsylvania Packet*, in which the writer tried to emphasize the "abject state of servitude" of the Catholic subjects of the king. Any serious study of history, this writer argued, should turn the mind of any Catholic away from allegiance to a government that had been so unrelenting in its bias and in its persecution of Catholics.[227]

David Dalton; Lieutenants Charles Vallancy, Charles Bingham, Edward Fitzgerald, James Moffat, Thomas Proctor, Samuel Bradstreet, William Gillespie, Herman Black; Ensigns John Jewell, John Stuart, Thomas Wilson, Edward Gillborne, Thomas Flynn, David Whitley, Joseph Thompson, John Cunningham, Thomas Serjeant; Adjutant John Jewell; Quartermaster John Stewart; Surgeon George Armstrong; surgeon's mate, John Hill. Sir Henry Clinton to Lord George Germain, *Sackville-Germain Papers*, October 23, 1778, cited in ibid., 251–252.

[226] Wilbur H. Seibert, *The Loyalists of Pennsylvania* (Columbus, 1905), 42, cited in ibid., 263.

[227] *Pennsylvania Packet*, January 28, 1779, cited in ibid., 263–264.

Other researchers have discovered that Pennsylvania Catholic Tory membership was not limited to one social class or ethnic background:

> It was a cross section of society; it embraced men of every social group, and men of English, German, and Irish extraction. Foremost was Alfred Clifton, classified as English and a "gentleman," but associated with him were Reynolds the looking-glass maker; Bernard Fearis, a vendor; Dennis Dougherty, a shopkeeper, who sold rum, sugar, and snuff; Joseph Griswold the distiller; and John Bray, schoolmaster. Of the same mind as Clifton the Englishman were John Campbell, John Maguire, Patrick Tonry, Isaac Lort, James Wirth, Bryan O'Hara, James Byrne, Patrick Hogan, George Connell, Timothy Carroll, John Tolly, George Spangler, and Michael O'Connor. Evidently Toryism knew no social classification, blood lines, or religious homogeneity, and Catholics were not impervious to its appeal.[228]

Perhaps the best way to think about Pennsylvania Catholics and the sides they took in the American Revolution is not in terms of who was categorically right or wrong, but rather in terms of how each person prudentially considered the anti-Catholicism—the legislation, the press, and even the violence—rampant on all sides. In many Catholic minds there was a real dilemma as to which side to support. But the fact that the majority went with the patriot cause provided a building block for future growth, both of the

[228] Ibid., 264. It would be difficult to determine if any of Philadelphia's Acadians were involved on either side of the conflict. They were greatly aided by the Quaker Anthony Benezet, as well as Father Robert Harding at St. Joseph's. Many left because of language barriers, as well as anti-Catholic prejudice. Those who remained were immortalized in Longfellow's poem *Evangeline*.

physical manifestation of the Church in the new nation and also of the preaching of the gospel and the great truths of the Catholic Faith. The American experience, with all the uncertainty in the country's foundational documents, still seemed to provide the safest atmosphere, in so many Catholic minds, in which to grow and to prosper.

Whichever way Catholics chose to go, their dedication to a cause was based not merely on what they felt would be the best political solution, but also on which faction would provide the freedom to practice, learn, and live the Catholic Faith.

Chapter 9

Catholic Colonial New York, New Jersey, and New England

Catholic history in the colony of New York long predates the British conquest of the Dutch in 1664. Though Catholic antecedents are scarcer than in either Maryland or Pennsylvania, the story in what became the Empire State remains significant.

We associate the beginnings of exploration with Henry Hudson, who, sailing in the service of the Dutch government, entered the harbor of New York in September 1609 in his small craft, the *Half Moon*, and traveled up the river that still bears his name. Hudson and his companions sailed north past what we now recognize as the Palisades, the Tappan Zee Bridge, Bear Mountain, West Point, and the capital city of Albany. A few months prior to Hudson's arrival, however, Samuel de Champlain, who had founded a small French settlement at Quebec the previous year, moved south from Canada, traveling into northeastern New York. The explorations of the two men bore significance for the next century and a half: The Protestant Dutch (and later the English) vied with the Catholic French for control of the upper reaches of New York State. The lakes and forests of upstate New York made for fertile battleground for the warring nations.

The Catholic history of the region begins with French Jesuit missionaries:

> The fur trade was not the only incentive that brought Europeans to New York. Among the French there was a small group of idealistic Jesuit missionaries who came to North America to convert the Native Americans to Christianity. The exploits of the Society of Jesus, which extended from Acadia to Wisconsin, and from Ontario to the Mississippi Valley, are one of the epic stories in the annals of colonial North America.... Between 1642 and 1649 no fewer than eight of these Jesuit missionaries died as martyrs, all but one of them at the hands of the Iroquois. Five were martyred in Canada and three in New York. Although the first priest to set foot in New York was probably Father Joseph de la Roche Daillon, a Franciscan Recollect who visited the Indians of the Niagara peninsula in 1626, the story of Catholicism in New York begins with the three Jesuit martyrs in the Mohawk Valley in the 1640's.[229]

This Catholic story runs in parallel with the story of Dutch colonization, which was sponsored by a Protestant monarchy with deep anti-Catholic motivations, though there were surprising moments of magnanimity between the religious and political factions.

New Netherland

Many private merchants in Holland had maintained an interest in the New World long after Henry Hudson's initial voyage. At least three such individuals in the Dutch cities of Amsterdam and Hoorn secured a trading monopoly in 1614, covering an ill-defined area between New France and Virginia. They became a loosely formed organization as opposed to a more traditional joint stock

[229] Thomas J. Shelley, *The Bicentennial History of the Archdiocese of New York: 1808–2008* (Strasbourg: Éditions du Signe, 2007), 14.

company. The life span of the partnership was limited, but they constituted the first organized economic interest in the region that would become New York.

Of much greater import was the Dutch West India Company, which was officially organized in 1621 and commenced operations two years later. It received an exclusive right to "trade, govern and colonize unoccupied land from Newfoundland to the Strait of Magellan and on the West Coast of Africa from the Tropic of Cancer to the Cape of Good Hope."[230] The company organization was complex, but real power was found in a group called the Board of Nineteen, who sat at Amsterdam.

There were no permanent dwellings on Manhattan Island until the coming of Peter Minuet in 1626. After his arrival, he based his expedition there, gathering his companions from the scattered areas where they had settled. Within two years there were 270 colonists in and around the fort at New Amsterdam, while to the north at Fort Orange, present-day Albany, there were only 14.

> Building the New Netherland population proved to be a slow process, because conditions in Holland did not favor any large exodus of people. The company endeavored to recruit emigrants, but industry and commerce were prospering in the homeland, and few were willing to go. At the same time, there were always dissatisfied or disillusioned settlers who wished for nothing better than to return to Holland.[231]

The Dutch West India Company was a different sort of enterprise from English efforts at colonization, fashioning a colony in the image of the fatherland: It was a group of well-to-do businessmen whose primary concern was a return on their considerable

[230] Pomfret, *Founding the American Colonies*, 280.
[231] Ibid., 281.

investments, not religious liberty or conversion of the natives or anything more elevated. The New Netherland colony had disadvantages and weaknesses from the start, and the scattered pattern of settlement did not help future growth:

> The territory itself was far from compact, and the nature of the economy resulted in the establishment of a series of trading posts: on the Hudson at Fort Orange, Esopus, and Manhattan; on the Delaware at Fort Nassau and Fort Casimir below it; and on the Connecticut at Fort Hope. All of them were widely separated and incapable of defense. Several of the posts lay within disputed territory and brought the company into conflict with the English in New England and on Long Island and with the Swedes and Marylanders on the Delaware. It should be recalled, too, that the Dutch West India Company held a patent for territory without definite boundaries such as were granted by the crown to each English colony.[232]

An Amsterdam jeweler and influential company director named Kiliaen van Rensselaer saw the futility of this approach, and, early on, devised a "patroonship" system, with the view that if the company granted large tracts of land to entrepreneurs who would develop them, the company would eventually be relieved of the expenses incurred from day-to-day operations. Each patroonship was envisioned as a mini feudal state, with the patroon possessing "the rights and jurisdictions common to the province of Gelderland in Holland."[233] Such fiefdoms began to dot the landscape the further

[232] Ibid., 283.

[233] Ibid., 285. The idea has characteristics similar to, albeit on a much smaller scale, the Bishop of Durham clause that Lord Baltimore received for his Palatinate of Maryland.

one traveled along the Hudson River, with Rensselaerswyck one of the most conspicuous.

From the outset, the colony of New Netherland contained a wide variety of classes, national origins, and religious groups. The diversity would be a helpful factor in the colony's later development, especially the degree of religious toleration that would find its way into colonial life.

Saints on the New York Frontier

Into this established colony came three Jesuit missionaries: Isaac Jogues, Rene Goupil and Jean La Lande. Goupil and Jogues were captured by Mohawk Indians in 1642. Goupil was quickly axed to death, but Jogues was blessed to have a fruitful thirteen months of imprisonment during which he baptized seventy Indians. Jogues managed to escape with Dutch help, though not before his left thumb and several fingers had been cut off. The Dutch commander at Fort Orange paid a considerable ransom to the Indians for the future saint and quickly saw to it that he got out of harm's way, sending him down to New Amsterdam.

St. Isaac Jogues was the first recorded priest to visit Manhattan Island; he spent a month there in 1643, but the Dutch governor, while polite to him, did not allow him to offer Mass. Jogues noted four to five hundred inhabitants on the island and a multiplicity of ethnic groups. There were very few Catholics, but the ones there enjoyed de facto religious toleration. He was surprised when he visited one home to find statues of the Blessed Virgin Mary and St. Aloysius Gonzaga; the owner explained that his wife was a Portuguese Catholic. The governor arranged for Jogues to be transported back to France, where he received a hero's welcome and might have settled into a comfortable life. But he later returned to the New World, making two voyages to upstate New York. On the second one, he was martyred by being tomahawked to death. The Mohawk Indians had discovered a box he had left behind in the present-day town of Auriesville; they believed it contained an evil omen that required its keeper to be killed.

Dutch authorities also saved two other Jesuit missionaries: Joseph Messani, who came to them with maimed fingers, and Joseph Poncet, who had been captured by the Indians but was able to survive the incident intact. By 1670, the Jesuits had reached the height of their missionary activity; many of the Hurons had been converted, and at least one-quarter of the Iroquois ultimately became Christians.

Among them was Kateri Tekakwitha, the daughter of an Algonquin mother and an Iroquois Mohawk father born in Auriesville, or, as it was then called, Ossernenon. Through her contact in present-day Fonda, New York, with a French Jesuit missionary, Father Jacques de Lamberville, she became a Christian, taking her Christian name after St. Catherine of Siena. She found it extremely difficult to practice her Christian Faith amid the paganism of the Indian tribes. Quite undeterred, she walked two hundred miles from her village to the Christian Indian village of Kahnawake on the south shore of the St. Lawrence River, south of modern Montreal. She lived only twenty-four years, dying in 1680, but was immediately venerated by the Christian Iroquois and French Canadian Catholics. Much of the reason for this reverence was her way of life:

> Kateri and other Christian Indians at Kahnawake were practicing a kind of "syncretistic asceticism." They wore hair shirts, kept fasts, exposed themselves to the cold, and performed other acts of self-abnegation. They did these things as good Iroquois would ... hardening themselves against pain, torture and starvation. They now engaged in such

asceticism as Christians, combining the native and Christian ethos of self-sacrifice.[234]

Missionary efforts in northern New York were especially noteworthy in two further instances. The first was the 1749 establishment of a mission called La Presentation by a French Sulpician, François Picquet, on the south shore of the St. Lawrence River. Described as an "avid French patriot as well as a dedicated missionary,"[235] Picquet also saw military action in Western Pennsylvania as a chaplain during the French and Indian War. A brief ten years after his mission's foundation, it was captured by the British and turned into a fort. Those still living on or around it were few and were eventually evicted.

A second enterprise, which survives to the present, was begun by a Jesuit missionary of unknown nationality—Father Antoine Gordon. His mission, St. Regis, was the last Jesuit mission in New France, straddling the modern border between New York and Canada. Over the years, it cared for the Kahnawake Indians, other Christian Indians, and French Canadian Catholics. In later years, Scottish Highlanders—Loyalists during the American Revolution—settled in the area of the St. Lawrence River on the Canadian side and became devoted parishioners, as did a large number of Irish who settled the surrounding area. The mission would become home to a Scottish priest, Father Roderick MacDonnell, who served St. Regis for twenty-one years and was enormously popular with the Indians. At their insistence, he was buried beneath the church, which, they always felt, he had built for them.

[234] Christopher Veesey, *The Paths of Kateri's Kin* (Notre Dame, IN: University of Notre Dame Press, 1997), 97–98, cited in Shelley, *Bicentennial History*, 17.

[235] Ibid., 18.

Transfer to British Control

Despite the reforms to Dutch colonial practices, the original settlers were quickly losing their hold on New Netherland. The West India Company had failed to prosper as expected, and at one point its very solvency was threatened. There was a pervasive feeling that a new, more competent governor was needed, and the company believed they had found one in Peter Stuyvesant. Unfortunately, his own severe disposition and intolerance of the slightest infringement on his executive authority stood in the way of his considerable administrative skills and was ultimately his undoing.

In addition, the Dutch faced competition from Swedish exploration under Peter Minuit in Delaware Bay. Minuit, who had served as a director for New Netherland, was now directing colonization efforts for the newly formed Swedish West India Company. His establishment of Fort Christina on the Delaware was short-lived, failing shortly after his own death in a West Indian hurricane. Despite this setback, Swedish competition took their toll on Holland's enterprises in New Netherland. By the mid-seventeenth century, it became obvious that Dutch efforts were bound to fail:

> The failure to attract colonists hurt Dutch prestige, but the deterioration of Anglo-Dutch relations in Europe had more immediate consequences. Determined to challenge Dutch commercial supremacy, England passed the "navigation act" of 1650, which prohibited foreign vessels from trading with its American colonies. A year later, Parliament took a big additional step, adopting a comprehensive Navigation Act which in effect excluded the Dutch from the carrying trade between England and other countries. Relations had been strained for years, and these new measures now precipitated the first Anglo-Dutch War, 1652–54. The English had the best of the fighting, and in the end the Dutch

> found it necessary to accept both the navigation restrictions and a settlement of English grievances. Dutch commerce with England was limited thereafter to direct trade, thus greatly reducing the opportunities available to the Dutch West India Company.... After 1654 the firm was wholly bankrupt.[236]

The English drift into Dutch territory had origins in the 1630s, but the accession of Charles II in 1660 revived interest in seizing New Netherland. The British had been suffering losses of revenue and of trade, with the Dutch purchasing as much tobacco as they desired in Maryland and Virginia and then shipping it to Europe by way of New Amsterdam. This circumvention reduced British income from duties and cut into the business that British merchants felt was by right theirs.

The actual British conquest in August 1664 was quite simple. The Dutch, outnumbered and outgunned, surrendered without any resistance, and their colony was immediately named New York. As far as Catholics were concerned, the change in the political circumstances would have been negligible. What was very significant, however, was the conversion of James, Duke of York, brother of the king, to Catholicism in the 1670s.

Even before the British conquest, Charles II had designated a huge swath of land between the Connecticut and Delaware Rivers as a personal colony for his brother, James. New York thus became the second proprietary colony in British America—and the second to be led by a Catholic.

> Like Maryland in its earliest stage, the fur trade dominated the economy. Like Maryland, too, many of the chief officials of New York, from governor to customs collector, were

[236] Pomfret, *Founding the American Colonies*, 297.

Catholic. And like Maryland under the Calverts, New York under the Duke enjoyed religious toleration. Catholics themselves were virtually a non-presence in the heterogeneous general population (approximately 10,000 in 1665), which included Flemings, Walloons, French, Germans, Scandinavians, English, Scotch and Africans. The province was heavily Dutch in the Hudson River Valley from New York City to Albany, mostly English in the smaller settlements on Long Island, Staten Island, Nantucket, and Martha's Vineyard.[237]

The Duke's conversion to Catholicism coincided with the Second Anglo-Dutch War, during which the Dutch briefly regained control of their former colony. When the English reconquered New York, a policy of religious toleration was enacted that would impact the Catholic population—both those present in the colony, and those who would soon be attracted to come.

Religious Toleration in New York

In 1682 James appointed a new governor for the colony, Thomas Dongan, who arrived in August of the following year. He would hold office for five years, and, by all accounts, was one of the more effective governors of colonial New York, despite the fact that he was an Irish Catholic. Born in Castletown, County Kildare, in 1634, he fled his native land after the Cromwellian invasion and served in an Irish regiment in the French army, where he rose to the rank of colonel. Dongan spent two years as lieutenant governor prior to his appointment to the top position in New York government. Never did he try to hide his religious convictions; at the same time, he was totally dedicated to the principle of religious

[237] Curran, *Papist Devils*, 121.

toleration. His arrival in New York, according to contemporary sources, was hailed with fanfare:

> Crossing the East River, Saturday, August 25 (1683), Dongan and his retinue entered the city. Crowds of English, Dutch, French, Indians and Negro slaves lined the streets between the walls and the fort, through which the cavalcade passed, and received the new Governor with vociferous expressions of delight, for it had been noised about that he came empowered by the Duke to adjust all the difficulties that racked the province. The little half-moon fort at the water gate, the rough stockade across the island, and the tattered soldiery must have brought an unusual smile to the soldier of Turenne, accustomed to the great fortifications and gorgeously clad and disciplined armies of Europe.... To the boom of cannon and the cheers of the people the Governor and his escort entered the fort. Next day was passed as became the Lord's day, and it is likely that the Holy Sacrifice of the Mass was offered within the walls of the fort by Father Harvey, assisted by Father Michael Forster (Gulik), Superior of the Maryland Jesuit Mission. On Monday morning the great room in the City Hall or Stadt Huys on Pearl Street was crowded by the provincial officials, civil and military, and the Mayor and Common Council of the city gathered to meet the Governor, who was escorted from the fort by the soldiery.[238]

[238] William Harper Bennett, *Catholic Footsteps in Old New York* (New York: Schwartz, Kirwin and Fauss, 1909), 86. Thomas Harvey was an English Jesuit whom Dongan brought with him. The governor then set up a chapel within the fort, and two other English Jesuits, Henry Harrison and Charles Gage, soon arrived. With Dongan's encouragement they opened a Latin School in 1687 in a building

The English provincial of the Society of Jesus foresaw a bright future for Jesuits in New York in light of the Catholic governor's arrival and the policies he quickly enacted. Writing to his superior in Rome, he argued that the city could soon support a Catholic college to which the scattered Catholics in Maryland could come. At such an early juncture, however, that was overly optimistic; Dongan himself noted that Catholics did not make up even 5 percent of the population:

> Here bee not many of the Church of England ... few Roman Catholicks; abundance of Quaker preachers men and Women especially; Singing Quakers; Ranting Quakers; Sabbatarians; anti-Sabbatarians; some Anabaptists; some Independants; some Jews; in short of all sorts of opinions there are some, and the most part, of none at all.[239]

Dongan's earliest measure, and the one for which he is chiefly remembered, is the passage of the Charter of Liberties. In this accomplishment, his record is comparable to other notable Catholics who had achieved political power throughout colonial history. Religious toleration seemed to be highest among their priorities, owing, no doubt, to the persecutions they had so often experienced in so many places.

The Charter of Liberties placed New York on unique footing. Though Catholics were still scarce, they would begin to profit from this document as their numbers increased. The Charter sought to secure the colonial government on a constitutional foundation so "that justice and right may be equally done to all persons." The

at what is now the corner of Broadway and Wall Street. See Shelley, *Bicentennial History*, 22.

[239] Jason Duncan, "A Most Democratic Class: New York Catholics and the Early American Republic" (doctoral dissertation, University of Iowa, 1999), 22., cited in ibid., 23.

powers of the colonial assembly were carefully stated, as were individual liberties that were to be protected. Liberty of conscience was ensured to all Christian peoples, and a specific provision was added for the benefit of some of the small Puritan towns on Long Island, that they could continue their form of worship totally unmolested. A great deal of understanding of English constitutional and legal thought went into the document; those who drafted the Charter "demanded for the inhabitants of New York rights fully equal to those enjoyed by Englishmen."[240]

It would not be long until the provisions of the charter were put to a very real test:

> In September, 1685, the Jews of New York City petitioned Governor Dongan for the right to trade and practice their religion. The Governor recommended their petition to the Mayor and Council of New York City. The petition was refused on the grounds that the Assembly intended freedom of worship and privileges of citizenship and trading only for those who professed faith in Christ. Governor Dongan obtained for the Jews the right to engage in wholesale trade and when the king extended toleration to people of all religious faiths the Governor made it his special purpose to see that the Jews secured their rights.... There was a Synagogue in New York before the end of Dongan's term.[241]

[240] Craven, *The Colonies in Transition*, 209.

[241] James J. Walsh, M.D., Ph.D., *American Jesuits* (New York: Macmillan, 1934), 49. Curiously, Walsh includes in his treatment of Thomas Dongan a comment from Theodore Roosevelt, the nation's twenty-sixth president, in a sketch of New York he once wrote. Roosevelt commented of Dongan that he was "an Irish Catholic gentleman of good family, the nephew of the Earl of Tyrconnell, [who] acted with wise liberality in matters political and in matters religious, towards the province he was sent to govern,

The Glorious Revolution Takes Its Toll

With 1688 came the Glorious Revolution in England, the overthrow of James II and the Stuart monarchy, and the accession of William and Mary. The effects of this in New York, as might be expected, were disastrous for Catholics and other religious minorities. The immediate outcome took the form of Leisler's Rebellion, led by Jacob Leisler, a populist with a strong aversion to Catholicism.

Prior to his overthrow, King James had dismissed Dongan and replaced him with Sir Edmund Andros, who would serve as governor of an entirely new geographic entity called the Dominion of New England, which included New York, New Jersey, and the entirety of present-day New England. In the midst of Leisler's Rebellion, Dongan fled for his life—first to Massachusetts and finally to London, where he arrived in 1691. Though he was given the title Earl of Limerick, Dongan was never able to win back his confiscated lands in Ireland. He died quietly in London in 1715.

Leisler and his compatriots held political power in New York for the next two years, during which protections for Catholics evaporated. But with the arrival of the new royal governor, Henry Sloughter, in 1691, Leisler was quickly arrested, and within a short time, he and his son-in-law were both hanged. To a certain degree, this ended the active harassment of Catholics—though that was not the British government's primary motive. Soon after, New York's Charter was amended to exclude "any person of the Romish religion" from the colony, which was in keeping with the instructions the governor had received from the mother country.

---

and was a man of high character and good capacity. He was also vigilant in preserving order, in warding off outside aggression and devoted to the well-being of the colony and proved himself the best colonial governor New York ever had." Ibid., 48.

In 1691, King William ordered the enforcement of the Test Act in the colony, requiring all office holders to deny any sort of belief in the Blessed Virgin Mary, the doctrine of transubstantiation, or veneration of the saints. In 1700, at the behest of the governor, Lord Bellomont, the Provincial Assembly passed An Act Against Jesuits and Popish Priests, carrying a penalty of life imprisonment for any priest setting foot in the colony and prescribing heavy fines for laypeople harboring priests. This legislation was to remain in effect for eighty years, until the outbreak of the American Revolution.

> If Catholics did not actually become extinct in New York in the middle of the eighteenth century, they certainly became an endangered species, who survived as isolated individuals, not as members of an organized community. Perhaps there were others like John Leary, the owner of a livery stable on Cortland Street. He attended services at Trinity Church on Sunday, but went to Philadelphia once a year to fulfill his Easter duty. He became a parishioner of St. Peter's Church, New York City's first Catholic Church, when it was opened in 1786. William Mooney is another example of an Irish Catholic who attended Trinity Church until the erection of St. Peter's and then became a parishioner there. An upholsterer with a shop on William Street, he is best remembered as the founder of the Society of Tammany or Columbian Order.[242]

[242] Shelley, *Bicentennial History*, 25. See also Michael J. O'Brien, *In Old New York: The Irish Dead in Trinity and St. Paul's Churchyards* (New York: American Irish Historical Society, 1928), 10–13. Trinity Church on Wall Street was the largest, most fashionable Anglican/Episcopalian Church in New York City. St. Paul's, a few blocks away, was its chapel.

New York Rejects Tolerance

By the era of the American Revolution, New York society had, as it had in all the colonies, taken on a very different cast. The number of Catholics in the colony increased during Dongan's tenure as governor, but that dried up with the passage of new anti-Catholic legislation. Further, there was attrition: The mere fact of a historically Catholic surname did not always indicate any affiliation with the Church. Hostility to the Church of Rome in New York generally came from a more educated, intellectual base by this time in the eighteenth century. One observer of the New York Catholic scene notes:

> The war had not been fought for religious liberty, which is not mentioned in the Declaration of Independence, but it was unquestionably one of its most important and enduring consequences. Suddenly and beyond all expectation, most of the legal barriers against Catholics and other religious minorities crumbled. No single reason or event explains the change. The aversion of the "founding fathers" from the prevailing European system, the indifference of many of them to organized religion and even to Christianity itself, the difficulty of deciding which if any group should be favored over another, and the fact that a very substantial proportion of the people were unchurched, all had a share in the shaping of the new situation. Certainly sympathy for Catholicism did not. It was a time when organized Protestantism was in a state of considerable disarray, and Deism and infidelity had spread widely among members of the small educated class.[243]

[243] Rev. Msgr. Florence D. Cohalan, *A Popular History of the Archdiocese Of New York* (Yonkers, NY: United States Catholic Historical Society, 1983), 12–13.

Proof of this description of secularism and anti-Catholicism came in the aftermath of the Quebec Act and the frightened reaction to it by the Continental Congress. The popular sentiments were echoed in New York by Alexander Hamilton and John Jay. Hamilton, who would do so much for the country in his position as secretary of the treasury and would become a prominent member of the Federalist Party, had a decided distrust of things Catholic. While still a young man studying at King's College (now Columbia University) in New York, he authored an anonymous pamphlet, *A Full Vindication of the Measures of Congress*, in which he asks of those who favor the policy of the British government, "Will they venture to justify the unparalleled stride by which Popery and arbitrary dominion were established in Canada?" Referring to the fate of Canada after the passage of the act, he again queries, "Does not your blood run cold to think that an English Parliament should pass such an act for the establishment of arbitrary power and Popery in such a country?" In another pamphlet, *Remarks on the Quebec Bill*, he sees another Inquisition coming in Canada and fears that "priestly tyranny may find as propitious a soil in Canada as it ever has in Spain and Portugal."[244]

Yet another, and even more strident, anti-Catholic outburst was to come later from New Yorker John Jay, destined to become the first chief justice of the Supreme Court of the United States. It wouldn't be too much to say that he was obsessed by anti-Catholicism. Take, for instance, events at the New York State Constitutional Convention in March 1777. Following his reading of a proposal granting liberty of worship to "all mankind," Jay offered an amendment that would exclude Catholics from this freedom by excluding "any sect or denomination of Christians" whose principles were "inconsistent with the safety of civil society." The state legislature was to be the judge of such inconsistency, but Jay knew

[244] Ray, *American Opinion of Roman Catholicism*, 289.

very well the temper of the times and the individuals making up the legislative body.

Those in opposition to Jay insisted that he be more specific, and so he introduced a new amendment that individuals be excluded from any consideration of freedom of religion until such time as they appear before the legislature and swear that they believe in their consciences that

> no pope, priest or foreign authority on earth hath power to absolve the Subjects of this State from their allegiance to the same. And further that they renounce and believe to be false and wicked, the dangerous and damnable doctrine, that the pope or any other earthly authority, have power to absolve men from sins . . . and particularly, that no pope, priest, or foreign authority on earth, hath power to absolve them from the obligation of this oath.

Jay's amendment was defeated by a vote of nineteen to ten.[245]

When another article for the New York Constitution, this one dealing with the naturalization of foreigners, was brought up for debate, Jay was again ready with an amendment that would deprive immigrant Catholics of citizenship and thus debar them from "all offices of trust and profit." Once more he was fought by political opponents with broader views, but the "forces of bigotry" won on this issue: When the Constitution was read, the forty-second article gave the legislature power to naturalize foreigners on the condition that they "take an oath of allegiance to this State, and abjure and renounce all allegiance and subjection to every foreign king, prince, potentiate and State, in all matters ecclesiastical as well as civil."[246]

[245] Ibid., 356.
[246] Ibid., 357.

Anti-Catholic diatribes did not come merely from politicians; the press also contributed, especially the Tory press in New York. James Rivington's *Royal Gazette* is a case in point. The paper argued that the revolutionaries were foolish to rebel against the king on the pretense that he was trying to introduce Popery into the colonies. To the contrary, Rivington asserted: It was the rebels who were in league with the perfidious Catholics, as they were allied with France, one of the most Catholic nations in the world.

The *Gazette* believed that a rebel victory would destroy the Protestant Church in America and establish that of Rome. The paper also blamed the Presbyterians in New York and throughout the colonies for instigating the rebellion as a backup plan for when their efforts to rid the colonies of the Church of England seemed to be of no avail. To those who followed his argument, Rivington offered a view of what would happen if the forces of rebellion were successful. He envisioned Spanish ships sailing to America with

> 50 tons of holy water for the use of the soldiers, 400 casks of consecrated oil for extreme unction; 10,000 cuts of various saints with brief accounts of the miracles worked by their reliques and at their shrines; 20,000 hair shirts, cowls and scourges and hempen girdles for the use of the religious orders to be established immediately; 3,000 wheels, hooks, pincers, knives, shackles and fire brands for the use of the Inquisition in converting heretics; 10,000 copies of a treatise called *Revelries or the Necessity of Extirpating Heretics*; 1,000 bales of indulgences; 20,000 copies of the Pope's Bull of Absolution of the French and Spanish armies for the massacres, burning of hospitals, butchering of infants, rapes and other crimes and cruelties committed in the reduction of Great Britain.[247]

[247] *Royal Gazette*, January 29, 1780, cited in ibid., 29.

Now, it was true that New York Catholics had every reason to celebrate the victory of independence: They could enjoy the highest degree of religious liberty they had until that time. Though their legal status was far from ideal, they would be unmolested in the free exercise of the Faith. New York made an exceptionally easy transition from British to American rule; there were no disturbances to speak of, and James Rivington's newspaper, renamed after the conclusion of the war, failed in subscriptions. It delighted the patriots to no end that the former Tory editor finished his life in debtor's prison.

The Rest of the Story

It is still very difficult to estimate the small number of Catholics living in New York City after the war. By 1783, however, there must have been a significant number because the idea of constructing the city's first permanent Catholic church began to emerge.

Some prominent Catholics in the city were Dominic Lynch, Thomas Stoughton, and Cornelius Heeney. Lynch was a native of County Galway, Ireland, and his family had long-standing commercial ties with Spain. He opened a branch of the shipping business his father had begun in Bruges, then part of the Austrian Netherlands, and made a considerable fortune before coming to New York in 1785. Thomas Stoughton, with whom Lynch would enter a business partnership, was also a wealthy immigrant. They would open a business in what is today Greenwich Village, selling imported wines, raisins, almonds, oranges, lemons, and the like; though they later had a falling out and the partnership dissolved, they remained active Catholics and were among the earliest parishioners of the newly established St. Peter's Church on Barclay Street. Stoughton would go on to become the Spanish consul in New York, remaining in that position until his death in 1826.

Cornelius Heeney, a lifelong bachelor and another Irish native, joined Lynch as the first two Catholics admitted to membership in the Friendly Sons of St. Patrick in the City of New York, an organization founded years earlier by Irish Protestants. Heeney made his fortune in the fur business and purchased a large estate in what was then called Brooklyn Heights. Heeney could be counted on throughout his life for large donations to St. Peter's as well as Catholic causes of many varieties.

The formal beginnings of Catholic life in the city can be traced to the occasional visits of Father Ferdinand Steinmeyer, S.J., also known as Ferdinand Farmer, from Philadelphia. He would offer Mass in the home of a Portuguese family in the city. There were also usually Catholic chaplains assigned to the French and Spanish embassies in the city. It was not until the coming of Father Charles Whelan, however, that the city had its first permanent priest. Whelan was an Irish Capuchin who had served as a chaplain in the French Navy during the Revolutionary War; he had been captured by the British and sentenced to Jamaica, but he escaped and ultimately arrived in New York. In February 1785, twenty-two laymen approached the French consul in New York, Hector St. John Crevecoeur, and asked him to help them secure a site within city limits from the municipal government. Both he and the mayor, James Duane, reacted positively, and Trinity Episcopal Church agreed to transfer several lots from their leaseholders at the corner of Church and Barclay Streets.

The Catholics formed themselves into a legal corporation consisting of four trustees and began an active fund-raising campaign. Interestingly, Governor George Clinton and Mayor Duane, both Protestants, contributed to the drive. The church, though not completely finished, was dedicated in November 1786; the cornerstone had been laid a little more than a year earlier, with a Spanish priest, Don Diego de Gardoqui, presiding. No sooner had parish life begun when a second Irish Capuchin, Father Andrew Nugent, arrived. Nugent, it appeared, was a far better preacher than Whelan and tension between the two soon became apparent. Bishop Carroll in Baltimore became aware of the growing conflict that split the parish into two factions, and so he intervened to try to get the priests to work together as co-pastors. Lay trustees had already emerged who would present their own difficulty in the early national years of the Church's life in the United States; here, even at this early date, the trustees at St. Peter's asked Carroll's permission to fire their pastor, Father Whelan. In a letter addressed to both Dominic Lynch and Thomas Stoughton, the bishop responded:

> If ever the principles there laid down should become predominant, the unity and Catholicity of our Church would be at an end; & it would be formed into distinct and independent Societies, nearly in the same manner, as the Congregational Presbyterians of your neighboring New England States.[248]

Whelan eventually resigned and went to Kentucky to do missionary work. Despite the turmoil, the parish had experienced significant growth. Whelan had reported that it was necessary for any pastor to know six languages: Those heard and used most frequently at St. Peter's were French, Spanish, Dutch, German, Portuguese, Gaelic, and English. Carroll later discovered that Nugent, now the parish's pastor, had previously been suspended by the archbishop of Dublin for sexual misconduct. Describing him as "a most infamous fellow,"[249] Carroll removed him as pastor and suspended him from

[248] John Carroll to Dominic Lynch and Thomas Stoughton, January 24, 1786, in *John Carroll Papers*, I, 200–206, cited in ibid., 40.

[249] Ibid., 40–41.

the priesthood. In his place came Father William O'Brien, an Irish Dominican.

O'Brien was among the first group of seventeen Dominicans who had presented themselves to Bishop Carroll for work in the United States. O'Brien had entered the Order of Friars Preachers at the ancient monastery of San Clemente in Rome, studied at Naples and Bologna, and easily met all the requirements Carroll might have presented. The journey from Baltimore to New York was an arduous eight days; nonetheless, the bishop made it to install the new pastor. He remained in the city for one month before returning, and sometime later wrote to O'Brien "not to lose courage; for if you should, I do not know where to find the clergyman in the U. States to replace you." He added that he really considered O'Brien's arrival in America "at so critical a period as a providential designation of you to repair so dreadful scandals & heal such dangerous wounds given to Religion at its first introduction into New York."[250]

O'Brien, who would go on to serve St. Peter's for thirty years, was able to open there the first free school in New York. He would also be the priest who received Elizabeth Bayley Seton, the first native-born American saint, into the Church. During a yellow-fever epidemic that struck the city in the final decade of the eighteenth century, the Dominican did commendable work as he encountered death daily among his congregation. He died in 1816, was buried in St. Peter's, and, in the view of at least one historian, "kept order and harmony in the Catholic body of the city and State."[251]

As to his predecessor, Nugent:

[250] *John Carroll Papers*, I, December 8, 1787, 271–272, cited in Mary Nona McGreal, O.P., ed., *Dominicans at Home in a Young Nation:1786–1865* (Strasbourg: Éditions du Signe, 2001), 34.

[251] *John Carroll Papers*, I, 526ff., cited in ibid., 35.

> Legally barred from using St. Peter's Church, Nugent continued to celebrate Mass for his followers in a private house, despite his suspension by John Carroll. He thus has the dubious distinction of creating the first schism in the history of the American Catholic Church. He seems to have become an embarrassment even to some of his former admirers, one of whom was James Shea, the father of the historian John Gilmary Shea. At the request of James Shea, in January 1790, the trustees of St. Peter's voted to provide Nugent with enough money to allow him to return to France. The money was well spent.[252]

Catholic New Jersey

When England conquered New Netherland in 1664, the Duke of York also ceded to a group of noblemen led by Sirs John Berkley and George Carteret a portion of the newly acquired territory named New Jersey that encompassed "the area bounded by Long Island Sound on the north, the Hudson and Atlantic on the east, the Delaware on the west, and the mouth of Delaware bay on the south."[253] Differences between the proprietors led to a division of the province into East and West Jersey, a split that remained until they were united as a royal colony in 1702. Initially, there appeared to be enough religious toleration to attract not only Protestant dissenters but a small number of Catholic workers:

> Catholics in the Jerseys as in New York, quickly rose to hold provincial offices; among them were Robert Vanquellen, who became surveyor general, and John Tatham, who served in several public capacities. William Douglas was elected to

[252] Shelley, *Bicentennial History*, 41.
[253] Curran, *Papist Devils*, 122–123.

> the General Assembly of East Jersey from Bergen County, only to be barred by his peers from serving when he owned that he was a Catholic.... Discretion was the price Catholics were expected to pay to practice their religion, and even more so, to participate in public life. Catholicism had only the most ephemeral institutional presence.[254]

Many factors went into the development of New Jersey. It was slower to develop than other settlements along the Atlantic seaboard because it lacked natural deep water harbors, and its heavily wooded areas were difficult to traverse. By the end of the eighteenth century, New Jersey's population was less than fifteen thousand, while neighboring New York and Pennsylvania had well over half a million each. Nonetheless, a wide variety of religions were present: Swedish Lutheran settlements along the Delaware River, Dutch Reformed Congregations west of the Hudson River, Puritans, Baptists, and Quakers from Long Island and New England, not to mention Anglicans, Presbyterians, Methodists, and a smattering of Catholics. Within most of these groups, "religious influences emanating from liberal New York and conservative Philadelphia left their marks on New Jersey."[255]

The initial broad assurances of toleration were not as realistic as supposed. *The Fundamental Constitution of the Province of East New Jersey* of 1683 explicitly excluded atheists from freedom of conscience and imposed a religious test for office holding that excluded all but Protestant Christians. After New Jersey became a royal colony in 1702, Queen Anne instructed the local government to extend a liberty of conscience to all except Papists. Some decades later, the colony was divided geographically into four spheres of religious influence:

[254] Ibid., 123.
[255] Quigley, *Catholic Beginnings*, 23.

> The Dutch Reformed Church members were predominantly along the Hudson River Valley; the heirs of the Puritan tradition ruled Newark and its environs; Perth Amboy and the central section contained a great mixture of sects; and the southern and western portions were dominated by the Quakers with small pockets of Baptists and Presbyterians.[256]

In the 1740s Catholics in Salem were visited by Jesuit Father Theodore Schneider, though his main base of operation was southeastern Pennsylvania. Later, Father Ferdinand Steinmeyer (Farmer), "one of the most beautiful priest characters of the American Church during the eighteenth century, whom all authors literally vie with one another to extol,"[257] made many missionary visits. From his native Württemberg, Germany, he arrived in Pennsylvania around 1751, spent several years in Lancaster, and took up where Father Schneider left off. His journeys every autumn and spring took him "along the Delaware River across country to Long Pond, ... Mount Hope, Macopin, New York City, Basking Ridge, Trenton, and Salem."[258]

Several decades later, when it came time for the writing of the New Jersey State Constitution, it is apparent that attitudes had changed little. There is no clear answer to the question of authorship of the document, though John Witherspoon was said to have been a guiding force, as was Reverend Jacob Green, a somewhat prominent divine.

> What is more important is that the New Jersey constitution was the first of the state instruments to discriminate

[256] Ibid., 26.

[257] Joseph M. Flynn, *The Catholic Church in New Jersey* (Morristown, NJ: n.p., 1904), 24, cited in ibid., 27.

[258] John M. Daley, S.J., "Pioneer Missionary: Ferdinand Farmer, S.J., 1720–1786", *Woodstock Letters* 75 (1946): 103–115, 207–231, 311–321, cited in ibid.,27.

against Catholics and that despite this bias it was praised for its liberality by some of the most distinguished personages of the time. Ezra Stiles, commenting on its religious provisions, records approvingly in his *Diary* "Universal Protestant Religious Liberty established."[259]

Empty New England

New England presented an entirely different set of circumstances from the rest of the American colonies. Throughout these stridently Calvinistic colonies, Catholics were either nonexistent or present in such exceedingly small numbers that neither individually nor collectively could much of a story be related. Nonetheless, some notes of significance are to be found in the mind-sets of the colonies' founders, their later ruling classes, and their state constitutions.

Massachusetts is a case in point, especially with its rather famous anti-priest law. Passed in 1700, the measure was largely the brainchild of the Earl of Bellomont, Richard Coote, whose father of the same name had committed many outrages against the Catholic population of Ireland under Oliver Cromwell. Bellomont had been appointed governor of Massachusetts, New York, and New Hampshire, and held a strong belief that Catholic missionaries were stirring up the Indians to attack British forces, who were then engaged

[259] Ray, *American Opinion of Roman Catholicism*, 355. Ezra Stiles (1727–1795) was a Congregational minister, author, and theologian. He served as president of Yale University and was one of the founders of Brown University in Rhode Island. Reverend John Witherspoon was Scottish born, became a Presbyterian minister, was a delegate to the Second Continental Congress from New Jersey, signed the Declaration of Independence from his adopted state, and was a professor and later president of the small Presbyterian College of New Jersey, which became Princeton University.

in one of their numerous wars with France. Massachusetts and New York both felt the repercussions of this law, which stipulated that any "Jesuit, seminary priest, missionary or any other spiritual or ecclesiastical person" had to depart the mentioned areas within a specified number of months; also, anyone of these categories who was apprehended "practicing or teaching others to say any popish prayers, celebrating masses, granting absolutions, or using any of the other Romish ceremonies and rites of worship" would, if apprehended, suffer "perpetual imprisonment." Any escape from prison, as well might be imagined, would result in death. Anyone caught harboring Jesuits or priests of any sort were to be fined two hundred pounds, and any justice of the peace before whom any of the aforementioned persons appeared had the power of immediate imprisonment pending a future trial if that individual could not give a satisfactory account of himself.[260]

Half a century later, Massachusetts was faced with a crisis for which the old anti-Catholic laws proved insufficient. During 1755 and 1756, six thousand Acadian refugees—French-Canadian Catholics—arrived in the English colonies. They refused to renounce their loyalty to France, and were seized, transported, and placed along the eastern seaboard of North America—Massachusetts by far receiving the largest number. Governor Thomas Hutchinson took a very kindly view toward them; in his history of the colony, he presented some interesting insights about these people and their fate.

Hutchinson related that these families, "being all Roman catholicks and great bigots," were often indiscriminately put on board vessels bound for one of the English colonies; parents and children were frequently separated. One of them told Hutchinson this was "the hardest which had happened since Our Savior was

[260] Ellis, *Documents*, 121–123.

upon earth." When about one thousand of them arrived in Boston the colonial assembly was in session, but several days passed before any determination was made about their fate. Many of the sick and elderly were received in houses along the coast; it was stipulated by the assembly that the entire group should be allowed to settle in such towns as would be most appropriate throughout Massachusetts, that they be employed in gainful labor, and that, in general, their support should be provided for. Hutchinson testified:

> The people of New England had more just notions of toleration than their ancestors, and no exception was taken to their prayers in their families, in their own way, which, I believe, they practiced in general, and sometimes they assembled several families together; but the people would upon no terms have consented to the public exercise of religious worship by Roman catholick priests. A law remained unrepealed, though it is to be hoped it would never have been executed, which made it a capital offence in such persons to come within the province. It was suspected that some such were among them in disguise, but it is not probable that any ventured.... They had it not in their power since they left their country, to confess and to be absolved of their sins, and the hazard of dying in such a state distressed them more than the fear of temporal sufferings.[261]

While there was considerable missionary activity in the area that would become the state of Maine during the period of French colonization,[262] this territory did not take on an English colonial

[261] Cited in ibid., 124–126.

[262] Ellis, *Catholics in Colonial America*, 125–146. Ellis treats the story of the Maine missions extensively, including the story of the first group of Anglo-American converts to Catholicism in New France. Between 1680 and 1760, approximately 1,200 captives were seized

configuration during the years prior to the American Revolution and did not enter the Union until 1820.

The neighboring colony of New Hampshire had a history of its own, though it is intertwined with Massachusetts. The colony was named by Captain John Mason, to whom the original land grant was given. Religious dissenters from Massachusetts led by Reverend John Wheelwright founded the town of Exeter. Massachusetts did lay claim to the region, fearing both the Anglicans as well as the members of dissenting sects who were settling there. Some religious concessions were made, and there was little religious persecution, except the hanging of a group of Quakers in 1659 or 1660. Farming, lumbering, fishing, ship building, and the fur trade attracted settlers early on, though Catholics were not to be found in any significant numbers.

New Hampshire was declared a separate royal province in 1679, with a governor appointed by the Crown. A colonial assembly also came into existence and, though Massachusetts took temporary control following the collapse of the Dominion of New England (of which New Hampshire was a part), it became permanently separate in 1692—though the area shared a governor with Massachusetts until 1741. Through the eighteenth century, immigration into the colony came chiefly from Massachusetts and Connecticut, with Scotch-Irish from Ulster making up the rest. By the time of the American Revolution, few, if any, Tories were to be found in the colony, and after the commencement of the War of Independence, New Hampshire, in January 1776, became the first colony to create a new government. The real manifestation of the New England

in the Maine territory and transported to New France. Among these, about 250 were eventually converted to the Catholic Faith, including one woman who became the maternal grandmother of a future bishop of Quebec. Ibid., 139.

religious mind was made apparent in the late 1780s and 1790s, with the many attempts to ratify a state constitution:

> In New Hampshire there were present all the elements of that politico-religious antipathy to Rome so characteristic of colonial British-America. There was in addition, an intensification of racial antagonisms due on the one hand to New Hampshire's proximity to the Canadian-French and on the other to the Scotch-Irish immigration. The frontier settlements of the province—itself an outpost of New England—thought of their Canadian neighbors almost solely in terms of the Indian raid. Such a medium was calculated to soften neither Protestant hatred of "French idolatry" nor republican contempt of "wooden shoes." The New Hampshire immigrants of the eighteenth century brought with them the heritage of economic, political and religious grievances common to all Scotch-Irish exiles of the period. In New England insult was added to injury when they were taken for native Irish, ostracized, and even forcibly ejected from their settlements. Given the historical background thus briefly sketched, the religious clauses of New Hampshire's constitution follow almost as a matter of course.[263]

The constitution was preceded by a bill of rights insisting on the right of conscience and the prohibition of any legislation "against the Protestant religion." On the third draft, after an attempt to ensure religious liberty to all in the colony failed, there still was a provision for accommodating exclusively "Protestant teachers of piety, religion and morality." Only Protestants were eligible to run for the major offices in the colony, and if by chance a Catholic should be chosen, he would be immediately confronted with a

[263] Ray, *American Opinion of Roman Catholicism*, 370.

test oath similar to that drawn up in England at the time of the Glorious Revolution. In fact, it was not until the mid-nineteenth century that religious qualifications for governor, senator, and representative were abolished.[264]

Rhode Island, founded by the religious dissident Roger Williams, and Connecticut present further and familiar stories. In the latter, dissenters were exempted from the payment of taxes benefiting the dominant Congregational church, and in 1784 an *Act for Securing the Rights of Conscience* stated that no Christian attending his own church should incur penalty for not attending the established church. All "Protestant dissenters" were to have the power to maintain their societies according to law. This left out Catholics and Jews, but in 1817 the constitution was amended to remove the adjective "Protestant." This was a small but sure victory for Catholics.

There was surely no great sympathy for Catholicism in Rhode Island either. Most laws dealing with religious matters contained the now familiar "except Papists" restriction. What did differ in Rhode Island, however, was that as soon as Catholics began to move into the colony in large numbers, steps were taken to remove their handicaps. The French army under Rochambeau had been much welcomed into the colony during the Revolutionary War, but it was quickly observed that the legal climate for the soldiers' faith was much less hospitable. Hence, in 1783 the assembly decreed

> that all the Rights and Privileges of the Protestant citizens of this State, be fully extended to Roman Catholic citizens, and that they being of competent estates and of civil conversation and acknowledging and paying obedience to the Civil Magistrate, shall be admitted Freemen, and shall have

[264] Ibid., 370–373.

liberty to choose and be chosen Civil or Military Officers within this state.[265]

No Home in Dixie

The Southern Colonies consisted of Georgia and both Carolinas. Interestingly, South Carolina's first constitution contained no provision regarding religion. In 1778, however, a newer state constitution declared Protestantism the state religion: Only Protestants were eligible to sit in the assembly or state senate.[266]

Though a considerable number of Scotch Highlanders, mostly Catholic, were found in North Carolina, the negotiators who drew up the state constitution were not inclined to be hospitable to them. Delegates gathered in 1775, many of whom had been given instructions from their constituents to avoid, at all costs, concessions to Catholics. One early state historian noted that the early settlers had brought with them "no kind remembrance of the popish clergy and their adherents." He added that each page of their history was stained with blood, for which the Irish Catholics and their clergy were responsible, and that granting any liberties or privileges to this sort would be to "cherish the very enemy from which they had fled." Therefore, the toleration of "popish idolatrous worship" was not to become a feature of North Carolina's landscape.[267]

[265] Ibid., 364.

[266] Curiously, even with such background, Charleston became a diocese in 1820, with County Cork–born Bishop John England presiding over an area covering both Carolinas and Georgia. Also, Charleston was to be the site of the publication of the first Catholic newspaper in the country, the *United States Catholic Miscellany*, edited by the bishop's sister, Johanna England.

[267] William H. Foote, *Sketches of North Carolina, Historical and Biographical* (New York: 1846), cited in ibid., 352. There is, however,

The deeper one traveled in the South, the fewer Catholics there were to be found. In Georgia, the system of land tenure until 1750 furnishes a key to understanding prevailing attitudes. Settlers were not permitted to "hold their lands in fee simple"—that is, they were not given the freedom to dispose of their land as they saw fit. There was a very real fear that landholders might sell their lands to either French or Spanish buyers. In that way, Catholics could get a foothold into the colony. In addition, Georgia colonial records show that in the encouragement of settlers, pitches were made solely to Protestant countries or to Protestant areas already existing in North America; the Georgia legislature even made appropriations to defray the costs of prospective Protestant colonists.[268]

The colonial mind, in so many instances, proves true the observation of the American historian Arthur Schlesinger Sr., that anti-Catholicism is the deepest bias in the American people. Though several other periods of United States Catholic history also prove this to be the case, the initial years of settlement and the formation of governments abundantly illustrate it. Remarkable, indeed, was Catholic forbearance in spite of it; still more remarkable was the Catholic growth that was to follow.

---

a well-established traditional opinion that the first governor under the state constitution, Thomas Burke, was a Catholic. Burke had been a member of the Constitutional Convention of 1776 from North Carolina and represented North Carolina in the Continental Congress from 1777 to 1780. Apparently, his religious views did not disqualify him in the minds of those who mattered.

268 Ibid., 252–253.

A Postscript

In 1784, just a few years before he was to be consecrated the first Catholic Bishop in the United States, John Carroll, superior of the American clergy, sent a detailed report to the Propaganda Fidei office in Rome. In it, he summarized the growth and progress of the Church in America since 1634; hopes for educational growth; the number of clergy, faithful, and churches; the location of Catholic settlements; and the like. The report sounds a note of great optimism for the future—with a bit of pride in what had been accomplished in the midst of substantial obstacles.[269]

It was this same spirit of optimism that prompted a group of Catholic laymen to write to George Washington, congratulating him on being unanimously chosen as the first president of the new nation. Under the clerical leadership of soon-to-be-Bishop Carroll, the letter was signed by the prelate's brother, Daniel Carroll of Rock Creek, Maryland, and his cousin, Charles Carroll of Carrollton. Dominic Lynch signed in New York, and Thomas FitzSimons in Pennsylvania. They confessed they would have written sooner, but their scattered condition delayed the collecting of sentiments

[269] James Hennesey, S.J., *American Catholics* (New York: Oxford University Press, 1981), 73–74; see also John Tracy Ellis, *American Catholicism* (Chicago: University of Chicago Press, 1969), 38–40.

for inclusion in the missive. They believed Washington's peculiar talent "in war and in peace" was to "afford security to those who commit their protection into your hands." In addition, they highly commended him for encouraging "respect for religion," and for inculcating "by words and actions, that principle, on which the welfare of nations so much depends, that a superintending providence governs the events of the world, and watches over the conduct of men." After summarizing the many ways in which national prosperity would benefit from Washington's administration, they ended with a salutation for "your health and life, in which are included the energy of your example, the wisdom of your counsels, and the persuasive eloquence of your virtues."[270]

Some months later, the chief executive responded: He demurred from their praise, and focused instead on the "prospect of national prosperity before us," describing it as something that ought to "excite the exertions of all good men to establish and secure the happiness of their Country, in the permanent duration of its freedom and independence." This would be accomplished under "the smiles of a Divine Providence—the protection of a good government—the cultivation of manners, morals and piety," all of which would ultimately ensure an "uncommon degree of eminence" in many areas. Perhaps most significant was the reminder that Washington gave the laymen of the part they had played in the Revolutionary War, and the aid to American independence that was received "from a nation in which the Roman Catholic religion is professed." In conclusion, he wished "the members of your society in America, animated alone by the pure spirit of Christianity, and still conducting themselves as the faithful subjects of our free government ... every temporal and spiritual felicity."[271]

[270] Ellis, *Documents*, 174–175.
[271] Ibid., 175–176.

Bishop John Carroll took possession of his cathedral, today Old St. Peter's in Baltimore, on December 12, 1790. He left little doubt about the responsibilities laid upon him, presiding as he did over a diocese extending from the border of Canada to the border of Florida, and from the eastern seaboard to the Mississippi River:

> It is no longer enough for me to be inoffensive in my conduct and regular in my manners. God now imposes a severer duty upon me. I shall incur the guilt of violating my pastoral office, if all my endeavors be not directed to bring your lives and all your actions to a conformity with the laws of God; to exhort, to conjure, to reprove, to enter into all your sentiments; to feel all your infirmities; to be all things to all, that I may gain all to Christ.... In God alone can I find any consolation. He knows by what steps I have been conducted to this important station, and how much I have always dreaded it. He will not abandon me unless I first draw upon His malediction by my unfaithfulness to my charge. Pray, dear brethren, pray incessantly, that I may not incur so dreadful a punishment.[272]

A prayer surely answered, to conclude a legacy surely worth telling.

[272] Ibid., 177–178.

Bibliography

A Declaration of the Lord Baltemore's Plantation in Mary-land: February 10, 1633. Baltimore: Maryland Hall of Records Commission, Department of General Services, June 20, 1983.

Agonito, Joseph. "St. Inigoes Manor: A Nineteenth Century Jesuit Plantation," *Maryland Historical Magazine* 72, no.1 (Spring 1977): 83–98.

Ahlstrom, Sydney E. *A Religious History of the American People*. 2 vols. Garden City, NY: Image Books, 1975.

Alden, John Richard. *The American Revolution: 1775–1783*. New York: Harper and Row, 1954.

Andrews, Charles M. *The Colonial Background of the American Revolution*. New Haven, CT: Yale University Press, 1924.

Andrews, Wayne, ed. *Concise Dictionary of American History*. New York: Charles Scribner's Sons, 1962.

Beitzell, Edwin Warfield. *The Jesuit Missions of St. Mary's County, Maryland*. Abell, MD: E. W. Beitzell, 1960.

Bennett, William Harper. *Catholic Footsteps in Old New York*. New York: Schwartz, Kirwin, and Fauss, 1909.

The Bicentennial Celebration of the Election of Archbishop John Carroll on May 18, 1789 at White Marsh. Bowie, MD: Sacred Heart Church, 1989.

Birzer, Bradley J. *American Cicero: The Life of Charles Carroll.* Wilmington, DE: ISI Books, 2010.

Brugger, Robert J. *Maryland: A Middle Temperament: 1634–1980.* Baltimore: Johns Hopkins University Press, 1988.

Calvert, Jane E., and Anthony K. Lake. "From Necessity, Not Choice: Lessons in Democracy from Maryland's Past." *The Occasional Papers of the Center for the Study of Democracy* 1, no. 1 (Spring 2005).

Chesterton, G.K. *A Short History of England.* Sevenoaks, Kent: Fisher Press, 1994.

Cohalan, Rev. Msgr. Florence D. *A Popular History of the Archdiocese of New York.* Yonkers, NY: United States Catholic Historical Society, 1983.

Connelly, James F., ed. *The History of the Archdiocese of Philadelphia.* Philadelphia: Archdiocese of Philadelphia, 1976.

Craven, Wesley Frank. *The Colonies in Transition: 1660–1713.* New York: Harper and Row, 1968.

Curran, Robert Emmett. *Papist Devils: Catholics in British America, 1574–1783.* Washington, D.C.: Catholic University of America Press, 2014.

Davis, Cyprian.*The History of Black Catholics in the United States.* New York: Crossroad Publishing, 1990.

Ellis, John Tracy. *American Catholicism.* Chicago: University of Chicago Press, 1956.

———. *Catholics in Colonial America.* Baltimore: Helicon Press (Benedictine Studies), 1965.

———. *Documents of American Catholic History.* Milwaukee: Bruce, 1956.

Farrelly, Maura Jane. *Papist Patriots: The Making of an American Catholic Identity.* Oxford: Oxford University Press, 2012.

Fink, Leo Gregory. *Old Jesuit Trails in Penn's Forrest.* New York: Paulist Press, 1936.

Gipson, Lawrence Henry. *The Coming of the Revolution: 1763–1775*. New York: Harper and Row, 1954.

Hammett, Regina Combs. *History of St. Mary's County, Maryland: 1634–1990*. Ridge, Maryland: Regina Combs Hammett, 1991.

Hanley, Thomas O'Brien. *Charles Carroll of Carrollton: The Making of a Revolutionary Gentleman*. Chicago: Loyola University Press, 1982.

Henessey, James, S.J. *American Catholics: A History of the Roman Catholic Community in the United States*. Oxford: Oxford University Press, 1981.

Hitchcock, James, *History of the Catholic Church from the Apostolic Age to the Third Millennium*. San Francisco: Ignatius Press, 2012.

Hoffman, Ronald. *Princes of Ireland, Planters of Maryland: A Carroll Saga, 1500–1782*. Chapel Hill, NC: University of North Carolina Press, 2000.

Hofstadter, Richard. *America at 1750: A Social Portrait*. New York: Alfred A. Knopf, 1971.

Hughes, Philip, *A History of the Church*. 3 vols. London: Sheed and Ward, 1934.

———. *The Reformation in England*. 3 vols. New York: Macmillan, 1956.

Jackson, Thomas Penfield. "Maryland Designe: The First Wall between Church and State," *The Occasional Papers of the Center for the Study of Democracy* 3, no. 1 (Fall 2008).

Kennedy, Paul, ed., *The Catholic Church in England and Wales*. Keighley, West Yorkshire: PBK Publishing, 2001.

Krugler, John D. *English and Catholic: The Lords Baltimore in the Seventeenth Century*. Baltimore: Johns Hopkins University Press, 2004.

Lawatsch–Boomgaarden, Barbara ed., *Voyage to Maryland (1633): Relatio Itineris in Marilandiam*. Wauconda, IL: Bolchazy-Carducci, 1995.

MacCulloch, Diarmaid. *Reformation: Europe's House Divided: 1490–1700*. London: Penguin Books, 2003.

Marlin, George, and Brad Miner, *Sons of Saint Patrick: A History of the Archbishops of New York from Dagger John to Timmytown*. San Francisco: Ignatius Press, 2017.

McAvoy, Thomas T., C.S.C. *A History of the Catholic Church in the United States*. Notre Dame, IN: University of Notre Dame Press, 1969.

McGreal, Mary Nona, O.P. *Dominicans at Home in a Young Nation: 1786–1865*. Vol. 1. Strasbourg: Éditions du Signe, 2001.

Melville, Annabelle M. *John Carroll of Baltimore: Founder of the American Catholic Hierarchy*. New York: Charles Scribner's Sons, 1955.

Metzger, Charles H., S.J. *Catholics and the American Revolution: A Study in Religious Climate*. Chicago: Loyola University Press, 1962.

Morris, Richard B., ed. *Encyclopedia of American History*. New York: Harper and Row, 1953.

Neusse, C. J., *The Social Thought of American Catholics: 1634–1829* Westminster, MD: Newman Bookshop, 1945.

Newman, Henry Wright. *The Flowering of the Maryland Palatinate*. Baltimore: Clearfield, 1961.

Newman, John Henry. *Lectures on the Present Position of Catholics in England*. London: Longmans, Green, 1908.

Norman, Edward. *Roman Catholicism in England: From the Elizabethan Settlement to the Second Vatican Council*. Oxford: Oxford University Press, 1986.

Norton, Mary Beth. *The British-Americans: The Loyalist Exiles in England: 1774–1789*. Boston: Little, Brown, 1972.

O'Collins, Gerald, S.J., and Mario Farrugia, S.J. *Catholicism: The Story of Catholic Christianity*. Oxford: Oxford University Press, 2003.

Parsons, Wilfrid, S.J., *Early Catholic Americana: A List of Books and Other Works by Catholic Authors in the United States: 1729–1830*. New York: Macmillan, 1939.

Peterman, Thomas J. *Bohemia: 1704–2004: A History of St. Francis Xavier Catholic Shrine in Cecil County, Maryland*. Devon, PA: William T. Cooke, 2004.

———. *Catholics in Colonial Delmarva*. Devon, PA: Cooke, 1996.

Phillips, Charles. *The Illustrated Encyclopedia of Royal Britain*. New York: Metro Books, 2009.

Pogue, Robert E. T., *Yesterday in Old St. Mary's County*. Robert E. T. Pogue, 2008.

Pomfret, John E. *Founding the American Colonies: 1583–1660*. New York: Harper and Row, 1970.

Ray, Sister Mary Augustina, B.V.M. *American Opinion of Roman Catholicism in the Eighteenth Century*. New York: Octagon Books, 1974.

Riordan, Timothy B. *The Plundering Time: Maryland and the English Civil War: 1645–1646*. Baltimore: Maryland Historical Society, 2004.

Rowland, Kate Mason. *The Life of Charles Carroll of Carrollton, 1737–1832: With His Correspondence and Public Papers*. 2 vols. New York: G. P. Putnam's Sons, 1898.

Shelley, Thomas J. *The Archdiocese of New York: The Bicentennial History: 1808–2008*. Strasbourg: Éditions du Signe, 2007.

Smith, Goldwin. *A History of England*. New York: Charles Scribner's Sons, 1966.

Spalding, Thomas W. *The Premier See: A History of the Archdiocese of Baltimore, 1789–1989*. Baltimore: Johns Hopkins University Press, 1989.

Steiner, Bruce E. "The Catholic Brents of Colonial Virginia: An Instance of Practical Toleration," *Virginia Magazine of History and Biography* 70, no. 4 (October 1962): 387–409.

Walsh, James J. *American Jesuits*. New York: Macmillan, 1934.
Who Remembers Long: A History of Port Tobacco Carmel. Port Tobacco, MD: Carmel of Port Tobacco, 1984.

Biographical Note

Fr. Charles P. Connor, S.T.L., Ph.D., is a professor of systemic theology and Church history at Mount St. Mary's Seminary in Emmitsburg, Maryland. He has previously authored books on several topics, such as *Classic Catholic Converts*, *Defenders of the Faith in Word and Deed*, *Meditations on the Catholic Priesthood*, *The Saint for the Third Millennium: Thérèse of Lisieux*, *The Spiritual Legacy of Archbishop Fulton J. Sheen*, and *John Cardinal O'Connor and the Culture of Life*. He has co-produced dozens of series for EWTN and is actively engaged in preaching retreats for priests and laity throughout the United States. A priest of the Diocese of Scranton, Pennsylvania, he served in diocesan parishes for eighteen years, including as rector of St. Peter's Cathedral in Scranton. Fr. Connor holds a B.A. and an M.A. in U.S. history from the University of Scranton, a Ph.D. from the Institute of Philosophy at the Catholic University of Louvain in Belgium, a doctorate in U.S. history from Fordham University in New York City, an S.T.D. from the Gregorian University in Rome, an M.A. from the Angelicum University in Rome, and an S.T.L. from the Pontifical John Paul II Institute for Studies on Marriage and Family in Washington, D.C.